The Oxford
Children's History

The Oxford Children's History

Volume 1: Earliest Times to the Last Stuarts

Roy Burrell

Oxford University Press

Oxford University Press, Walton Street, Oxford OX2 6DP

Oxford   New York   Toronto
Petaling Jaya   Singapore   Hong Kong   Tokyo
Delhi   Bombay   Calcutta   Madras   Karachi
Nairobi   Dar es Salaam   Cape Town
Melbourne   Auckland

and associated companies in
Beirut   Berlin   Ibadan   Nicosia

Oxford is a trade mark of Oxford University Press

©Roy Burrell 1983
First published 1983
Reprinted 1986

British Library Cataloguing in Publication Data

Burrell, Roy
  The Oxford Children's History.
  Vol. 1: Earliest Times to the Last Stuarts
  1. Great Britain – History – Juvenile literature
  I. Title
  941   DA30

ISBN 0-19-918186-1

Typeset by Tradespools Ltd., Frome, Somerset
Printed in Hong Kong

Contents

Chapter Sixteen   The Restoration

Chapter Seventeen   The Last Stuarts

Family Tree of the Kings and Queens of England

- ■ Anglo-Saxons
- ■ Danes
- ■ Normandy
- ■ Plantagenet
- ■ Lancaster
- ■ York
- ■ Tudor
- ■ Stuart
- ■ Hanover
- ■ Saxe-Coburg Gotha
- ■ Windsor

Egbert 802–839 ■

Ethelwulf 839–856 ■

Ethelbald 856–860 ■

Ethelbert 860–866 ■

Saint Ethelred 866–871 ■

Alfred 871–899 ■

Edward the Elder 899–924 ■

Athelstan ■ 924–940

Edmund the Elder ■ 940–946

Edred ■ 946–955

Edwy the Fair ■ 955–959

Edgar the Peaceful 959–975 ■

m 1st wife

m Elfrida (stepson)

Edward the Martyr 975–978 ■

Ethelred the Unready 978–1016 ■

Edmund Ironside April–Nov 1016 ■

Ethelred the Unready

Canute the Great 1016–1035 ■
m Elgiva

m Emma (widow of Ethelred)

Harold Harefoot ■ 1037–1040

Hardicanute ■ 1040–1042

Edward the Confessor 1042–1066 ■
nominated

Harold II Jan–Oct 1066 ■
defeated by

William I 1066–1087 ■
(Conqueror)

William II ■ (Rufus) 1087–1100

Henry I ■ 1100–1135

Matilda *m* Geoffrey of Anjou

Adela *m* Count of Blois

Stephen 1135–1154 ■

Henry II 1154–1189 ■
m Eleanor of Aquitaine

Richard I (Lionheart) 1189–1199 ■

John 1199–1216 ■

Henry III 1216–1272 ■

Edward I 1272–1307 ■

Edward II 1307–1327 ■

Edward III 1327–1377 ■

Edward III

Edward, Black Prince

Lionel, Duke of Clarence

John, Duke of Lancaster

Edmund, Duke of York

Thomas, Duke of Gloucester

802 to the present

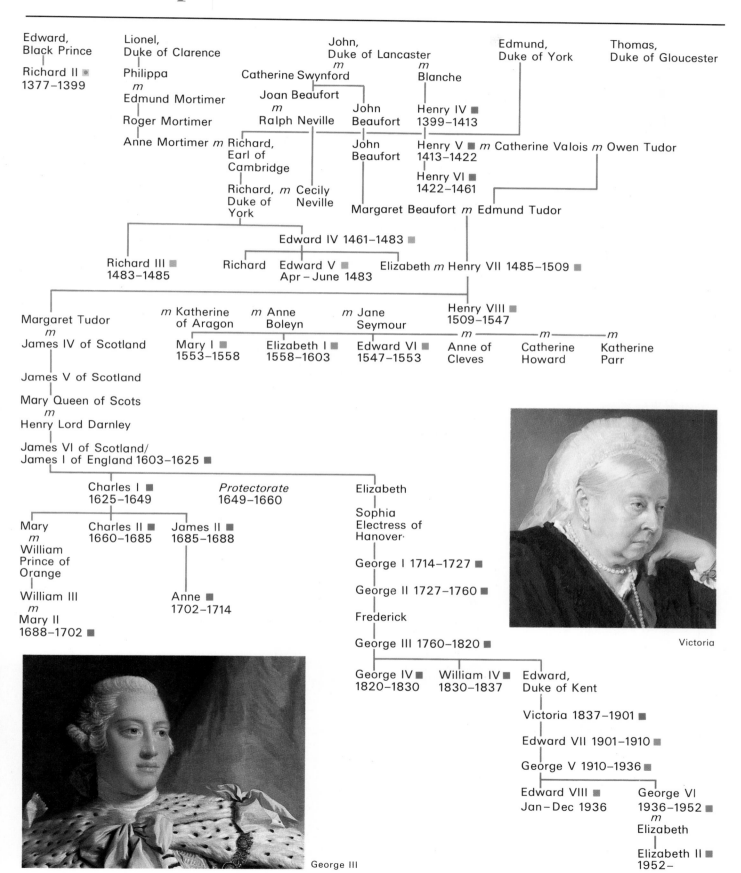

Edward, Black Prince
Richard II 1377–1399

Lionel, Duke of Clarence
Philippa
m
Edmund Mortimer
Roger Mortimer
Anne Mortimer *m* Richard, Earl of Cambridge

John, Duke of Lancaster
m
Catherine Swynford
Joan Beaufort
m
Ralph Neville
John Beaufort

John, Duke of Lancaster
m
Blanche
Henry IV 1399–1413

Edmund, Duke of York

Thomas, Duke of Gloucester

Richard, Duke of York *m* Cecily Neville

John Beaufort

Henry V 1413–1422 *m* Catherine Valois *m* Owen Tudor
Henry VI 1422–1461

Margaret Beaufort *m* Edmund Tudor

Edward IV 1461–1483

Richard III 1483–1485

Richard

Edward V Apr – June 1483

Elizabeth *m* Henry VII 1485–1509

Margaret Tudor
m
James IV of Scotland

James V of Scotland

Mary Queen of Scots
m
Henry Lord Darnley

James VI of Scotland/ James I of England 1603–1625

m Katherine of Aragon
Mary I 1553–1558

m Anne Boleyn
Elizabeth I 1558–1603

m Jane Seymour
Edward VI 1547–1553

Henry VIII 1509–1547
m —— *m* —— *m*
Anne of Cleves   Catherine Howard   Katherine Parr

Charles I 1625–1649

Protectorate 1649–1660

Elizabeth

Sophia Electress of Hanover

George I 1714–1727

George II 1727–1760

Frederick

George III 1760–1820

Mary
m
William Prince of Orange
William III
m
Mary II 1688–1702

Charles II 1660–1685

James II 1685–1688

Anne 1702–1714

George IV 1820–1830

William IV 1830–1837

Edward, Duke of Kent

Victoria 1837–1901

Edward VII 1901–1910

George V 1910–1936

Edward VIII Jan – Dec 1936

George VI 1936–1952
m
Elizabeth

Elizabeth II 1952–

Victoria

George III

The Reigns of the Kings and Queens of England

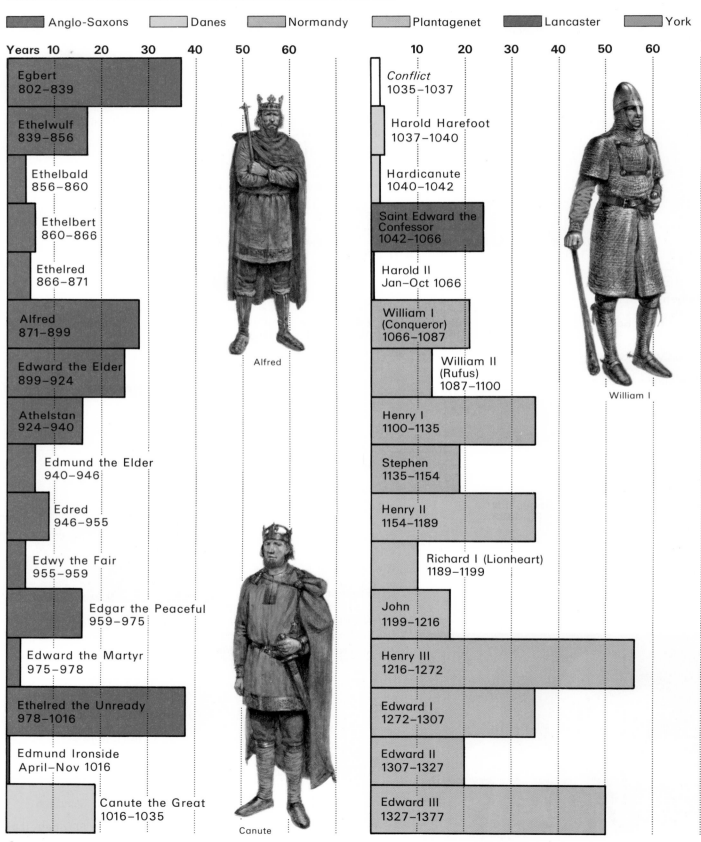

Anglo-Saxons · Danes · Normandy · Plantagenet · Lancaster · York

Years 10 20 30 40 50 60

Egbert
802–839

Ethelwulf
839–856

Ethelbald
856–860

Ethelbert
860–866

Ethelred
866–871

Alfred
871–899

Edward the Elder
899–924

Athelstan
924–940

Edmund the Elder
940–946

Edred
946–955

Edwy the Fair
955–959

Edgar the Peaceful
959–975

Edward the Martyr
975–978

Ethelred the Unready
978–1016

Edmund Ironside
April–Nov 1016

Canute the Great
1016–1035

Alfred

Canute

10 20 30 40 50 60

Conflict
1035–1037

Harold Harefoot
1037–1040

Hardicanute
1040–1042

Saint Edward the
Confessor
1042–1066

Harold II
Jan–Oct 1066

William I
(Conqueror)
1066–1087

William II
(Rufus)
1087–1100

Henry I
1100–1135

Stephen
1135–1154

Henry II
1154–1189

Richard I (Lionheart)
1189–1199

John
1199–1216

Henry III
1216–1272

Edward I
1272–1307

Edward II
1307–1327

Edward III
1327–1377

William I

802 to the present

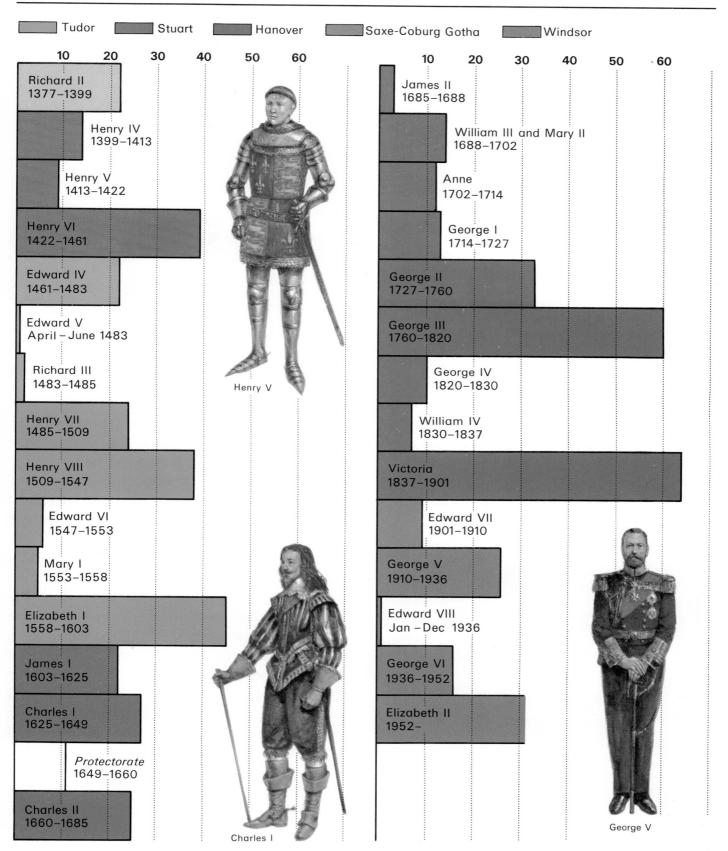

Tudor □ Stuart ■ Hanover ■ Saxe-Coburg Gotha ■ Windsor ■

10 20 30 40 50 60

Richard II
1377–1399

Henry IV
1399–1413

Henry V
1413–1422

Henry VI
1422–1461

Edward IV
1461–1483

Edward V
April – June 1483

Richard III
1483–1485

Henry VII
1485–1509

Henry VIII
1509–1547

Edward VI
1547–1553

Mary I
1553–1558

Elizabeth I
1558–1603

James I
1603–1625

Charles I
1625–1649

Protectorate
1649–1660

Charles II
1660–1685

Henry V

Charles I

10 20 30 40 50 60

James II
1685–1688

William III and Mary II
1688–1702

Anne
1702–1714

George I
1714–1727

George II
1727–1760

George III
1760–1820

George IV
1820–1830

William IV
1830–1837

Victoria
1837–1901

Edward VII
1901–1910

George V
1910–1936

Edward VIII
Jan – Dec 1936

George VI
1936–1952

Elizabeth II
1952–

George V

Chapter One   The Celts

1 The People

Have you ever been to London Airport? It is hard to imagine what this busy, bustling place with its roaring airliners has to do with history. Yet, many centuries ago, long before aeroplanes had been invented, Heathrow was a quiet country area.

During the Second World War, something was found there which showed that Heathrow had an interesting past. It was a Royal Air Force station in those days and needed a longer runway. Bulldozers scraped away the grass and soil and as they did, a strange pattern appeared.

There were lots of little dark circles in the lighter earth. Men from the museum came to look at them. They said that the circles had once been holes in which wooden posts had stood.

Everyone wanted to know how old they were and what they were for. The airmen were surprised when they were told.

'There was once a wooden building here,' said one of the museum men. 'It was most likely a temple and could have been put up more than 2,000 years ago.'

'Can holes tell you that?' asked an airman.

'Yes. The shape of the building is shown by where the holes are. We know that the holes had big posts in them. From this we think we know what the building was. Pieces of pottery can also help us to put it in the right period. If no one touches a spot where a hole has been dug, the signs of its position and shape will stay there almost for ever. You could dig a pit in your garden, fill it in, and thousands of years in the future someone could find it and even say how deep it had once been.'

'Who made the holes?' asked the airman.

Iron Age horse harness

Iron Age pottery

'We think it was the work of the Celts, who lived all over Britain in those days. They lived in Europe too, and wherever they settled, they left things which tell us something about them.'

The museum man was right. There was once a whole Celtic village near the temple and remains of the Celts are to be seen almost anywhere in Britain.

Sometimes there are simple finds like those above from Essex.

A lot of the remains are surprisingly large and much too big to put in a museum.

The Celts were noisy and quarrelsome according to their neighbours, the Romans. This is why they were nearly always fighting each other. When the Celts came to Britain, there was plenty of land available, even if the people who owned it had to be driven out first.

The earliest Celts in Britain made themselves villages of little round huts. Later on, when there was not enough land to go round, they began to fight amongst themselves.

Villages were started on islands, in lakes and marshes, on tongues of land sticking out into the sea, or on the tops of hills. The villagers would have felt safer behind the stronger defences of a hill fort. There are still scores of these to be seen in Britain.

above Remains of an Iron Age hill fort at Morvah in Cornwall
below The village at Heathrow

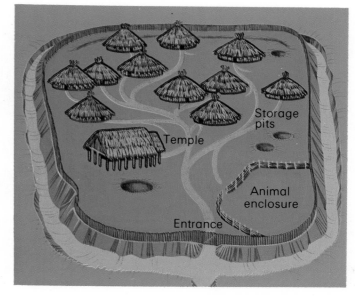

Temple

Storage pits

Animal enclosure

Entrance

2 A Hill Fort

Model of a chariot from Llyn Cerrig Bach in Wales

Whenever a tribe went hungry, there were always men who would try to talk the others into moving to a new home. Sometimes they had their way, and the tribe went off, taking their animals and seed corn with them.

The warriors rode in their war chariots and behind them came flocks of sheep, herds of cattle and ox waggons laden with all that the tribe owned. Those with no carts had to walk.

When they came to a place they liked, they would try to drive out the people who lived there. If they managed to do this, they were lucky. If not, they had to move on.

Some tribes crossed from France to England in boats. Wherever they went, they found people already living. Land was not easy to capture. They did not always have the chance to strike the first blow. Often, the attack came from the owners of the land through which they were passing. The warriors would put on their helmets and take up their shields, swords and spears.

When both sides were ready, they whipped up their horses and drove their chariots towards each other. They hurled their spears and then jumped down to fight on foot. The rest of the newcomers watched from the ox waggons.

If the newcomers lost, they tried to get away as fast as they could. It wasn't always easy after this sort of battle.

Attacking a hill fort might be a simple matter if those who lived there had not kept the defences in repair. All the same, the invading warriors had to run uphill, while the defenders could hide behind the banks of earth and only show themselves to hurl stones.

The attackers could shelter behind their shields but they found it much harder to fight up a slope. Those at the top of the hill had no trouble in throwing stones downwards.

Almost 2,000 years ago a wandering Celtic tribe made war on the people who lived in Maiden Castle. This huge hill fort is in the West Country. At that time its defences were not as strong as they should have been.

The Celts were too impatient to camp round the hill and wait for those inside to run out of food and water. They moved towards the fort and were met with a hail of stones which most of them managed to take on their shields.

After a while, there were fewer stones because the men inside had been too lazy to collect enough. The leader of the attackers shouted to his men to move faster. They ran up the slopes and a lot of them climbed over the walls and into the ditches where they fought with their swords.

As soon as they had cleared the first ditch, they scrambled up to the next one and then the one beyond that. Finally they came out on the flat top of the hill and there was little more fighting.

The chief told everyone what to do so that the fortress would not be taken so easily the next time. The ditches would have to be made deeper, more stones must be added to the walls and new posts cut to stop them sliding down the hillside. The huts on the hilltop had to be tackled next. A few could be used but most had to be rebuilt. While this was going on, the farmers were sent to take over the fields in the lowlands.

When the repairs had been completed, sacrifices were made to the gods. They hoped that the gods would help them when their new home was next attacked.

3 The Family

Imagine that it is now ten years since the Celtic tribe captured Maiden Castle and they have settled down a little. They still go on raids for cattle from time to time but there are no more full-scale wars. The warriors practise with their weapons. The craftsmen make things and the farmers grow food.

Let us visit a farm. The children live in the round farmhouse. They sleep on springy piles of heather or bracken laid on the hard dirt floor. Their parents' bed is a pair of wooden benches draped with sheep skins.

The children don't wear pyjamas or nightdresses. If it is very cold, they keep their

day clothes on and snuggle under sheep skins, but most nights they pull off their clothes before they lie down to sleep. The house is usually warm because the fire is never allowed to go out.

A little while after the sun has risen, Briacan wakes up. He is thirteen. He pulls on his long trousers and wakes his younger brother, Awyl, who is ten. Awyl yawns and goes with Briacan to fetch wood for the fire. He will dress later.

The fresh air from the open door wakens their sister, Clawen, who is eight. She puts on her blouse and skirt and is surprised to find her parents are still asleep. Usually Baban, the baby, wakes everyone up.

'*Does Baban always cry in the mornings?*' we ask Briacan when he and Awyl come back with the wood for the fire.

'No, not always. Mother is often the first to wake. Then Clawen goes to get water from the spring.'

'*What do you do all day?*'

'Well, we don't have much time for playing because we have to help our parents. Clawen has to do what Mother tells her. She seems to like looking after the baby best.

'She also has to get Grandmother her food. Granny is too old to move about much. She sleeps with my two aunts in a space at the back of our round house.'

When Clawen comes back with the water, everyone is up and even Awyl is dressed. No one washes unless they are very dirty. Everyone sits to eat the oat cakes mother has cooked and Briacan wants to know what he must do today. Father brushes crumbs from his long, reddish moustache and thinks.

'We have finished the ploughing,' he says, 'and now the sheep must be brought to the top field for shearing.' The boys like this. If they can get the sheep in quickly, there will be time for games.

left Bronze dish
above Iron Age pottery from Maiden Castle

4 The Children

It takes all the morning to collect the sheep. Then they eat the dark bread and goat's cheese mother has given them. They wash it down with weak beer from a goatskin. After a rest they will play. They have to make the toys they need.

Briacan sharpens both ends of a short piece of wood and lays it on the grass. He tries to hit one of the sharp tips with the butt of his spear. The 'rat', as they call it, will fly away if he gets it just right.

'*Do you have any other games, Briacan?*'

'I like our next game best. Last year one of us used the spear to bat away a stone thrown by the other. Awyl missed and the stone hit him instead. So I had an idea. We collected tufts of wool from gorse bushes, twisted them into a long thread and wound it round the stone. The ball was much better. In fact it was too good. It bounced and rolled so much that we lost it.'

It is very warm for springtime, so the boys have a splash in a nearby pond. While they are drying off in the sun, they play 'knife-cloth-stone'. On the count of three, each player brings his hand out from behind his back. One pointing finger is a knife, a fist is a stone and a flat hand a cloth.

A knife beats cloth because it can cut cloth, but loses to the stone which can blunt it. Cloth is better than stone because it can wrap round the stone. Before long they argue over

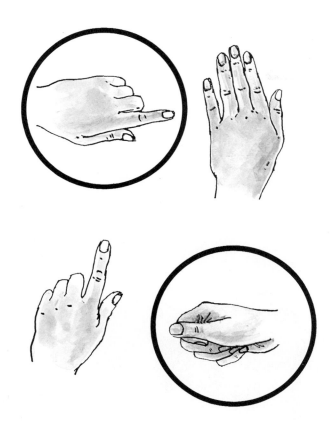

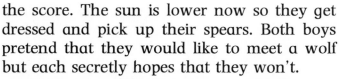

the score. The sun is lower now so they get dressed and pick up their spears. Both boys pretend that they would like to meet a wolf but each secretly hopes that they won't.

Briacan wishes he was a chief's son, learning to fight with real weapons and driving a chariot. Then he would not have to go with the other children collecting mushrooms and berries or gathering the seeds of wild plants for making into porridge. He wouldn't have to work on the farm either.

When they get back, Clawen tells them that she is learning to weave. She can cook already. Grandmother and her aunts show her what to do whenever they have time.

5 The Tribe

The king and his warriors practised chariot driving and different kinds of fighting. They were interested in breeding and training horses but they left the care of the other animals, such as sheep and cows, to those who did not fight. Because they kept the rest of the tribe safe from its enemies, they expected the farmers to work hard and grow extra food to feed them.

Briacan's father is a farmer who has only a few small fields. Some of his father's friends have farms so big they have to have slaves to do the work. There were many different kinds of jobs which had to be done throughout the year.

Briacan's mother looks after the children, gets the meals ready and makes the clothes from thread which she has spun herself.

Every grown-up had to be able to earn a

living by doing these simple tasks. People with special skills were looked up to by the others. They were the craftsmen of the tribe. They spent most of their time doing the one thing they were good at.

In every tribe the blacksmith is the leading craftsman.

'*Why is your job so important?*' we ask him.

'Because we are a tribe of warriors,' he answers proudly. 'We Celts have won a lot of battles with our iron swords. Many of our enemies have to make do with bronze ones. Bronze is not as good as iron and much harder to get.

'I don't just forge good swords. I also make spear and arrow heads as well as other things.

'When we find the iron, it is mixed in with rock and has to be dug out of the ground in lumps. It is called iron ore. The ore is brought to the smithy where I heat it in a fire. My helpers blow air into the fire with bellows to make it hotter.

Iron Age spearheads

'I grip a glowing lump with my tongs, lay it on the anvil and hammer it. Specks of hot rock fly away in showers of golden sparks. When most of the rock has gone, I put the iron that is left back in the fire. After a while it's soft enough to be taken out again. I beat it out on my anvil into the shape I want. A tribe is as good as its weapons and that's why we smiths are so important.'

6 Festivals

Let's ask Briacan about the holidays he has.

'Holidays? What are holidays?'

'*When you don't go to school or do any work*,' we explain.

'Oh, I see. You mean *holy* days. I don't know what you mean by school, but we do have festivals four times a year when work stops.'

'*Like our Easter, Whitsun and Christmas?*'

'I don't know what they are. We call our festivals Samhain, Imbolg, Beltane and Lugnasa. Samhain is the most important. It comes in the late autumn and really marks the start of winter. It's the first feast of the year.'

The Celts were mostly farmers and warriors. When the crops failed or the cows fell ill, they did not know why. They thought that someone had cast a spell, or more likely, that the gods were angry. They held feasts throughout the year to please the gods and put them in a good mood.

They held great religious services in honour of the 'Other-world', as they called the place where the dead went and the gods lived. They made sacrifices both of animals and human beings. The chants and prayers had to be said in exactly the right way or they thought their plants would not grow in the fields and the animals would give no milk or even die.

The Celts didn't know about the germs which were the most likely cause of these things so they tried magic. Most of us don't really believe in magic, although we would like to. When you have been in trouble, have you ever said to yourself, '*If I touch every lamp post on the way to school, I won't be punished*'?

You know in your secret heart that it doesn't work but you've got to do all you can. The Celts knew that they couldn't do much about disasters, so perhaps magic was the answer.

Every three months there was a festival. Samhain came on the first of November and marked not only the onset of winter but also the beginning of the Celtic new year.

The magic rites started the evening before. They were meant to protect the people and bring them good luck. It was the time when the Other-world spirits could be seen by ordinary folk and this could be dangerous, as the following story shows.

Wooden idol from Dagenham

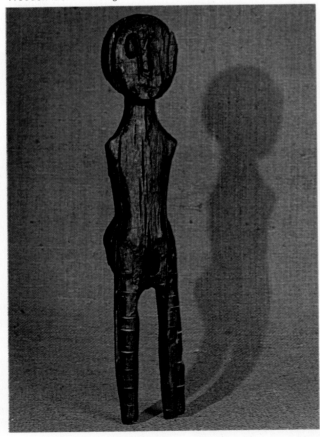

On the Eve of Samhain one year, a handsome stranger came to the village and asked to meet the best harpist in the area, a man named Culag. The stranger offered Culag a bag of gold if he would come and play at a feast. At first Culag refused but a sight of the gold tempted him and at last he went with the stranger to a large hall not far away where there were over a hundred guests. Culag played music for them all night until he became so tired, he fell asleep.

When he awoke the next morning, he found himself lying on the grass at the foot of a little hill near a small lake. He was still clutching his harp and the leather purse he had been given. Alas! There were only stones in it.

As he stumbled to his feet, he caught sight of his reflection in the lake. He was amazed at the face which stared back at him. The skin was wrinkled and both his hair and beard were long, tangled and snow-white. When he got home, he found that thirty years had passed. His wife had died and his children were grown and did not know him.

The story of Culag was told to the children as an awful warning of what could happen on the Eve of Samhain. Memories of the festival of Samhain have come down to us through the ages. Today we know it as Hallowe'en.

By the first of February, the earliest flowers were in bloom and the young lambs were being born. Sheep were very important to the Celts because their wool was needed to make clothes. February the first was called Imbolg. The goddess of the feast was Brigit. People prayed to her and made sacrifices on her altars. By doing this, they were hoping that she would give them large and healthy flocks.

7 Beltane and Lugnasa

Three months later came Beltane which was held on the first of May. The name may have come from the god Belenos, or it may mean 'bright fire'. It was yet another chance for the Celts to pray to the Other-world to send them luck and riches. Two huge bonfires were lit and the cattle were driven through the flames to make them clean and pure. In many parts of Europe, including Scotland and Ireland, the custom of May Day bonfires survived until modern times.

The last period of the year started on August the first. Its name was Lugnasa and it went on longer than the other festivals. The day of Lugnasa came in the middle of a month of feasting and merry-making. It was in honour of the god Lugus. There were often sports, fairs, games and 'pretend' fights.

It was a custom to hold an enormous get-together to which all the people of an area were invited. It was the one time in the year when people could enjoy themselves with their relations and friends.

8 The Druids

All the festivals were run by the Druids. These were the priests of the tribe and only the king came above them. Sometimes they lived away from the tribe in holy places in the forests. They held ceremonies in clearings in the forest, particularly where there were oak trees. The oak was believed to be a holy tree and so was the mistletoe which grows on it. The Druids thought mistletoe was a powerful medicine. The Roman writer Pliny describes how they gathered it.

'The mistletoe is rarely found, but when it is, the Druids gather it with solemn ceremony. They do this on the sixth day of their first month. After the preparations have been made for the sacrifice or feast under the tree, they bring two white bulls. A priest dressed in a white robe climbs the tree and cuts the mistletoe with a golden sickle. The plant is caught in a white cloth. Then they sacrifice the victims and pray to their gods for good luck. They believe that a potion made from mistletoe is a remedy against all poison.'

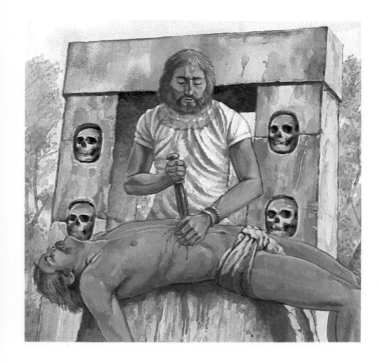

The Druids were medicine men and magicians. Woe betide anyone who annoyed a Druid. A spell said properly could ruin his crops or stop his cows giving milk. If the Druid were really cross he might curse the man until he died.

Druids did not fight but they sometimes went to a battle to put spells on the attackers. If an enemy were frightened enough, he would be easier to beat.

Even when there were no wars, a man might quarrel with his neighbour, perhaps about the boundary between their farms. The Druid would decide who was right and that was an end of the matter.

A few Druids could read and write but none of them really trusted books – they preferred to keep everything they had to know in their heads. They started their training as boys and were taught by an older man. They sat on the floor of his hut and listened as he recited the piece for that day. It might be a spell, a family tree or a list of laws. The teacher said a line and the class repeated it after him. They went on doing this until they knew the piece by heart. They had no need of pencils, exercise books or satchels.

Some tribes had a wise man or woman who could tell what was going to happen in the future. If the king wanted to know whether he should fight against another tribe, he would ask the Druid. An animal, or even a human being, would be sacrificed. The body was then laid out and the Druid looked at it carefully. The Celts believed that he was able to see things which had not yet happened by doing this.

The Celts thought nothing of sacrificing a captured enemy so that they would know if it was to be a lucky day for them. They might burn him to death or cut off his head. The heads were sacred and kept in a shrine in the forest. Sometimes a clever carver made a full-sized model of one of these heads, either in wood or in stone. Here are pictures of these statues. The word Druid may mean 'wise man of the oak trees', so it isn't surprising to find that the wooden statues are nearly always made of oak.

Druids' shrine from France; stone head from Gloucester

Chapter Two   The Romans

1 Fishbourne

No one lives in this house. No one wants to any more. The windows are broken. Tiles have slipped off the roof. The rain will soak the wooden beams until they rot and fall down. After a long while, the walls will crumble and there will be nothing left but a heap of bits and pieces.

Dust will blow across the heap and bury it. Weeds will grow so thickly that you would never know that a house once stood there. Because it is too much trouble to clear away the rubble, it will be left. A new house might be built on top of it or someone might find the remains hundreds of years later. If someone did not paint and repair the house you live in, the same thing could happen.

In 1960 a workman was digging a ditch in a field at Fishbourne, near Chichester in Sussex. He found some strange pieces of broken tile like these:

He called the foreman to come and look at them and asked him what they were. The foreman shook his head. 'I don't know,' he said. 'I've never seen anything like them before.' The workman said, 'They could be old. What should we do with them?' 'Perhaps we should take them to a museum,' the foreman replied.

Mrs. Rule, the lady from the museum, was very excited by the pieces of tile. She asked if she and her helpers might come and dig in the field. She thought that the pieces were most likely Roman and nearly 2,000 years old.

The diggers from the museum soon found the remains of a house. The wood and most of the plaster had rotted away. But there were enough tiles, bricks and stones for them to work out what it had once looked like. It turned out to be very large and must have belonged to someone very rich and important.

The house and all the objects were indeed Roman and many centuries old. The diggers

above A reconstruction of Fishbourne Palace

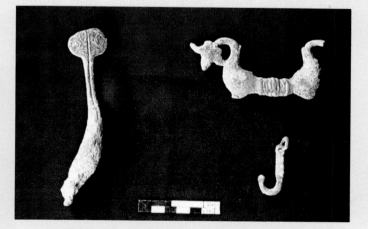

also found a great many everyday things. These have been put in a museum made specially to hold them. They tell us a lot about the way people lived in those days. Perhaps you can guess what they were.

2 The People

Julius Caesar   Claudius Caesar

What were the Romans doing in Britain? Why did they build the house at Fishbourne?

Rome is a town in Italy and had started as a village of mud huts nearly three thousand years ago.

The earliest Romans were farmers and shepherds. When they were raided, they hid in the hills around the village. To make themselves safer they built a wall round their hills. It's easier to fight your attacker if he is below you.

The Romans quickly learned that the best way of dealing with an enemy was to attack him before he could attack them. So they left their farms, took their weapons and raided the most dangerous of the nearby villages.

Before long, they had captured all the towns and villages in their area. They trained men to be full-time soldiers. Before this, the Romans had fought only when there was danger. Now, the full-time soldiers could conquer even more land. At last Rome ruled the whole of Italy. The Romans went on fighting until they owned all the land round the Mediterranean Sea.

One of the army leaders was called Julius Caesar. He conquered the land of Gaul which today we call France. Some of the prisoners he took in France were from Britain. So Julius Caesar made up his mind to find out what that country was like. He crossed the Channel twice but he did not conquer Britain. That was

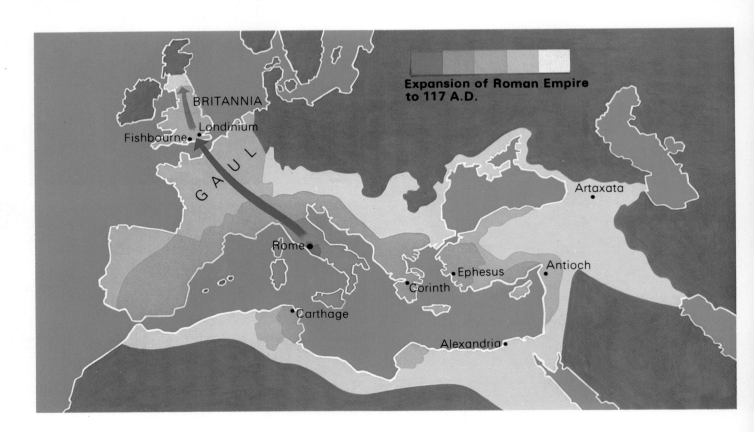

Expansion of Roman Empire to 117 A.D.

BRITANNIA
Londinium
Fishbourne
GAUL
Rome
Carthage
Corinth
Ephesus
Antioch
Artaxata
Alexandria

How Rome may have begun

done by the armies of Claudius Caesar nearly a hundred years later.

The legions which Claudius sent here gradually pushed the Britons back. One by one the chiefs of the tribes gave in. But the Romans showed the beaten tribesmen how much better it was to live in towns and well-made houses. In a few years, Britain was dotted with towns and villas, as the large houses were called.

There were many reasons why the Romans came. They wanted corn, leather, wool, tin, copper, lead, gold, silver and slaves. They made sure that those who helped them to get these things were well paid. The house at Fishbourne was probably a reward given to one of their British friends. And perhaps they came to Britain because once you start conquering, it's hard to stop.

The army of Claudius invades Britain

3 The Family

This picture shows excavations on the site of a Roman country house. Let's imagine what it looked like when the Romans were here. You can see into the bedroom of Marcus and his younger brother, Lucius. There is not much furniture, just two beds, a stool each and a chest for clothes.

The boys have to get up early. They go to school in the nearby town. They don't have much of a wash because they will bathe in the afternoon. They do this every weekday. You can see them putting on their tunics and sandals.

Look at the lavatory. It is next to the bathroom. The used bath water can flush the toilets. When the boys have washed their hands and faces, they go and meet their parents and their sister Julia in the dining room.

After breakfast, all three children must go off to school. Usually they have to walk but

Key to Roman Villa **1** main reception room **2** living room **3** boys' bedroom **4** cold bath **5** hot room **6** lavatory **7** smoke-stack of hot room furnace

this morning they can get a lift on a cart. Their mother's name is Marcia. She tells them to put on an extra cloak. The main part of the villa has central heating but outdoors thick clothes have to be worn.

School starts at eight o'clock and goes on until after midday. The fathers of the pupils have to pay the magister or teacher. Poor people can't afford to send their children to school after they are about eleven or twelve. It costs more then. More boys go to school than girls. Most girls stay at home to help their mothers.

below and right Roman tableware

31

4 School

There are only about ten pupils at the school. It is at the back of a shop in the town square. As you can see, it is rather bare. There are no charts or pictures on the walls. The lessons are mostly reading and writing, with a little arithmetic.

The children have to copy pieces from books by famous writers. The language they use is Latin. Paper and parchment are too dear so they use a little wooden board covered with wax. Each child writes with a sharp piece of wood. If he makes a mistake, he uses the other end of his pen to rub it out. You can see that the Romans didn't use our modern numbers. They find it hard to do sums with letters. They are doing arithmetic with pebbles and bead frames.

I	II	III	IV	V	VI	VII	VIII
1	2	3	4	5	6	7	8

IX	X	XI	XII	XIII	XIV	XV
9	10	11	12	13	14	15

XX	L	C	D	M
20	50	100	500	1000

Roman writing materials

When Marcus, Lucius and Julia have finished their lessons, they put their things in their satchels and go home for the midday meal.

Father's friend, Maradus, is visiting and the two men lie on couches. The slaves bring in the cold meat, salad and sausages and later, pancakes with honey. The three grown-ups drink wine. The children drink a mixture of wine and water.

above Slave at work in a Roman kitchen
left Reconstruction of a kitchen in a Romano-British house

5 Making a Living

Father's name is Cornelius. He has to earn money to keep his family in comfort. He owns a large stretch of land around the villa. He is head of the family so no one argues with him. Cornelius runs the family business and sells things from the farms on his land. The farm work is done by slaves.

Cornelius is in charge of religion on the estate as well. Romans have many gods. Some of them are famous and important. Others are not so well known. There are gods to look after everything, even the house, the fields and the food stores. The villa has a small temple or shrine on the far side of the garden.

Let's ask Cornelius what the shrine is for.

'It's where I make my offerings of corn and wine to the gods. I must get their advice and blessing before anything is decided in the family. I wouldn't plant my corn, start a journey or do a business deal until I'd been to pray at the shrine.'

Remains of the shrine at Lullingstone villa

owners got theirs free as a reward for serving in the army. Some owners rent their land to farmers; they say they don't have time to spare from their duties as town councillors. But Maradus and I prefer to run things personally. I manage to help run the town as well. I'm also a magistrate. At my court in the forum I hear cases and try to settle the townspeople's arguments.'

'*Does everyone do this?*'

'Most people do. In the family it's the father who is in charge of religion. My friend Maradus is a Briton who has learnt our ways but he isn't quite as careful about these things as a proper Roman would be. Mind you, he doesn't have to worry about Ceres, the goddess of harvests. The slaves at his villa don't grow crops, they make things out of clay.'

'*What things?*'

'Tiles and bricks for buildings; cups, beakers, bowls, jugs and jars for the kitchen and dining table. Maradus is lucky. He can tell his workers what to do in their own language but he speaks Latin almost like a Roman. He had to buy his land, although most villa

6 In the Town

In the afternoon, Cornelius has to go back to the town. Marcia is going with him and they will take the children as well. Marcia wants to get some material for making clothes. The house slaves do the everyday shopping. They buy most of the food from the market stalls. For special things, however, Marcia goes herself.

Stone carving of a Roman shop

Julia likes shopping too. The boys are being allowed to go to the gymnasium at the public baths where they can meet their friends and play games.

They will all meet in the forum afterwards.

Remains of Roman shops in Italy

Some soldiers are expected to arrive in an hour or two and everyone wants to be there when they come. The soldiers are part of a legion which has been sent to the town. One of the officers is Marcia's brother, Gaius. The children are looking forward to seeing their uncle again.

Cornelius joins his family just in time to see the officers ride into the square. These are followed by the legionaries on foot. An orderly leads Uncle Gaius's horse away and he is soon surrounded by the family. Everyone is laughing and talking at once. The ordinary soldiers are marched off to camp by the centurions.

Back at the villa everybody wants to hear what the news is from Rome. Gaius Julius Decuminus, to give him his full name, will take a bath after his long journey. Cornelius and the boys have not yet bathed today, so they will join him.

7 A Story

Marcus was told not to play with his uncle's sword. But he did, and that's how he cut his hand. 'Sit down Marcus,' says his father. 'I'm going to tell you a story.

'Once upon a time when the world was young, the gods moved about their business, keeping the earth a pleasant place to live in. Neptune ruled the seas, Diana lit the different faces of the moon and Phoebus drove his sun chariot across the sky every day.

'Phoebus was a magnificent god, dressed in gold and silver with a shining crown on his head. Few could look at him without being dazzled. Every morning his slaves decked him in all his finery whilst those in the coach-house cleaned and polished the chariot. The stable boys groomed the four strong and spirited horses, ready for the time when their master would take his place at the start of the day.

'And every morning, Phoebus drove the glittering team up the steep slope of the sky, bringing light, warmth and life to the people below.

'Phoebus had a son named Phaeton, whom he had never seen. Many times the boy had asked his mother to take him to meet his father but she had always refused. The journey to the east was far too long and difficult she said.

'The boys at his school jeered at Phaeton and told him that they didn't believe his father was a god. He was so upset that at last his mother said she would take him to see Phoebus. Perhaps the god could think of some, way to prove to the boys at school that Phaeton's father really was the sun god.

'Many weeks later, they arrived at the magnificent eastern palace. Phoebus was overjoyed to see his son and when he heard what the trouble was, he offered the boy his crown. Phaeton was not sure that anyone would believe him just because he had a golden crown.

'"Father," he said, "Would you let me drive your chariot across the sky? If the boys saw me doing that they would have to believe me."

'Both his parents tried to turn him aside from this mad idea. "It takes all my strength to control the horses," said his father. "How do you think you will manage?" But nothing they said could put the boy off. Sadly Phoebus dressed his son in a suit of armour to protect him from the heat and told him what to do.

'"Don't swerve away from the track," he said, "and don't, whatever you do, use the whip or the horses will bolt."

'Phaeton was pleased and proud to be driving his father's chariot across the heavens but the heat bothered him and it was all he could do to hold the team on its course. Time after time he was only just able to keep them on the track. It seemed to be taking ages to get to the highest point. After a more violent swerve than all the others, Phaeton forgot his father's words and flicked at the animals with his whip.

'The horses went crazy, plunging and rearing wildly. The more the boy tried to rein them in, the worse things got. When they soared high above the track, he became dizzy looking down at the vast depths below. When they shot down earthwards, they got so close to the ground that the grass was scorched. Lakes dried up, rivers changed their courses and forests caught fire. The Sahara was turned in an instant from a pleasant area of farmland to the desert we know today.

'Now, totally out of control, the chariot lurched along the paths of heaven. To prevent any more damage Jupiter, the lord of the gods, took a thunderbolt and hurled it at the terrified horses. The missile destroyed the chariot and cut the horses free, but Phaeton,' Cornelius paused and looked at his son, 'Phaeton was killed.'

There was a short silence and then Marcus said in a small voice, 'Sorry Father; I won't do it again.'

8 Maiden Castle

This man's name is Vespasian. He was the commander of the Second Legion, the *Augusta*, as it was called. His legion was sent to Britain to conquer the tribes in the southern part of the country. Suetonius, a Roman writer, tells us that Vespasian's legion captured over twenty fortified towns. One of these towns was Maiden Castle in Dorset.

This is Maiden Castle. Apart from its great ditches it doesn't look much like a stronghold. But here is what it must have looked like in AD 43 or 44 as it faced Vespasian's soldiers. You can see that it is not as big as a modern town. But it does have streets, houses and barns.

Between 1934 and 1937 a team of archaeologists began to dig at Maiden Castle. The team was led by Sir Mortimer Wheeler. From the skeletons and objects the archaeologists found, we know something about the

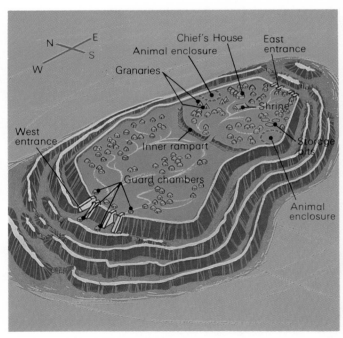

fierce battle Vespasian fought here.

The tribesmen were not afraid of the legions. Their stronghold had always kept them safe from their enemies. From the ditches their warriors could hurl pebbles as big as apples. They used slings to throw them further. Above all, the tribe would be fighting downhill whilst the enemy was struggling up. But the town had never faced a well-drilled Roman army; nor one with siege weapons.

9 The Attack

When the legions arrived they did not begin to fight straight away. Vespasian and his officers rode round the hill several times looking for the weakest place to attack. They decided on the eastern gates.

Next day the chief of the tribe and his men looked down from the gates. They saw the Romans slowly wheeling their siege engines into position. The catapults and ballistas came near enough to hurl rocks and shoot bolts at the Britons. But the Romans were out of range of the British slings.

Soon the bombardment began. It drove the defenders out of the lowest ditch and splintered one of the big wooden gates. Then some of the legionaries formed themselves into a 'testudo' or tortoise. You can see from the picture on page 39 why it was called a tortoise. The men fought their way through the maze of ditches towards the damaged entrance. Those in the middle of the tortoise carried a huge log. They would use it to batter down the broken gate.

While this was going on the Romans were hurling javelins and more stones at the Britons. Every time a defender showed his head above the ramparts he was risking his life. At last the trumpets sounded the advance. The main body of the legionaries put their shields above their heads. Led by their officers they charged towards the town. Soon the Romans were swarming up the slope. They captured ditch after ditch, leaving dead and wounded tribesmen behind them. In the last ditch they came to some huts and quickly set them on fire. As the smoke and flames rose into the sky the legionaries burst through the great gates.

The tribesmen and even their wives fought fiercely but they were no match for the Romans. By the late afternoon the few remaining defenders were forced to give up and the battle was over.

The next day the prisoners had to bury

their dead. There was no time to hold proper burial ceremonies. Food and drink were put in most of the graves to help the dead warriors in the afterlife. The Romans pulled down the massive gates at the west end of the town. Then they destroyed the rest of the defences. Vespasian selected hostages and his army moved off to their next battle.

Here are some of the things that were found by the archaeologists. They are now in the museum at Dorchester. Many of the skulls had been split by Roman swords. One man must have died during the first bombardment of the gate. You can see a catapulta bolt sticking in his spine. This man below is holding a joint of lamb. Somebody must have thought he might get hungry on his way to the next world.

10 The Signifer

This tombstone is from Caerleon on the Welsh border. It tells us about a Roman soldier. The writing means: 'To the Gods of the Underworld. Gaius Valerius Victor, son of Galeria of Lugdunum,* standard bearer to the Second Legion, *Augusta*. He served seventeen years and died aged forty-five.'

A legion had a brass eagle as its main emblem. It was carried by a senior officer and always had a small group of men to guard it. It was a disgrace to lose the eagle in battle. Romans often fought for years to get back one which had been captured from them.

Gaius did not carry the legion's eagle. He was a Signifer, or standard bearer. Every legion had several cohorts, each divided into centuries. Every group had its own standard so there must have been about sixty of them in a legion.

A Signifer had to be brave but not so brave that he led his men into danger when there was no need. Gaius had joined the legion in France, the country where he was born. He trained under strict centurions. Soon he became a good soldier and was promoted.

In the year AD 43, the Emperor Claudius ordered the Augusta and three other legions to attack Britain. The commander of the Augusta was Vespasian. He later became emperor himself.

Vespasian led his men to victory in thirty

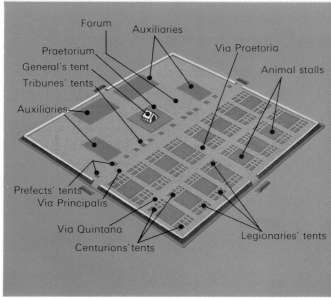

A Roman marching camp

Forum
Auxiliaries
Praetorium
Via Praetoria
General's tent
Animal stalls
Tribunes' tents
Auxiliaries
Prefects' tents
Via Principalis
Via Quintana
Legionaries' tents
Centurions' tents

*Lugdunum was the Roman name for Lyon in France.

battles. The legion captured the Isle of Wight and over twenty hill forts. You can read on pages 38 and 39 how they took Maiden Castle.

Every time a legion stopped for the night, the soldiers made a camp. They set up the tents and made a wall of earth all around them. Four years after they landed, the Romans had overrun most of south-east England. Some of the camps were rebuilt in wood, brick and stone. One of these camps became the fortress of Glevum (Gloucester) and another became Isca (Caerleon).

The soldiers made roads to join the forts. The Second Legion made Caerleon its base. Some of the soldiers left it from time to time to do other jobs. Some started a lead mine in Somerset. Some built part of Hadrian's wall.

Gaius, as a sort of senior sergeant, had to look after his men when they were at Isca. He held inspections and helped train the new recruits. He saw that each soldier got his pay and he ran the camp savings bank.

We don't know how or when Gaius died. There are not many records of the period. Tombstones can give us a few facts with which to make a picture of life in those days. For example, this stone, bearing the unlikely name of Longinus Sdapezematygus, tells us that he was a Greek, aged 40, who had served as a horse soldier. Those who dug up the stone in Colchester say that it was probably knocked over and damaged by some of Boudicca's rebels.

11 Roman Ships

We don't know as much about the ships the Romans used as we do about the villas and towns in which they lived. The remains of Roman buildings are often found. Ships are made of wood and wood quickly rots away in the salt sea water. But the Romans did write about their ships. Sometimes they carved pictures of them on buildings and monuments. Here is a picture of the types of ship Vespasian would have used to bring his legionaries and their baggage from Gaul to Britain.

Remains of a Roman ship found at Blackfriars in London

12 The Ninth Legion

It is AD 61. Let's visit the Ninth Legion at Lincoln, or Lindum, as it was called then. The legion should have between five and six thousand men but a number of them are away in the north of Britain, some are on leave and a few are in hospital.

The legionaries are on parade. One of them is called Gaius Saufeis. When the roll-call is complete, the centurions tell the tribunes, or junior officers, that there are only about fifteen hundred foot-soldiers plus a few mounted men. The tribunes report this to the legate, or commanding officer.

The legate's name is Quintus Petillius Cerialis. He pats his horse's neck and speaks to the legion. 'Men of the Ninth,' he says, 'You bear a proud name – "Hispana". In the next few days you will have the chance to bring it even more honour. This morning news reached me that the Iceni tribe to the south of here have revolted. We must teach Boudicca, their queen, a lesson. Be ready to march in an hour.'

Gaius Saufeis

The men go to fetch what they need. They will have to carry two fencing poles, a spade, cooking pots, food and spare clothes, as well as their armour and weapons.

It is an unlucky expedition. Boudicca has more than 100,000 men and the legionaries of the Ninth stand no chance, in spite of their better discipline and training. Gaius falls with a sword-cut in his leg and cannot move. Towards the end of the battle hardly any of the foot-soldiers are left alive and the cavalry are forced to break off the fight and escape. A horseman hauls Gaius on to his saddle and gallops away. Gaius does not live long after the battle. Although the doctors at the camp hospital do what they can, he dies from his infected wound.

His body is buried alongside a road leading out from Lindum and this is the tombstone his friends put over the grave. The words are hard to read but this is what they say: 'To Gaius Saufeis, son of Gaius, of the Fabian

Tribe, born in Heraclea, soldier of the Ninth Legion, aged forty. He served for twenty-two years. He lies here.' The stone was dug up on the west side of Lincoln High Street in 1865 and is now in the British Museum.

There is a mystery about the Ninth. Early in the second century all trace of it vanishes. Some people say that it left Britain for another part of the Roman Empire and that it is the records which have disappeared, not the Legion.

Rosemary Sutcliff in her book, *The Eagle of the Ninth*, tells an exciting story of how it might have been cut to pieces while fighting in Scotland. We just don't know the truth.

Eagle from a Roman standard found at Silchester

13 An Unsolved Murder

This is Hadrian's wall. It was built about eighty years after the first Roman landing in Britain. It marked the boundary of the Roman empire and ran for 73 miles right across the north of England. Housesteads is one of the largest of its forts and stands about half-way along the wall.

Many people go to see what is left of it and there is still much to look at. The visitor ought to try to picture what went on in a Roman border fort, otherwise he will see no more than a jumble of stone blocks. We know a great deal about Housesteads fort and how it was run. But we have few details about any of the people who lived there.

The soldiers slept in the barrack blocks and spent much of their time drilling, marching, patrolling and parading. Their commander liked to keep them busy because he knew that boredom is a soldier's worst enemy. The legionaries might be fed up with all these tiresome duties but they would feel worse with nothing to do at all.

Perhaps the commander got his junior officers to organize a sporting contest or two. A boxing or wrestling tournament might take the men's minds off their dreary army life. The fort is miles from civilization and the men had very little to spend their pay on — small though it was. Let's imagine a story about two of the legionaries.

Gambling is one way soldiers have of getting rid of their money. The commander knows that this leads to quarrels and fights so he has banned it but it still goes on secretly. One of the places he suspects is a shop in the civilian settlement. This settlement grew up just outside the south gate and has

houses, shops and wine bars. The commander turns a blind eye to what goes on outside the fort provided that there is no trouble. One unpleasant incident he never found out about.

Late one morning, two legionaries who are free from guard duties for the day stroll over to the shop in the settlement. We may imagine them trying their luck with the dice. We can picture the British husband and wife who run the place serving them with drinks as the afternoon wears on. Darkness falls outside and in the dimly lit back room, the woman switches the dice for a pair which are loaded with lead.

The soldiers are not too drunk to realize they are being cheated. A quarrel flares up. One of the soldiers demands his money back. The Britons refuse and then try to bundle him out of the hut. As he pushes the woman away she stumbles, falls and hits her head on the sharp corner of a stool. Her husband bends over her.

'You've killed her!' he shouts. 'I'll call the guard. Murder! Mur –.' He never finishes. One of the soldiers tries to frighten him into silence by drawing his sword.

The man closes with him, grabbing for his right arm. As he does so, the soldier's sword goes into him. He chokes and slips to the ground. The legionaries gaze in horror at the two corpses, one of them with a sword sticking out of its chest. Between them, they wrench the sword out of the body but the end breaks off as they do so.

The murderers decide to try and hide the evidence of their crime. One of them has noticed a pile of fresh clay at the back of the shop. He finds a shovel and the two men dig a hole in the floor of the hut. They cram the bodies into it, cover the entire area with the clay and stamp it down.

Somehow or other, one of them manages to get a replacement for the broken sword and no one finds out about the killings.

'But,' you will say, 'how do we know if no one ever found out?' Well, you were warned that this was an imaginary story.

However, parts of it are true. A team of archaeologists were digging up the fort and its surrounding buildings in 1932. In the foundations of one of the shops they found, underneath the clay floor, the skeletons of a middle-aged man and woman. What is more, the man's remains had the sword point broken off in its ribs.

14 Roman London

This is what London looked like in Roman times. It was called Londinium. We can't be sure the map is right in all its details because the bricks and stones the Romans used are now buried under modern pavements. They only come to light when old buildings are pulled down.

There were streets, houses, shops, temples, hotels, offices and baths. Some people lived in flats and had to go to the public baths. Richer families had big houses with enough space for their own private set of bathrooms.

This picture shows all that is left of the baths belonging to a large house in Londinium. Back in 1848, when workmen were knocking down a row of old houses, they found a lot of Roman tiles. They showed them to Mr. Bunning, the man in charge, who told them to dig carefully. Soon they had uncovered the hot room of the baths.

Over a century later, the offices which Mr. Bunning's workmen had put up were knocked down. More rooms of the Roman baths were found. They took up a larger area than most modern houses.

15 The Baths

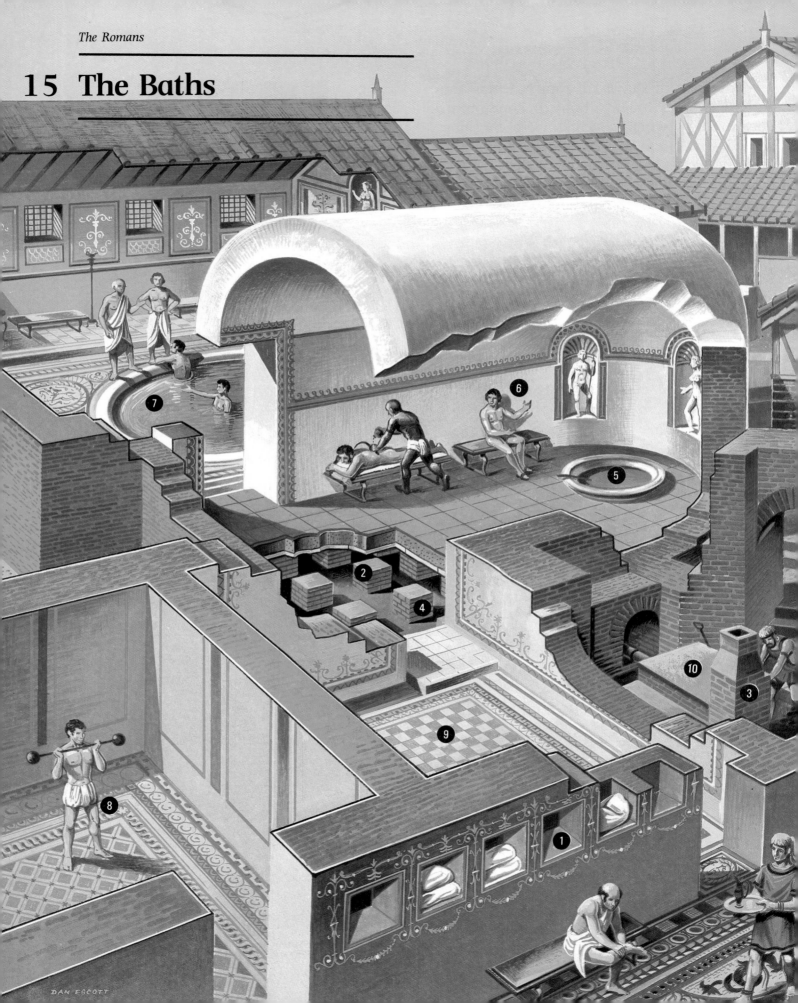

Some Roman houses had Turkish baths and others had saunas. Very rich families might have had both. A Turkish bath will steam you, the sauna uses dry heat. In both cases the idea is to make you perspire. Let's pretend you are going to have a Turkish bath.

You leave your clothes in the first room (1). In the second one you might do some press-ups or weight-lifting to start you sweating. At a public bath, there would have been a gymnasium where you could join in a ball game. Roman children were fond of playing 'touch' or leapfrog there.

The next room is warmer and the last one hotter still. The Romans kept up the heat by means of a hypocaust (2), which you can see in the picture.

Look at the slaves stoking the furnace (3). The gases from the fire are swirling round the brick pillars (4) and making the tiled floor hot. There is a huge basin of water in the corner (5). If you splash the water on to the tiles, it will cause clouds of steam and make the air misty.

There wasn't any soap in Roman times, so you will probably get a slave to rub you down with olive oil (6). You feel yourself getting hotter. All the little pores in your skin open, and the oil and perspiration carry away the dirt. Then you have to scrape off all the dirty oil with an implement called a strigil.

You walk to the next room and dive into a cold plunge bath (7). You swim a few strokes and climb out, shaking the hair out of your eyes. A good rub down with a rough towel makes you glow all over. All you have to do now is pull your tunic on and slip your feet into your sandals.

Key to Roman Baths **1** lockers for clothing **2** hypocaust **3** chimney **4** pilae, **5** bowl of cold water **6** caldarium **7** cold plunge bath **8** gymnasium **9** tepidarium **10** furnace

Strigil and oil pot

We don't know who the people were who lived in the house at Lower Thames Street, nor do we know how it came to be in ruins. By AD 450 the remains of the bath house seem to have been used as a rubbish dump. By that time, the soldiers had gone home to defend Rome from its enemies. The Saxons invaded most of south-east England.

A Saxon warrior, wandering through the half-empty city, noticed water gushing up through broken bricks. He wondered where it was coming from. He did not know that it was the spring which had fed the baths. He climbed on to the heaps of rubble, searching for the source. Unluckily for him, one of the two brooches which fastened his cloak came undone and dropped down out of sight. He couldn't find it.

The brooch didn't see the light of day again until 1968 when the rest of the Roman building was dug up. Not far from where the Saxon had lost his brooch, the diggers also found a number of Roman coins. The family had most likely hidden them when the Saxons first attacked London. They were no doubt hoping that the invaders would go away and that they would be able to come and live in the house again.

1 Romans and their Gods

This is a scene in a Roman temple in London. It is the temple of Jupiter, the most important of the Roman gods. The visitor prays to Jupiter that he will have a safe journey. He pours a little wine on the altar in front of the statue as an offering.

He could choose to go to any of the temples in Roman London, each built to house the statue of a different god. On the opposite page are some of the gods.

The Romans don't mind how many gods the people worship. Just as long as no one says that his is the only god, he can pray to dozens of different ones on the same day if he wants to. The Romans have even brought back a few gods from abroad. They have built altars and

temples to these gods too. The law says that
the citizen must also bow down to statu of
the emperor. The emperors of Rome do ot
like the gods of Britain. This is prob y
because the Druids refused to let the C s
make peace with the legions. However, Ce
gods are still worshipped in some plac
sometimes by Romans themselves.

1–3 C
left P Mercury; *5* Mars; *6* Mithras; *7* Mars
r from the Temple of Jupiter in London

2 The Christians

Christian secret sign from Ephesus

There is another group the Romans cannot stand. These are the Christians who will not bow down to any statue at all. The emperors put them in prison, flog them or throw them to the lions in the arena. Even in Britain the Christians have to keep their beliefs hidden.

They meet where and when they can. For safety's sake, they have to have passwords and secret signs. This is so that a Christian will know if a stranger is a friend or an enemy.

For three hundred years Christians were arrested, tortured and killed. The Romans thought they were trouble-makers but the more they tried to stamp out the followers of Christ, the more of them there were.

Roger Payne

3 St. Alban

Have you ever been to St. Alban's in Hertfordshire? It was an important town in Roman times and some ancient parts of it can still be seen. If you travel by coach, you will probably get out in the car park and go to look at the finds in the museum. Here are pictures of some of them.

Shell mosaic

Statue of Venus

Lamp chimney

They give you an idea of what life must have been like for the people who lived in Verulamium, as they called it, nearly 2,000 years ago. These museum objects are not all that there is to see. You can go and look at the ruins of a Roman villa with its underfloor heating still in place. You might like to trace the remains of the town walls and gateways and see what is left of the Roman shops and the theatre. If you did all that, you would probably be tired out with walking. You won't have the energy to do more than look at the church in the distance. It's too far away and it isn't Roman anyway.

But why isn't the modern town still called Verulamium? The reason is quite interesting.

When the Romans had been in Britain for over two hundred years, a man named Diocletian became emperor. He found the empire too big to run all by himself, so he split it into two halves, the Eastern and Western Empires. Then he turned to the problem of the Christians.

There were more of them than ever. There were Christians in the army and even in the emperor's own palace. The trouble was that they seemed to be willing to die rather than give up their beliefs. This made many ordinary Romans think that it must be a fine religion if men and women would sooner face death than give it up. So more people became followers of Jesus.

In the year 303, Diocletian gave an order that everything the Christians owned was to

Reconstruction of the forum at St. Albans

A town house

The theatre

be taken from them, their churches torn down and the people themselves made into slaves.

A Christian in Verulamium was warned one night that the soldiers were coming to arrest him. Someone had told the officer that he was not only a Christian but a priest as well. He decided that the best thing he could do was to try to get away from the town as quickly as possible.

Unluckily for him, the soldiers saw him as he was leaving the house and they gave chase. He ran as fast as he could, down streets, across squares and through narrow alleys. He doubled round the side of the theatre and along the back of the silent, empty shops.

He stopped to listen and catch his breath. A door opened near him and a slave girl beckoned him in. She had heard the sounds of people running and had come to see what was happening. She was also a Christian, a slave working for an army officer named Albanus, or Alban. She recognized the priest but before she could hide him, Alban himself appeared.

They had to tell him the truth and he asked why the priest didn't give up his faith and save himself from death. The priest replied and they went on talking for most of the night. Then the soldiers started a house-to-house search. When they came to Alban's house, he had changed clothes with the priest and taken his place. The priest escaped but Alban was put to death.

In later years, Christians were allowed to worship openly and their religion became the official one for the whole empire. The Christians in the town built their new church on the spot where Alban had been executed. The Church in Rome made him a saint. A new town grew up round the local church. It was called St. Albans in his memory. St. Albans is still there but Roman Verulamium lies in ruins.

A modern representation of St. Alban

4 Saxon Raids

At the time that Alban was born, a danger appeared to those who were Christians and those who were not. To find out what it was, let us pretend we can go back into the past and watch what is happening. We are looking at a fishing village in Roman Britain. The year is 285. The village is in ruins. Everything seems to have been smashed, stolen or burnt. Let's ask one of the boys from the village how it happened.

'*What's been going on here, Tiso?*'

'I'm not sure myself yet. The men were loading their nets on to the boats, ready to go fishing, when I spotted three ships making for the shore. I knew they were not our ships. They weren't Roman ones either. They were long and wide and had neither mast nor sail. The crew were all rowing with long oars. Our

above and right Weapons of the time

men were not sure what to do. They didn't know if the strangers were going to be friendly or not. Most of our men went up to the village to find what weapons they could. Marwed has gone to the fort to fetch the centurion.'

'*What happened next?*'

'Well, the strangers ran their ships on to the beach and started to walk towards us. They were quite tall with fair hair and they were all carrying shields and swords or axes. My father tried to talk to them but they just knocked him down. There was nothing we could do except hide. There were far too many of them.'

'*What did they want?*'

'Anything they could get. They loaded their ships with our corn, sheep and valuables. I think they even took some of the older children. My friend Dracus was carried off. Then they set fire to the village. We're bound to starve'.

As Tiso is talking, a column of legionaries with their centurion is marching down to the beach. They are far too late. The three Saxon ships are black specks on the horizon.

'Saxons, eh?' says the centurion. 'Don't worry, we'll have a working party sent out to help rebuild the village and we'll send some rations over. Next time they dare show their

faces, we'll be ready for 'em'.

Unluckily for the Britons, more Saxons came in the next few years. Once in a while the Roman soldiers caught them but most of the time, the raiders attacked so quickly that they were gone before anything could be done.

5 The End of the Empire

Collapse of the Roman empire

Britain was not the only part of the empire to be attacked. Every few years, news would arrive that enemy tribes had broken through the frontiers. The commander of the British legions would then have to take his soldiers to help defend the empire against the hordes of wild tribesmen who wanted to smash it.

When that happened, the Saxon raiders had more time to murder and plunder. They knew that there were no troops about so they moved further inland. They brought more

ships from their homelands in Germany and Denmark. There were plenty of Saxons willing to row hundreds of miles across the North Sea if there were easy pickings to be had at the end of the voyage.

Nearly all of the Britons who had lived in villages on the coast thought it better to move away to where they felt safer. The Saxons followed them up the rivers leading inland. Then they would fill their ships with loot from places ever farther from the sea.

Sometimes the Saxons would come upon a small town. They were not interested in the underfloor heating of the houses, nor in the temples, churches and baths. All they wanted was the treasure inside them. They smashed down doors and stole whatever they fancied. When they had got all they wanted, they often had a feast. A few of the cattle they had taken would be killed, roasted and eaten.

They did not admire the fine villas. They were just as likely to break up tables and stools to make a fire in the middle of a beautiful mosaic floor.

When the legions had dealt with the troubles in the empire, they came back to Britain and drove off the Saxons once more. Many years later, the tribes in Europe broke through the frontiers in several places at once. The Roman troops had to leave yet again.

If you had been down in the docks at Dover on a spring morning in the year 410, you would have seen more soldiers than you had ever seen before. They are being marched on to the ships.

The little girl does not know it but this time the legions will not be coming back. Before her life is over, Rome itself will have been conquered and the empire will be at an end.

6 Saxon Settlements

When the Saxons found that the legions did not come back, they spread further into England. Then they heard that Rome itself had been captured. Now they could stay here for good, provided they could beat the Britons.

One thing was sure. If they stayed, they would have to change their way of life. It was all very well raiding villages and towns but they couldn't keep on doing this. Once they had driven out the Britons, there was nothing left to steal because there was nobody to raise cattle or plant corn.

A few Saxons came as families with wives and children. Others married young British women. The settlers gave their villages Saxon names which often end in 'ing', 'ham' or 'ton'. The only British words they took over were the names of nearby hills and rivers which they may have learned from their British wives.

The Britons called all the invaders 'Saxons' but there were many different tribes, such as Jutes, Angles and even Franks.

What did the Britons do without the legions to help them? We can't be sure but there are legends, or stories, told. One of these says that the Britons found a man to train them and lead them against the Saxons. The legends say his name was Arthur. If he existed,

this is what Arthur might have looked like. Later, all sorts of wild legends were invented with Arthur as their hero. Most of them couldn't have been true.

It is possible that there was a great fighter called Arthur and that he fought many battles against the Saxons. He may have stopped them taking over the whole of England – for a time. The Saxons gave up trying to push westward and seemed content to stay in the lands they had already taken. Then, perhaps a hundred years after Arthur's time, they were on the move again.

This time there was no great leader to stop them. They beat the Britons and drove them into the mountains of the west and north. They set up their own Saxon kingdoms and began farming the land.

Do you remember the Saxon warrior who

The Saxon's brooch

Suthrige kingdom

lost one of his cloak brooches while he was wandering over the ruins of a Roman bath house? We don't know his name but we think we know where he went. He belonged to a band of Saxons which set up a kingdom to the south of the River Thames. It was actually named 'The South Kingdom'. In the Saxons' own language it was 'Suth Rige'. It sounded, perhaps, like 'Soo-three-er'. If you don't say it carefully, it ends up as 'Surrey'.

Our Saxon died and was buried at Mitcham in Surrey. Of course, we can't be completely certain that it was the same man but a brooch was buried with him. It was the twin of the one found in London.

7 Angles or Angels?

When the Saxons first came to Britain, they had gods and goddesses of their own. We know some of these because most of the days of the week are named after them. Tiw, the war god, Woden, the father of the gods and Thor, the god of thunder, gave their names to Tuesday, Wednesday and Thursday. Friday comes from the goddess Frig. The Saxon days of the sun and moon are our Sunday and Monday.

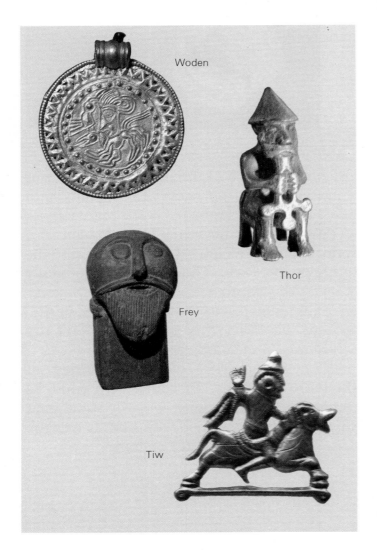

Woden

Thor

Frey

Tiw

Pope Gregory

Christianity died out in England with the coming of the Saxons. There were of course a few Christians among the Britons who had been driven westward to Wales and Cornwall or northward towards Scotland. In these British lands the knowledge of Jesus was kept alive.

Gregory was the son of a rich Christian family in Rome. He became a judge. Then his father died and left him a fortune. He gave it all away and went to live as a poor monk in a monastery. In a few years, he was put in charge of the monastery as abbot. The Bishop of Rome asked him to help organize the Church which was growing fast.

Rome had once been the capital of a great

empire. Now it was becoming the chief city of the Christians. Sad to say, there was at least one thing that had not changed since the days of the emperors. This was slavery.

One day Gregory was passing the slave market when he saw some boys with fair hair who were about to be sold. Their skins were pale and Gregory was puzzled. Most slaves were dark haired and brown skinned. He asked a man where they came from. 'Angle land,' said the man. 'They are Angles.'

Gregory said, 'They look more like angels than Angles.' The man looked surprised.

'They are nothing like angels,' he said. 'They are fierce, savage heathens.'

'Are they indeed?' said Gregory. Then he added, half to himself, 'How wonderful it would be to go to Angle land and tell them about Jesus Christ.'

He put this idea to the bishop and to his surprise, he was allowed to go. Joyfully, he got ready. There was little to pack. He and the monks he chose to go with him took only a little food. They would be staying in a different monastery each night and walking all day.

They had travelled for only three days when they were overtaken by a messenger on horseback. He told them that the bishop was dead and that they must return to Rome. Gregory found that the old man had died of the plague. Christians were beginning to look up to the bishop as head of the whole Church, or Pope, which actually means 'Father'.

Gregory realized that everyone wanted him as the next leader. He tried to say he was not good enough to be Pope but there was no one else to take on the job. He was so busy in his new position, he knew he would never go to the land of his 'angels'. He didn't forget them, though.

In the year 596 he sent for Augustine, a monk from his old monastery. Augustine was told that he had been chosen to lead a team of monks to rescue the Angles from their heathen ways.

8 The Missionaries

Early in the spring of the year 597 Augustine left Rome for Angle land with forty monks. The first part of their journey followed the footsteps of Gregory, but soon they had passed the place where he had turned back. They pressed on, talking excitedly of what they would do when they got to Angle land.

They met a cloth merchant leading a train of horses with packs on their backs. He asked them where they were going. He seemed surprised when they told him, 'Angle land'.

'I wouldn't go to England if you paid me a fortune,' he said. The monks wanted to know what he meant. He told them that the English were cruel, bloodthirsty savages who hated strangers. 'They won't let you land,' said the merchant, 'or, if they do, you won't get a chance to tell them about Jesus. They will kill you, most likely.'

The monks were frightened and refused to go on. After an argument, they went back to Rome where Gregory tried to calm their fears. 'Of course they are savages,' he said. 'That is why they need the word of God. They will let you land and they will listen to you. Go and do God's work.'

The little band set out again, not very willingly, and after a long journey they landed in east Kent. Augustine held a short service to thank God for their safe arrival and to ask His help in the task before them. It seemed to him that their prayers had been answered when a message arrived from Ethelbert, the King of Kent.

The king ordered Augustine to come and see him. To Augustine's delight, he found that King Ethelbert's wife, Berta, was already a Christian. She persuaded her husband to let the missionaries preach and even to build churches. The first church the monks put up was near the place where they had landed. Its foundations can still be seen amid the ruins of the Roman fort at Richborough. The second tiny chapel was built in Canterbury, the king's chief town. There is a church there to this day. It is called Canterbury Cathedral. Of course, the cathedral wasn't started until long after.

Queen Berta's daughter, Ethelburga, went to the north of England to marry Edwin, King of Northumbria. With her she took Paulinus, one of Augustine's monks. Paulinus did his best to talk Edwin into becoming a Christian but the king was not sure.

One night, after supper in the king's great wooden hall, the talk turned to religion. Edwin asked his thanes, or lords, what they thought. Some were for Paulinus, some were for the old gods. In the silence that followed a bird flew into the hall. It was lit for a moment by the candles and the bright firelight and then it was gone.

Remains of St. Augustine's Church in the Roman fort at Richborough

An old man who had not spoken until then raised his head. 'It seems to me,' he said, 'that the life of a man is like the flight of that bird. No man knows where it came from nor where it has gone. Is my life no more than a few moments in the light and then darkness without end?' No one spoke and the old man went on. 'I say that if Paulinus and the god he serves can give us hope of a life after death, we should listen to him.'

Paulinus converted many of the northerners and became England's second bishop, with his cathedral at York.

There were many setbacks but slowly the Saxons were converted. So were many of the Britons in Ireland, Wales, Scotland and Cornwall. Nearly all the missionaries were later honoured by being made saints. They are Saints Aidan, Augustine, Patrick, Columba, David, Wilfrid, Cedd and Chad.

9 A Ship Burial

The children in this picture are dressed as Vikings. They look as though they are burning a longship. They aren't Vikings and the boat is only a model. The men are celebrating the end of winter at Lerwick in the Shetlands. They call what they are doing 'Up-Helly-Aa' and the reason for the Viking dress is that the Shetland Islands to the north of Scotland once belonged to both Norway and Denmark.

The flaming ship may remind you of the old Norse custom of putting a chief's dead body on his ship, setting fire to it and sending it out to sea. Another kind of ship burial came to light in 1938 when a Suffolk lady named Mrs. Pretty decided to have a closer look at some strangely shaped mounds on her land. She lived close to the River Deben at a place called Sutton Hoo, near Ipswich. The man in charge of the digging was a Mr. Basil Brown.

The diggers cut their way into three of the little hillocks and found that they all contained burials. One was very interesting as the body had been put in a boat before being covered with earth. Unluckily, all three graves had been robbed and there was little to show for the work done.

The following year Mrs. Pretty made up her mind to dig into a new mound, the highest one on her land. No sooner had the digging started, when rows of iron rivets came to light. It was plainly another ship, and a big one at that. Like the other vessel, it showed signs of having been attacked by grave robbers, so Mr. Brown wasn't too hopeful.

However, he went to work, carefully removing the sand from the inside of the ship. Almost all the wood had rotted away and the only way he could tell where it had been was the pattern of iron rivets. The diggers had just enough time to take out the things they found in the bottom of the hole before the Second World War broke out and the dig had to be filled in again to protect it from enemy bombers.

The objects found in the ship were cleaned and are now preserved at the British Museum. They proved that the ship burial at Sutton Hoo was the richest and most important Saxon archaeological find ever made in Britain.

Belt buckle

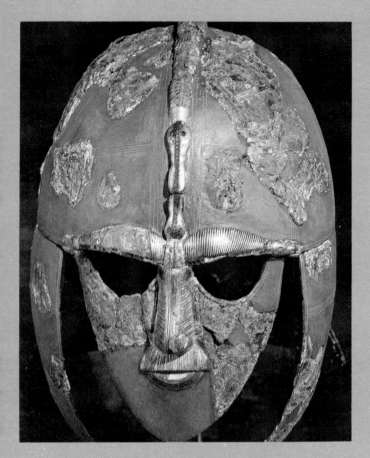

Objects found in the Sutton Hoo ship-burial

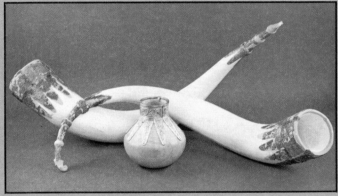

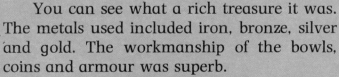

You can see what a rich treasure it was. The metals used included iron, bronze, silver and gold. The workmanship of the bowls, coins and armour was superb.

The value of these things was so great, the experts believe they must have marked the grave of a king. They even think they know which king it was. The coins gave a date in the early 7th century, so it is quite likely that the ruler was Raedwald, Saxon King of East Anglia, who died about 624.

Most of the grave goods show the burial to be that of a pagan chieftain. Most, but not all. There are two silver spoons with Christian markings. Could it be that Raedwald was trying to make sure he went to heaven but was uncertain whether this would be the Christian paradise or the Valhalla of the old Norse gods?

Chapter Four   The Saxons

1 The Family

Wulfstan is a thane, or lord. He is going to tell us why his people came to England and a little about his family.

'They came in great ships,' he says, 'from the other side of the North Sea, where our home once was. The land there was poor and would not grow very much. We were hungry a lot of the time. We got better at building ships and taking them to sea. If we couldn't grow enough food on our farms we could at least catch fish to eat. It isn't easy to catch fish and it's a lot more dangerous than growing oats.

'After a while, we decided to try to find a better land to settle in. That was years ago, of course, soon after the Romans left Britain. I was born here and so were my three children.

'Cedfric is my eldest child, and Athelm my youngest. Edbur, the only girl, comes in between. Their ages are twelve, nine and seven. Cedfric is already learning to be a thane like me. He is being taught how to use sword and spear so that he can take my place one day.

'As one of the king's chief soldiers, I have to fight for him when there's a war. In peace time I try to protect the villages in this area. I help the farmers by hunting down the wild animals which would eat or damage their crops. All these things Cedfric will have to do when he grows up.

'My other two children are different from Cedfric. Edbur is practical and Athelm is a dreamer but both are clever. No one could say that about Cedfric!

'Edbur is good at embroidery and sewing and she mustn't waste her life married to some farmer. Athelm will never earn his living by farming or fighting. He does nothing very much except stare and wonder. I shall soon have to tell Athelm what I have planned for him. The boy doesn't know it yet but the king has offered him a place in his new school at Winchester.

'Our king, Alfred, thinks that some of the brighter children ought to know how to read and write. I wasn't educated myself; nor was anyone else in this village. I'm not sure whether it's a good thing or not. Look at Eswy, the swineherd's son. Far from reading, he wouldn't even know what a book was. Yet he seems happy enough to look after the pigs and help his father on the farm.

'Now I think of it, none of the children here seem unhappy. Would they be better off if they could speak Latin? All the same, I can't see Athelm ploughing a field. These things may be fine for most of the other children but I suppose he will be better off at school. I'll tell him tomorrow when the king and the bishop come to see how we're getting on with the building of the new church.'

2 A Saxon Village

After the Saxon raiders had driven the Britons away into the hills, or even captured some of them, they set about making their own villages. Often they chose places fairly near river banks.

Much hard work was needed. Trees were chopped down and their roots pulled out by men using teams of oxen. The branches were lopped off the tree trunks. The wood was used to build the first houses.

When the land was cleared, the men shared it out. There were two or three very large fields for crops such as wheat, barley, oats, peas and beans. Most of the animals were kept together in another field where they could eat fresh grass. The men saved some of the grass from part of the field. They dried it and fed it to the animals in the winter. On the edges of the forest, pigs ate acorns and roots.

There were pits for the digging of stone, chalk and clay. Some of the women had beehives for honey. Near the small houses a few vegetables were grown. The women cut reeds from the river's edge. They were for thatching the roofs of the houses and barns. There were very few stone buildings in Saxon England. The thane's house was the biggest in the village but it was made of timber like all the others.

The small huts of the poorer peasants were crowded in the winter. Some farm animals had to be brought inside during the worst of the weather.

The farmers ploughed their long, thin strips of land with oxen. The soil was then raked with a harrow to break up the lumps. When it was fine enough, the seeds were scattered by hand and covered with soil. In the late summer the crops were harvested. It was hard, tiring work.

While the men worked in the fields, the women were busy too. They had to look after the young children and get the meals ready. Peasant women fed chickens, kept bees, milked goats, made cheese and brewed beer from barley. All women, whether rich or poor, had to be able to sew and spin, to weave cloth and make clothes. The poorer wives spent most of their time doing these things. The richer ones had slaves to do much of the work.

3 Saxon Churches

You can see how far the building of the church has got.

4 King Alfred

When the church is nearly finished, the bishop arrives with a lot of important-looking people. He goes to the stone cross to say prayers for the people of the village. They all kneel down while he is speaking. Athelm keeps staring at the bishop and those who have come with him. Most of them are splendidly dressed. Athelm doesn't know that one of the strangers is King Alfred himself.

The king is pleased to see how Wulfstan's church is getting on. Let's ask him why he is so keen on churches and learning.

'Well,' he says, 'I was taught to read and write when I was a child and later I learned Latin. I love books and I don't think we'd be any better than the Danes* without them. Nor can we be proper Christians unless some of us can read and learn how we are supposed to behave.

'You know that the Danes have taken half of this land? Well, I got to know them early in my life and I tell you that the way of learning is better than that of barbarism.'

We ask him about the Danes. 'My father was Ethelwulf, King of Essex, Kent and Wessex. When I was about twenty, the Danes attacked our neighbours, the Mercians. My elder brother and I took our soldiers to help them hit back. We won that time but in the next six years a lot happened. The Danes turned on us and when my father and brothers were all killed, I became king.

'We had beaten the Danes and they left us alone for a while. We used the breathing space to build up a fleet of fast, strong ships and

*'Danes' was Alfred's word for the Vikings.

A Saxon church today

strengthen the towns, or 'burghs', as we call them. It was just as well we did, for in the seventh year of my reign, the Danes came back.

'I was driven westward with only a few followers and had to hide for months among the islands of the Somerset marshes. I managed to raise a new army and we beat the Danes so soundly that it was years before they returned to the fight. When they did, we won again.

'Finally, their leader, Guthrum, agreed to sign a treaty with me at a village called Wedmore. I told him he must become a Christian and then promise not to attack us any more. In return, we Saxons let them keep the eastern part of England, or Danelaw, as they called it. They haven't bothered us since!

'We can now turn our minds to thoughts of peace. I want to make our laws fairer and simpler so that everyone knows where he stands. My school at Winchester is a beginning but I'd like to see more of them.

'That reminds me: where's your son Athelm, Wulfstan?'

Athelm is brought before Alfred and Wulfstan tells him he is to be sent to the king's school at the royal town of Winchester. He is too excited to thank the king properly, but the boy's smile shows how pleased he is.

5 Alfred's School

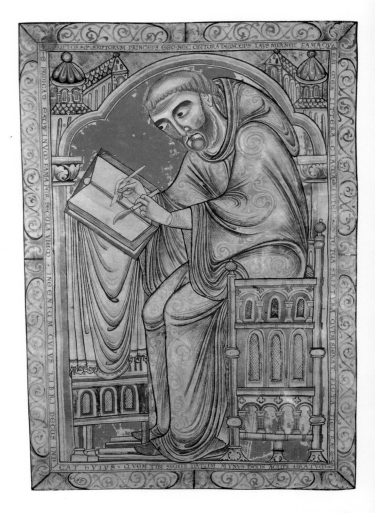

In the years after the Saxons had first become Christian, there were many churches and monasteries built. They needed prayer books and Bibles. The new schools also wanted books. In the days before printing had been invented, every single volume had to be copied out by hand. The Saxons were very good at doing this and soon monasteries in Europe were sending to England for their books. The Saxons had started out as pirates, become farmers and then found themselves the best copiers and artists in the whole of the Christian world.

The monks wrote the words out carefully in ink on parchment. To make the page more beautiful, they painted a coloured design or picture around the first letter of a chapter. Some Saxons did more than copy. They wrote their own books or translated Latin ones into English. A monk named Bede, who lived at Jarrow on the River Tyne, wrote a history of England in Latin. King Alfred himself learned Latin when he was nearly forty so that he could translate works by Latin authors for his people.

During the time of the Danish raids, the Saxons were too busy fighting to worry about books. Now that Alfred had made the Danes agree not to attack his lands, he could think about church matters and teaching the children once more. Let's visit Alfred's new school in his court at Winchester.

It is very early in the morning. The sun is not yet up. A monk goes round the dormitory waking the boys. They wash their hands and faces in cold water and get dressed. There are eleven boys, the youngest only five years old. Two of them are relations of King Alfred. The others, like Athelm, are boys who might make good priests or monks.

The priest blesses the children in Latin and they go off for their first lesson. Their classroom is a monk's cell. It is rather cramped and bare. The teacher sits on the only stool and the children on the floor. The first hour is spent on plain reading and writing in the Saxon language. The second hour is for Latin. They learn Latin prayers by heart but Alfred wants them to be able to understand the language. Then they can write to scholars abroad, no matter where the scholars live, and no matter what language they were brought up to. All educated men know Latin.

After two hours of lessons it is time for breakfast. The children go to a dining room with trestle tables and wooden benches. There is rye bread with goat's cheese, followed by a

bowl of porridge. To wash it down, there are cups of water. Then they must go to their third lesson.

Alfred wants them to be taught about the stars and planets. Those who will be priests when they grow up will then be able to work out the right times for holding the important feasts and fasts of the church year.

After dinner, the children go to another reading and writing lesson. Once the Saxons used letters called runes. By Alfred's time, everyone who can write at all uses the Roman alphabet, both for Latin and Saxon. The children start copying words and sentences on to a writing tablet, rather like the ones Roman schoolboys used.

Other lessons follow as the day goes on. The children are taught about the music used in church and spend a lot of their time studying the Bible itself. So many books are needed that the monastery has its own library. New books and copies of old ones are made in the scriptorium, or writing room.

Pages from two Saxon manuscripts

When the children can write really well, they may be allowed to use quill pens, ink and sheepskin parchment, as the monks do. The copies which the monks make are sent to churches all over Alfred's kingdom and even abroad.

At the end of the children's day, there is a light meal and another service in the chapel. Then, quite early in the evening, they go to bed.

6 Law and Order

Alfred made a new set of laws for his people. Each village held a court every month. The thane was in charge of the moot, as it was called. The court met outdoors on the top of a small mound. If the weather was bad, they met in the thane's house or in a barn.

We would not think the cases the court heard very important. They were mostly quarrels between neighbours. One man might complain that the thatcher had cheated him. Another might accuse a peasant of stealing his chickens. Then the peasant would have to bring his friends to tell the court that he was an honest man. If it was the first time he had been accused, the court would most likely believe them.

More serious cases were heard at the king's court. Punishments were much harsher than those in our time. A man who went on stealing might be branded or have his hand cut off. Hanging was the reward for a long list of crimes. Other wrongdoers were even burned or boiled to death.

If a man killed another in a fair fight, it was not thought of as murder, but a fine had to be paid to the dead man's family. This was done to stop blood feuds dragging on for years. The Saxons had a scale of fines to be paid if the fight ended with a wound rather than death. These fines were called 'wer-gild' ('man money').

Saxon coins

Sometimes the king, or the thane, could not make up his mind about a case. Then there would have to be a 'trial by ordeal'. Let's watch such a trial at Wulfstan's moot and ask him to explain what is happening.

'In this case,' explains Wulfstan, 'a man has been stabbed to death with a dagger. Witnesses say that the dagger belongs to Hod. One says he saw Hod near the dead man's house at the time of the murder. Hod says that everyone knows he and the dead man were friends. Another swears that Hod was mending a barn a mile away when the killing took place.

'I just couldn't decide,' says Wulfstan, 'so I talked it over with the elders. We have agreed to put Hod to the ordeal. He will have to walk three steps holding a bar of hot iron. Then his hands will be bandaged. If the burns are healing three days later, we will let him go. If they aren't, he will be found guilty. Sometimes the accused has to take a stone from the bottom of a cauldron of boiling water. The rest of the trial is the same.'

'What does this kind of trial prove, Wulfstan?'

'It shows God is watching,' he replies. 'God alone can heal a man's hand. He won't do that if the man is guilty.'

'What about the police?' we ask.

'Police?' says Wulfstan. 'I don't understand.'

We explain what police are and the thane nods. 'I see what you mean but we don't have anything like that. We have the tithing system. Each area has ten householders. They and their families form the tithing group. Every boy has to join a tithing when he is twelve. Each member keeps an eye on the others. A man isn't so likely to break the law if he knows he is being watched.

'Of course, men do commit crimes. When that happens, the suspect's tithing members must make sure he turns up for his trial. If he doesn't, they may have to pay a big fine. On top of this, the accused man is outlawed.

'I expect you know that an outlaw has no protection. He is outside the law. Anyone can kill him on sight without paying wer-gild or having to stand trial for murder.'

7 A Story

This is Wayland's Smithy near Ashbury in Berkshire. Today we know that it is really a burial chamber from the New Stone Age. The same area has many such reminders of our prehistoric past. Centuries ago, local people made up stories to explain things they didn't understand. This is the story they told about Wayland the Smith.

Some said he was a god. He was a brave warrior, a good hunter and a fine smith. Everyone wanted the beautiful things he made out of iron, silver and gold.

One day he fell in love with a girl and married her. He didn't know that she was really a goddess. After a few years, she grew tired of pretending to be human. When Wayland came home, she was gone.

Thinking she would come back, he made a fine gold ring to give her when she returned. The next day he made another ring, for she was still missing. The weeks turned to months and each day he fashioned a gold ring. He hung them all on a string in the smithy.

News of this strange smith reached the ears of King Nidud, a cruel and greedy man. He sent some of his soldiers to find out if the stories were true.

When the soldiers got to the smithy, Wayland was out hunting. They saw the rings and counted them. 'Seven hundred!' cried one man. 'The smith will never miss one.' When they gave the ring to Nidud, he ordered them to go back and fetch the smith himself. 'If he struggles,' he added, 'tie him up and carry him here.'

Bound hand and foot, Wayland was brought before the king. 'Did you make this?' asked Nidud, holding up the ring. Wayland called him a robber and asked for the ring back. 'Wayland,' said the king, 'we shall have all your rings and anything else you can make.' The furious smith shouted that he would make nothing for a thief.

The king grew angry and gave orders that Wayland's legs should be broken. The king's two sons laughed when this was done. Wayland was kept prisoner in a smithy on an island in the middle of a lake. When his legs had healed, Wayland could scarcely walk. The king told him he would get no more food until he began to make jewellery again. Wayland had to do as he was told or he would have starved but in his heart he planned his revenge.

Secretly he stole small pieces of the metals the king gave him to work with and began to make a pair of wings. If he couldn't escape on foot he would learn to fly.

One night the king's two sons rowed over to the island. They were as cruel and greedy as Nidud himself. They wanted Wayland to hand over some of their father's gold which had been given to the smith for him to use. Wayland asked them if anyone knew they had come. Naturally, they had told no one. Wayland then said that the gold was in a large chest in the corner. As they bent over to lift the lid, he killed them both with an axe.

He cut off their heads, buried the bodies and burned their boat. Using all his skill, he

turned the skulls into silver bowls. Nidud thought the boys were away hunting and suspected nothing. He even admired the new bowls which Wayland had made.

Then Nidud's daughter also paid Wayland's smithy a secret visit but for a very different reason. She told him that she was ashamed of what her father had done. Wayland knew that his vengeance was almost complete when she went on to say that she now hated her parents.

She said that she had fallen in love with Wayland and wanted to go with him. They could use her boat, she suggested. Wayland was sorry for her but had to say that he was already married. She watched in amazement as he strapped on his wings and flew to Nidud's castle.

The king was furious when Wayland told him that his sons were dead and that his daughter hated him. Nidud's archers tried to shoot Wayland as he flew away but they missed. Ever since, he has searched the whole world, looking for his beloved wife.

Chapter Five   The Vikings

1 Viking Ships

It is a misty autumn day in 1955. A fishing boat is just coming into port. The port is Roskilde in Denmark. The engine is puttering happily. As the skipper takes the ship through the narrow channel leading to the harbour, another boat begins to overtake him.

The skipper looks at it angrily. 'The fool,' he mutters, 'there isn't room for two vessels here.' He has to move over and as he does, he feels and hears the bottom of the ship scrape on something under the water. He is lucky that they don't go aground.

When the ship is safely in port, he complains to the harbour master. 'Someone ought to do something about it,' he says. Two years later someone does.

In the summer of 1957, a team of divers went down to see what the trouble was. They reported that it seemed to be a long ridge of stones. A few of the stones appeared to be unusually large, so the team decided to move some of them to one side. When they did, a number of pieces of wood were uncovered.

People in the town said that they looked like bits of a shipwreck. Experts came down from Copenhagen's National Museum. They surprised everyone by saying that the remains were those of a Viking ship. They wanted to see some more of the fragments but it's hard to dig under water.

A metal dam was driven into the sea bed right round the ridge. Then the water was pumped out. By the summer of 1962, the diggers were able to go to work.

In less than five months, tens of thousands

top Parts of Viking ships
above Digging inside the dam

of pieces were rescued. For a while they had to be kept in special tanks. If they had been allowed to dry out, they would have shrunk and twisted. After this they were soaked in chemicals so that they would keep their shape.

It took a while for the chemicals to work but at last the men from the museum could try to fit the pieces together. It was like doing a giant jigsaw puzzle. It will take them years to finish the job. A special display hall has been built in Roskilde so that the public can see the work going on.

Enough has been done already to show that there were five wooden ships. They all date from Viking times and are probably over a thousand years old. No two of them are alike. There was a small ferry or fishing boat. Almost three quarters of this ship has been found. It is nearly forty feet long and eight feet wide.

One of them was a merchant ship which carried cargoes across the North Sea and the Baltic. It is about three and a half feet longer than the ferry. The larger merchantman was built for crossing the Atlantic to Iceland. It measures fifty-two feet from stem to stern.

There were two warships as well. The smaller one is only half complete. Even so, it was sixty feet long when it was first made. The largest one of all was so big that the diggers thought at first it must be two separate vessels. Then they realized that they had found a Viking longship. This was the kind of ship the Vikings used for their greatest voyages. It was the type they chose when they were not just raiding but coming to conquer and settle in new lands.

Most of the ships found once had a mast and sail and also a row of holes in the top planking for the oars to go through. The smallest ship could be managed by only four or five men but the longship carried fifty rowers. It was more than ninety feet long and nearly fifteen feet wide.

All the vessels seem to have been weighted with stones to make them sink. Perhaps the people of Roskilde had tried to block the harbour entrance to keep out raiders.

The ship museum at Roskilde

2 The People

No one knows where the name 'Viking' comes from. It may mean someone who lives by a 'vik', or creek. The word is often used for those people from the northern lands who sailed, raided and traded in ships like the ones found in Denmark. They travelled all over Europe and a good distance outside it as well. Saxons called anyone a Viking, or a Dane, if he had come here to raid or conquer, whether he came from Sweden, Denmark or Norway.

Life was hard in those countries. A lot of the land was mountainous or sandy heathland. None of this is good for farming. The people had a job to grow enough food for themselves. If we take a look at a village we can see something of what their lives were like.

It is a morning in early summer at Tarby. The villagers are busy. Women are washing clothes or making them, preparing meals, carrying water from the stream and doing lots

of other kinds of jobs. It is strange but there don't seem to be very many men about. There are plenty of children but the only men around look rather old.

The reason is that most of the younger men have gone to sea. The fields near the village don't grow very much food so the villagers have to make up the difference with fish. Sometimes they catch a seal; if not, the children gather shellfish and birds' eggs.

One of the children shouts from the beach. The fleet is coming in. Soon they are unloading the catch. Some will be cooked in the long-house kitchen for the feast. This will be done by thralls, as the Vikings call their slaves. The rest of the fish will be cleaned and then salted down or smoked so that it will keep.

When the fishermen have eaten and drunk, the chief tells them that he would like some of them to come on a raiding party with him. The target is a monastery in England.

Einar, one of the warriors, agrees to go in the chief's longship. They will leave in a week's time. Einar decides to take his son Thorkel with him. It will be Thorkel's first raid.

3 Life at Sea

The figurehead of a Viking ship

A week later, the Tarby men are joined by Vikings from three or four other villages. There are to be three longships, two from the villages up the coast and one from Tarby itself. The Vikings are very good boat builders and sailors. They have to be. Those seamen and ships which were not good enough never came back home from fishing or raiding.

Sea Foam is the name of the Tarby boat. It is the largest of the three. It is built of thin, springy oak planks. These overlap slightly and are fastened to the ribs with nails or wooden pegs. Any gaps have been filled in with lengths of tarred wool. The hull is painted all over with tar to keep the water out.

Thorkel and Einar are helping to load the ship with the things they will need. Thorkel is almost a grown man and makes light of the loads. There are barrels of smoked fish and meat, sacks of oats, bags of salt, casks of water, barrels of ale, tents, oars, cooking pots, tools, weapons and armour.

The *Sea Foam* has no cross seats, or thwarts, so each man sits on a chest while he rows. In the chest he will put his own belongings, such as spare clothes, chain mail coat, helmet, sword and axe. Einar and his son do not wear their war things but are dressed in everyday clothes. Each has trousers of animal skin, belted at the waist. Thorkel wears a green woollen tunic while his father's is red. Each has a sleeveless sheepskin jacket with a cloak on top. They have round leather caps. Their boots are also of leather.

The crew say their goodbyes and push the *Sea Foam* into the waves. They scramble aboard. There are forty men in the crew and about thirty in each of the other boats.

The oars are pushed out and the men begin to row. The ship is steered with a large paddle at the stern. The steersman calls out the time so that the men can row together.

The wind is blowing off the shore, so as soon as the ship is far enough out, the oars are pulled in and the single mast hauled up into its place. Then the sail fills with air. The men will not row again until they are near the end of their journey – unless the wind drops or changes direction.

A lot of Viking raiders keep in sight of the coast until they can see England across the Channel. Einar's chief means to go straight across the North Sea.

Vikings know how far north or south they are, even if they haven't seen land for days. They use the sun and the stars to help them. They can also tell the time from the sun and stars to within a quarter of an hour.

The chief divides the crew into two groups. One group cooks some food and then sleeps. The other men bale out water, trim the sail and act as look-outs. They musn't get separated from the other ships. These are not easy to see on a dark night, especially if the weather is bad.

They take it in turns to eat, sleep and be on watch. More than a week goes by before they are in sight of land. One of the crew knows the coastline. They are only five miles from the monastery they are going to attack.

4 A Viking Raid

Sometimes the Vikings take horses with them on a raid. When they beach the ships the horses can get over the low sides and the riders urge them on through the water. The *Sea Foam* doesn't carry horses this time. The raiders are unlikely to do much fighting. Monks don't usually meet them with swords.

When they get to the right place the sail is furled and the mast is lowered. The oars are untied and pushed out. The men row hard for the beach. As the keel grates on the sand, most of them are ready to jump over the side and wade ashore. A few will be left to guard the ship and drive wooden stakes into the sand. The ship will be tied to these to stop it floating away.

The fighting men are now dressed for war. Their round leather caps act as padding for the metal helmet which goes on top. A small piece of iron from the helmet rim protects the eyes and nose. Each man has a thick leather tunic. Those who can afford it have softer leather coats with little iron rings sewn on them. They carry wooden shields with iron edges. Each man has either a sword or a battle axe.

Let's hear from Thorkel what it was like to go on a raid. We'll ask him if his first one was exciting. 'Yes it was,' he says, 'and it might have been more exciting if there had been any berserkers. I looked round to see if there were any as we were trudging up the beach.'

'What are berserkers?' we ask.

'Warriors who work themselves into a rage with oaths, chanting insults until they

are blood mad. From then on, they don't care about their own safety, nor even if they get killed.

'As I say, I looked round but no one was shouting anything. All was quiet except for the waves, the seabirds and the crunch of our feet on the pebbles.

'Then we scrambled up some rocks, over the fields behind and on into the woods, where the chief told us what to do. Once through the belt of trees, there was open farmland in front of the monastery. The chief divided us up into groups and told us to wait when we got to the edge of the wood. I wanted to get a better look and I peered through the bushes.

'One of the monks who was working on the farm must have seen me because he raised the alarm. The monks dropped their spades and hoes, tucked up their robes and ran. There was nothing else to do but give chase. I remember one monk stood his ground with a hoe in his hands. A Viking cut him down with a sword blow and I knew that he was dead.

'I had seen men killed before but not like this. I was half-ashamed and half-excited. I suppose I'd have done the same in his place –

but he shouldn't have got in our way. He wasn't the last monk I saw killed that day, although I think most of them got away.

'I know I stood staring at that first dead body until my father shouted at me. We broke into the buildings and took whatever we could find. The church had the most treasure. There were gold and silver ornaments such as crosses, plates and candle holders. We had sacks to put the things in. Before we left, some of the wilder ones overturned the altar and set fire to it.

'As soon as we were sure there was nothing else worth having, we made our way back to the boats. I expect I'll go on other raids as I get older but I'm sure I'll never forget this one.'

Years later, Thorkel will come back on a different kind of voyage. This time there will be hundreds of longships, not just three. The Vikings will be coming to England, not to steal ornaments but land.

Long after his time, the Vikings from Denmark will have conquered all of northern and eastern England. The country will be divided between the Saxons in Wessex and the Vikings in the Danelaw.

5 The Vikings in Normandy

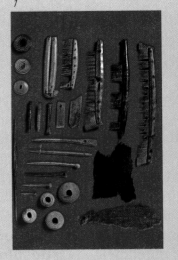

The Vikings raided, traded and conquered in many places. They settled in the islands to the north and north west of Scotland. They set up trading posts in towns such as Dublin and York. They reached the Mediterranean by travelling along the rivers of Russia. They attacked France, southern Italy and even Africa.

They were so feared that Christians used to end their prayers by saying, 'From the fury of the Northmen, Good Lord deliver us.' Some Christian kings paid them to go away. The money was called Danegeld. Some kings gave them land to settle in, hoping they would drive off any other raiders.

Their manners were rough. A story is told about Rollo the Ganger. Rollo was the leader of a Viking band of warriors. They were allowed to settle in north west France. He was such a tall man that his feet dragged on the ground when he rode his pony. His men said he was 'ganging', or walking.

King Charles of France knew that he was both cruel and proud, so he ordered the

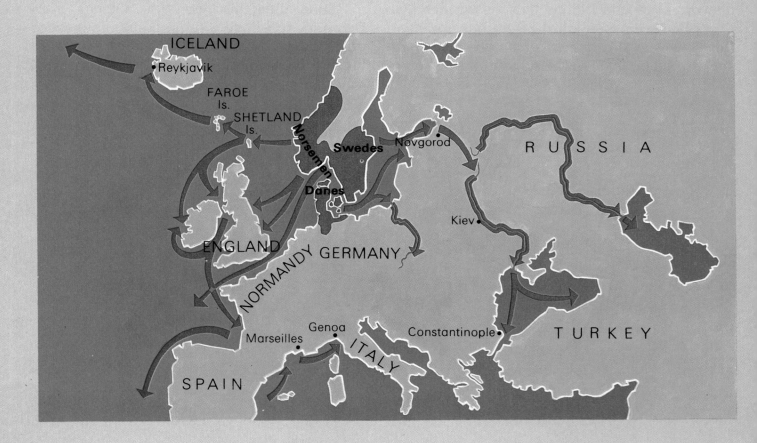

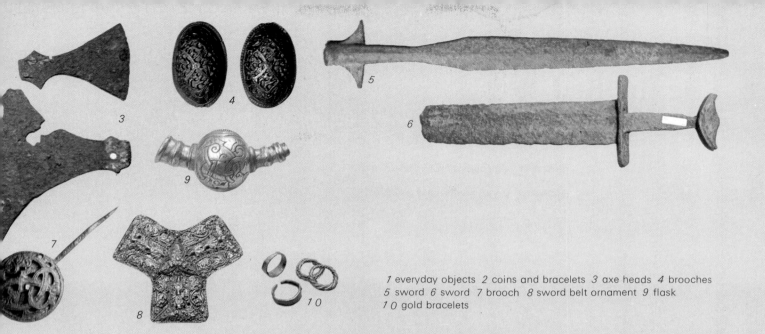

1 everyday objects 2 coins and bracelets 3 axe heads 4 brooches
5 sword 6 sword 7 brooch 8 sword belt ornament 9 flask
10 gold bracelets

Viking to kiss his foot. Rollo bent down and took the king's foot in his hand. Instead of kissing it, he heaved with all his strength. The astonished king flew through the air and landed on his back behind the throne. Rollo had too many Vikings with him to be punished. In fact, he later took the title of Duke.

Because the area he ruled was owned by Northmen, the French called it 'Normandy'. It was from here that the Vikings, or Normans, were at last to launch a successful attack on England.

Not all the Vikings had settled down by this time. Many went on exploring. Some got as far as Baghdad in the Near East, others went in the opposite direction.

6 Eric the Red

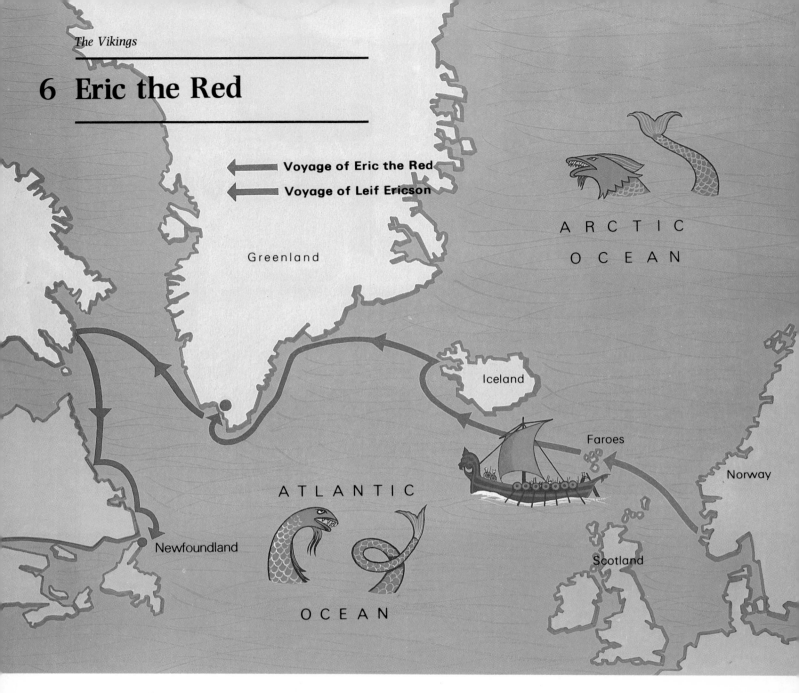

Voyage of Eric the Red

Voyage of Leif Ericson

Greenland

A R C T I C

O C E A N

Iceland

Faroes

Norway

A T L A N T I C

O C E A N

Newfoundland

Scotland

Perhaps the most surprising voyages were made by Eric the Red and his family. Eric killed a man and was told to leave Norway. He sailed for the Faroe islands and then on to Iceland. Irish monks had discovered Iceland but it was the Vikings who settled there. When Eric landed in 982, he was told of a great land to the west. A sailor named Gunbjørn had once been driven ashore there.

Eric set sail for this new country with his wife and children, plus a few friends. They rowed and sailed westward for several days before sighting land. It didn't look very inviting so they went round the bottom of the island and up the west coast where they landed. Eric called it Greenland.

The country was rather like north Norway but it had no trees. A man called Bjarni tried to bring them a cargo of timber but he was blown off course by a gale lasting several days.

When the weather cleared he saw land. He didn't stop to see what it was. He sailed the hundreds of miles back to Greenland. When he reached Eric's house, he told him what he had seen. Eric's son Leif made up his mind to look for this strange place as soon as he was old enough.

His chance came in the year 1001. He set sail for the west and found Bjarni's land. A landing party explored but there were too many rocks and stones so they sailed south. Twice more they went ashore. Finally they found a good place with trees and grass. They called it Vinland. They built huts and spent the winter there, bringing the timber back to Greenland in the spring.

Other members of Eric's family went to Vinland and tried to make their homes there. They were attacked by the natives and had to leave. Vikings went on trying to live in Vinland for years.

Most of this story was not written down for centuries. When it was, some people said that Vinland must have been America. Others said the story was all lies and the Vikings could never have got so far. In modern times, men

These houses in Iceland today are similar to the ones Eric the Red would have known

have dug up the remains of a blacksmith's forge in Newfoundland. They also found traces of some buildings.

There is no doubt they were the work of Vikings. Nor is there any doubt that men from Europe had landed in America almost five hundred years before Columbus set sail.

Excavation of a Viking site in Newfoundland

7 Saxon and Dane in England

We read earlier how Alfred had beaten the Danes and made them keep to their own part of the country. Unfortunately for the Saxons, Alfred died in the year 901. The Anglo Saxon Chronicle, which he ordered to be kept, gives us many facts from the period. Some of the books which he translated from Latin himself can still be read.

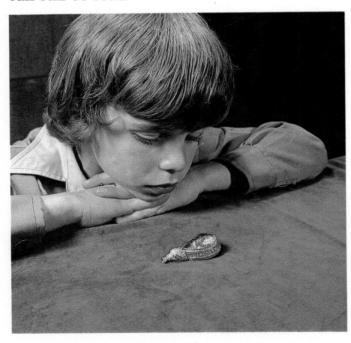

In the Ashmolean Museum at Oxford is a reminder of the gentler side of King Alfred. It is a beautiful gold brooch with what may be a picture of Alfred himself on it. Around the edge it says, 'AELFRED MEC HEHT GEWYRCAN', which means 'Alfred had me made'.

Alfred was called 'the Great' by his fellow Saxons. This was not only because of his learning but also because he stood up to the Danes. He raised an army which beat them on land and he made an English navy which

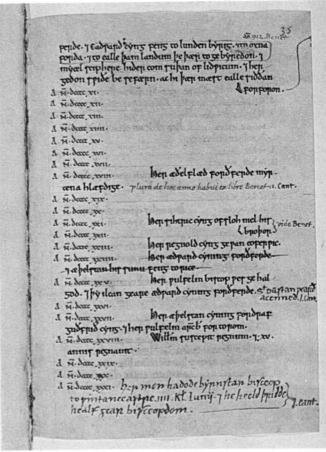

A page from the Anglo-Saxon Chronicle

Alfred's introduction to a book by Pope Gregory

beat them at sea.

The kings who came after him were not all so good at fighting invaders. Athelstan was the best of them. He was Alfred's grandson and was crowned at Kingston in 925. He called himself 'King of Britain' and he won a great battle against a huge army of Vikings, Scots and Britons at Brunanburh.

No matter how many times the Saxons beat the Danes, they were never able to drive them out completely. Many towns in the north and east of England keep their Danish names to this day. You can be fairly sure a place was once a Danish settlement if its name ends with 'by', 'thwaite', 'thorp' or 'toft'.

In the year 980 a new Danish threat appeared. This time there were not just little groups of raiders but a large army. They had been gathered together in camps in Denmark. Their leaders didn't just want plunder, they had come to conquer the whole country.

The Saxon King Ethelred tried to buy them off with Danegeld. The people of England had to hand over more than 150,000 pounds of silver. It did no good. In 1013 another Danish army arrived. Their leader was Swein Forkbeard. The Danes captured London and Ethelred fled to France. Swein was accepted as king but died shortly afterwards. His son came over to take his place. Ethelred also died, leaving a son named Edmund Ironside to carry on the fight.

Swein's son, whose name was Canute, beat Edmund in East Anglia and became the first Dane to rule the whole of England without argument. He tried to reign as Alfred had done and it seems that the Saxons were willing to have him as king. The Danes still call him 'the Great,' as the Saxons had once called Alfred.

When Canute died, his sons were not nearly such good rulers. The last of them, Hardicanute, left no son to reign in his place. With the help of Earl Godwin, Edward the Confessor became king in 1042. He was another son of Ethelred and therefore a Saxon.

It seemed that the threat of the Norsemen was ended. It was not so. The descendants of Rollo the Ganger in Normandy were already beginning to look at England with greedy eyes. The last great invasion of England by the men from the north was not too far off.

Manuscript illustration of King Canute

8 A Story

Here is a story that the Vikings used to tell about their hero-god, Thor.

He was big and strong. He had a magic belt and a magic hammer. If he pulled the belt tight he became twice as big and twice as strong. His hammer never missed its mark when he threw it and it always came back to his hand. One day Thor was told that there was a land of giants who were much bigger and stronger than he. He thought he would challenge them to see who was the stronger. He set out for giant land with a boy as a servant and a friend named Loki.

When they had been walking for a long while, it grew dark. Thor spotted a great hall in the forest, so they went in through an enormous doorway and lay down to sleep.

In the middle of the night the ground heaved under them. They started to their feet and Thor took up his hammer. 'Quick!' shouted Loki, 'into this small side room. It will be easier to defend if we are attacked.' They stayed on guard all night but nothing happened.

In the morning they found the cause of the noise. It was a giant snoring. They woke him up and he told them his name was Skrymir. Then he asked for his glove back. It was a moment or two before Thor realized that it was the giant's glove in which they had passed the night. The side room was one of the fingers!

Skrymir offered to show them the way and carry their bundles inside his own. When they stopped to rest, the giant fell asleep again but Thor was hungry. Alas! Skrymir had tied the knots on his bundle so tight, Thor could not undo them. He tried to wake the sleeping giant but Skrymir did not stir. Thor shook him and punched him. Then he hit him with his magic hammer. The giant brushed the hammer away, muttering, 'Must have been an insect,' and snored on. Again Thor hit him. 'Must have been a twig dropping,' mumbled Skrymir without waking.

For the third time Thor raised his hammer. Then he brought it down with all his might on the giant's head. Skrymir woke up and said sleepily, 'It's time we were on our way, friend Thor. This place is uncomfortable. An acorn has just dropped on my head.'

When they came to the castle of the king of the giants, Skrymir told Thor to be careful. 'You think I'm a giant,' he said, 'but here I'm just a little one. Farewell, friend Thor.'

The gates were locked but Loki scrambled through the crack under the door, followed by Thor and the boy. The king of the giants was waiting for them. 'Welcome to my home,' he said, 'but you can only stay one night. Of course, you could stay longer if any of you is a champion.' He looked at them. 'What can you do, each of you?' he asked.

The boy said he could run fast but the giant's butler beat him easily. Loki boasted that he could eat more than anyone. The king laughed and ordered a servant to bring a wooden trough of meat. Loki ate his half but the servant ate not only the meat but the bones and the wooden trough as well.

Thor said he would try a drinking contest. The king had a horn brought in and told him that most giants could drain it in one go. Thor found that the level had only fallen an inch after his third swallow. He tried to raise the castle cat off the floor to prove his strength

but could only lift one of its paws.

To cover his shame, he boasted of his skill at wrestling but the giant's old nurse pinned him to the ground.

The next morning the giant king led them to the gate of the castle. 'Don't be downhearted, Thor,' he said. 'Now that you are safely out of my castle, I can tell you that I wouldn't have had you as a guest at all if I'd known how strong you were.'

'Strong?' exclaimed Thor, in surprise. 'You mock me, giant.'

'Indeed not', said the giant. 'I can see I must confess, Thor. I played a trick on you. Several tricks, in fact. I was Skrymir and you very nearly killed me. I put a spell on my bundle. No wonder you could not loosen the knots.

'My butler, the one who outran your boy, was none other than Thought. Nothing is faster than Thought, Thor. Why do you think Loki was outeaten? My servant was Fire

himself in disguise. Fire eats almost as fast as Thought moves.

'Now we come to your part, Thor. When you could not drain the horn, it was because one end of it dipped down into the sea. The levels of the oceans all over the world have dropped because of what you did. The cat you could not lift was the serpent which binds the whole world together.'

'But what about the wrestling?' asked Thor. 'To be beaten by a woman! And such an elderly one!'

The giant laughed so loudly that the stones shook. 'Haven't you guessed? The nurse was Old Age, against whom no one can win.'

Thor smiled for the first time since they had started out. 'Farewell, Thor,' said the giant. 'You did too well! Please don't come back here again!' With that, he slammed the gates shut. Thor laughed and went away with his two companions.

Chapter Six   The Normans

1   Two Battles

A scene from the Bayeux Tapestry

This is part of a piece of embroidery. It is rather special. To start with, it is over 900 years old. It is called the Bayeux Tapestry.

The Saxon king, Edward the Confessor, had ruled England for nearly a quarter of a century. As he lay dying, he sent for Harold, the son of Earl Godwin. He had enough strength to tell Harold that he was to be the next king. Then he died. Harold was crowned king without delay.

At least two other men thought they should be King of England. One was Harald Hardrada, King of Norway. The second was Duke William of Normandy.

William always said that Edward had promised the English throne to him. He also said that Harold Godwinson had sworn to help him become King of England. It seems likely that Harold was tricked into doing this when he had been shipwrecked in Normandy some years before.

King Harold's brother, Tostig, had been Earl of Northumbria. He was a cruel man and was ordered to give up his earldom and leave the country. He had gone to Norway and urged Hardrada to attack England. If the Norwegians won, he would get his earldom back.

Harold knew there would be an invasion so he got his army ready to beat off the attacks. He didn't know which one would come first. It might be the Norwegians if the wind was from the north. If it was a southerly

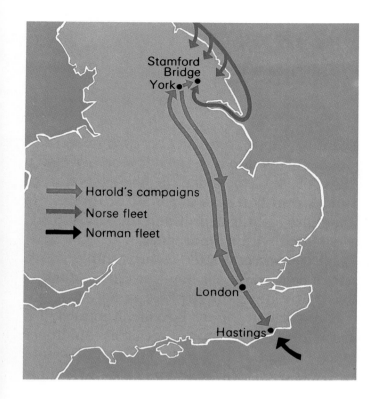

wind then the Normans would win the race.

Harold kept his army near London ready to march north or south. Throughout the summer of 1066 they waited and nothing happened. At last the men grew impatient. They wanted to go home and help gather in the harvest. Harold gave in and let half of them go.

The wind was wrong for Duke William. Day after day it blew steadily from the north, keeping his ships in port. Unluckily for King Harold, it was just right for the Norwegians.

News reached Harold that Hardrada and Tostig had landed in Yorkshire. The message said that there were 300 ships and thousands of Vikings. Harold set off with his army to walk the 180 miles to York, which the Vikings had captured.

When he arrived, a messenger from the Norwegians said that Hardrada demanded the land of England. 'Tell your king,' said Harold, 'he shall have just six feet of our land. For his grave,' he added. Then he said thoughtfully, 'Hardrada is a tall man and his

body will not fit a normal grave. You had better offer him seven feet!'

We do not know what Hardrada said when he heard the reply but Harold's words came true. Both Tostig and the Norwegian king were slain in the Battle of Stamford Bridge, which the Saxons won.

Harold had no time to enjoy his victory. News reached him that the wind had changed and that Duke William had landed on the south coast. The Saxons made the long march all the way back again to fight another battle.

Harold put his army of 7,000 men at the top of a slope about seven miles from Hastings. There was a marsh on each side. Harold made some of his men line up across the front of the army with their shields touching. At about nine in the morning, William's archers fired arrows but few of them got past the shields. Then he attacked with men on horseback but still the line held. Every time the Normans came up the hill, the Saxons drove them back with spears, axes and swords.

One group of Norman raiders scattered and some of the Saxons made the mistake of leaving the shield wall to chase them downhill. Norman arrows came flying down over the shields that were left and Norman horsemen poured through the gap. Harold was slain — some say by an arrow in the eye. The fighting went on until it was dark. When it was done, Saxon rule was over for ever.

Battle Abbey

2 A Castle

Before William left Normandy, he had a wooden fort made. His men took it to pieces and carried it in their ships to England. There they rebuilt it. They might have lost the Battle of Hastings and would have wanted somewhere to shelter.

William's knights knew that they would have to have castles too. Their reward for helping the new king was often a piece of land. Although they had won a battle, they had not conquered all of England. Some Saxons would fight to try to stop the Norman knights taking their land. The safest thing for William's men to do was to put up forts straight away.

Of course, it would have been nice to build a big, strong castle out of stone. But this would have taken a long time, perhaps years. Let's imagine how one man, Baron Roger de Lô, solves the problem. Roger wants something that will be ready much more quickly. He looks round his new lands for a small hill.

There isn't one, so he sets his men to work to make one. On top of it they fit together heavy slabs of oak to make a box-shaped fort. Stables and barracks are built at the foot of the motte, as it is called, and the whole thing is enclosed with a stout fence.

A few years later, when things have settled down a bit, Sir Roger wonders what he can do to make his castle stronger. A friend tells him about Maitre Basville, a man skilled in the art of making stone castles. Sir Roger sends for him.

First of all, Maitre Basville wants to know

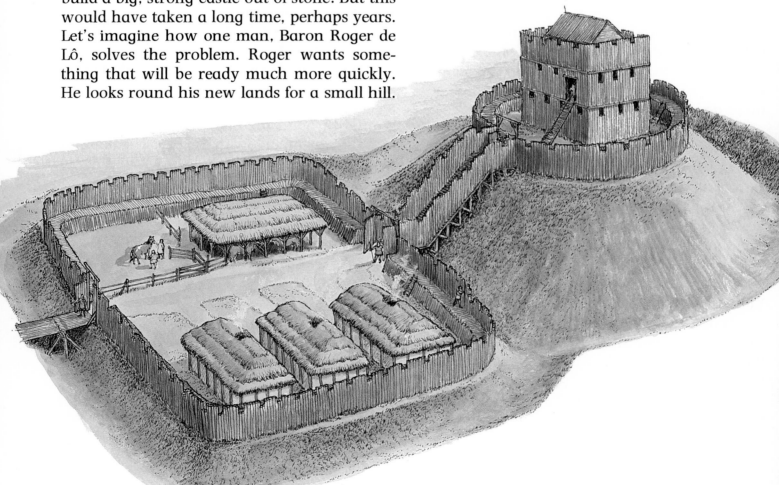

what Sir Roger has in mind and how much he can spend. Sir Roger has large estates and money to spare. They get down to details. The builder tells the Baron not to have a heavy stone building on top of his motte. 'I have seen them,' he says, 'and they are not safe.' They speak in French, for the Vikings of Normandy had long given up their own language.

When they have agreed, Maitre Basville leaves for Normandy. The labourers will be found in England but he has to take on many stone masons, stone cutters, engineers and scaffolders, together with their apprentices. He also has to buy the stone and get it shipped across the Channel to England. Everyone agrees that limestone from Caen in Normandy is the best you can get for castles.

In the meantime, Roger has to get the site ready. It has been decided that the wooden fort must be pulled down but that the new castle should go somewhere else. The builder says there is no longer any need for a motte. Stone castles can be very high, so any flat ground will do.

There is a level place near the bridge over the river. Men on top of a castle roof will be able to stop an enemy crossing the bridge with their arrows. The water from the river can be used to fill the moat.

The chosen place is not empty though. There are several small Saxon houses in the way. This doesn't worry the Baron. He sends his soldiers to turn the peasants out of their homes which are then pulled down. The Saxons are angry but can do nothing.

3 A Baron

Baron Roger de Lô really has only one name. The word 'Baron' is a title. The 'de Lô' part means 'from Lô'. Lô is a town in Normandy. Very few lesser men had more than one name.

Roger is very pleased with his castle. When it is almost complete he walks round it. He sits on a saw bench in the main hall. He and his family have come quite a long way in a short time. His grandfather's grandfather was one of Rollo's Vikings. Before that time, they had scratched a hard living from poor soil. Now he is one of William the Conqueror's trusted men.

Here is a picture of the Baron dressed for war. His helmet has protecting pieces at the front and back like the earlier Viking pattern. He wears a coat of chain mail from neck to knees. It has slits so that he can sit comfortably on his horse. The sleeves are short to leave his arms free to use weapons.

It is a long and difficult job to make a coat of chain mail. The Normans call it a hauberk, which really means 'neck cover'. To start with, that is all it was. Later it became a coat. Some even look like old-time bathing costumes with short arms and legs. All are made of stiff linen or leather. The smith has to make thousands of little iron rings. Some of them are left open so that they can be joined up. Every ring is linked with four others. The rings are fastened to the leather backing. A hood of chain mail goes on Roger's head and his helmet on top of that.

right Falconer from a medieval manuscript
below One type of Norman helmet

Roger's day can be a very long one sometimes. He has to make sure that his officers are doing their jobs properly. They have to see him regularly to let him know what is going on. He has them in one at a time to make their reports.

There are men in charge of collecting rents. Others look after the stables, horses, soldiers, storehouses and the armoury. These are his stewards and bailiffs. Before long he will have to appoint a man to look after the castle. He will be known as the Constable and will tell Roger when repairs are needed or where the defences can be made stronger.

Every now and then he holds a court to try those who have broken his laws. Otherwise he will ride round his estates to make sure that things are going well. If he has nothing else to do he likes to go hunting. Large animals such as deer and wild boar will be hunted with dogs and finished off with spears. He uses a tame falcon to chase smaller game such as hares, rabbits and birds.

4 Life in the Castle

The key for this illustration is on page 112

Life in the Castle

Key to the Norman castle on previous page:
1 drawbridge 2 gate house 3 moat or fosse
4 stables and smithy 5 barrack house 6 open back square tower
7 forebuildings 8 dovecote 9 haystacks 10 store shed
11 buttery 12 removeable planks 13 main entrance to keep
14 guard room 15 chapel 16 moveable partitions
17 private apartments 18 mural passages 19 latrines
20 well on first floor 21 stores on ground floor
22 entrance stairway to first floor of forebuildings 23 merlons
24 crenellations 25 curtain wall 26 arrow slits
27 pigeon roosting holes 28 double-pitched copper-covered roof
29 church 'without the castle' 30 priest's house

The great hall is the most important place in the castle. While all the other rooms in the keep, or donjon, fit between the floors, the hall is two floors high. This is where the main meals are taken. Nearly all those who live in the castle eat together in the hall.

Roger and his wife, the Lady Alicia, sit at the high table which stands on a platform in front of a huge open fireplace. They are warm. So are the important people who are eating at the same table. Those at the far end of the hall can scarcely feel the fire, although they know it is there because the air is full of smoke.

The wooden floor is covered with rushes. There are some bright, coloured hangings on the walls and over the doorways. These help to brighten the greyness which is everywhere. The only light comes from the fire and dozens of rushlights or candles.

The castle is a cold and draughty place. The window spaces have no glass in them. The only way you can keep out most of the rain and snow is to close the wooden shutters. As this also shuts out the daylight, it is only done after sunset.

Although Roger's stewards might buy some of the food they eat, the Baron expects most of it to be grown on his own farms. The Normans don't go shopping for bits and pieces as we do. Everything has to be planned for several months ahead. If things are bought at all, they are bought in bulk.

A lot of food, such as meat and fish, is smoked or salted and packed away by the ton in the storehouses. There has to be enough to go round if there's a siege. By the time the enemy army is camping round your castle, it's too late to think of going out for tomorrow's dinner.

In the summer time there is plenty of fresh food – pork, beef or a little mutton. In the winter, the Baron will get tired of eating meat which has not kept too well. One of the stewards will order his men to go fishing in the river. Some castles have their own ponds which are stocked with live fish.

The salted meat has to be eaten, even if it is going bad. Norman lords often smother it with peppery spices to hide the taste of the meat. Fresh meat is sometimes roasted but more often it is boiled. It is served on stale slices of bread. The leftovers are given to the poor when the meal is over. Roger and his guests drink wine brought over from France. His men have to make do with ale. A cup is filled and passed along the table. Each one takes a sip as it goes by.

The children don't eat with their parents. The boys don't even live with them. At the age of seven or eight, a boy is sent to the castle of a friend or relation to be trained as a knight. In his turn, Roger is training the son of a friend. The boy's name is Hugh. He is about eleven. He passes food to the guests and helps pour out the drinks. As the diners eat mostly with their fingers, Hugh brings them a bowl of water and a towel.

After the fruit and nuts have been eaten, the meal is over. It started at ten in the morning and has lasted well over an hour. It seems rather early to us but everyone has been up since sunrise. Most people sleep in the great hall. They stretch out on the benches or even on the floor, wrapped in woollen cloaks.

Roger and his wife sleep in the solar. This is a small private room above the hall. It has its own fireplace and even a wooden bed screened off with a curtain. Not a lot of hand and face washing is done but Roger has a bath in the solar once a week.

There are lavatories in the corner towers. They are very rough and ready. There is just a wooden seat balanced over a chute leading out to the moat. You have to take a bucket of water with you to flush the toilet.

Lady Alicia spins, weaves and sews for part of the day and so do her two daughters, Adela and Betlindis. The women are expected to make some of the clothes, although the servants do most of the work.

Lady Alicia and her daughters wear the same kind of clothes. They have woollen stockings and soft leather slippers. Alicia wears a slip or undershirt which comes to her feet. A gown goes over this and on top is a cloak or mantle. Her headdress is called a wimple.

In the afternoons, Roger sees to Hugh's training if he has no important business. The boy is taught to use weapons. He can ride already. The second meal is taken at about four or five o'clock. Everyone goes to bed soon after dark.

5 Hugh's Day

1 HUGH RISES EARLY AND, BEFORE BREAKFAST, ASSISTS THE LORD TO BATHE AND DRESS.

2 AFTER A SIMPLE BREAKFAST, HUGH CLEANS AND POLISHES THE LORD'S ARMOUR.

3 HUGH TAKES LESSONS WITH THE PRIEST FOR THE REST OF THE MORNING.

5 EVERY DAY HUGH SPENDS SOME TIME AT WEAPON TRAINING.

6 IN THE EVENING HUGH SERVES HIS LORD WITH MEAT AND WINE AT DINNER.

4 IN THE AFTERNOON, HUGH AND THE
OTHER SQUIRES GO HUNTING WITH FALCONS.

AFTER THE MEAL HUGH PRACTISES PLAYING HIS HARP.

CARRYING A RUSHLIGHT, HUGH MAKES HIS
WAY TO HIS BED CHAMBER. →

6 King William and the Feudal System

William said that he owned all the land because he had conquered it. He gave about half of it to those who had fought for him at Hastings. He made sure that the pieces of land were well scattered so that anyone who wanted to rebel against him would find it hard to get an army together.

The men who received land from William were called 'tenants-in-chief'. There were about 200 of them. They were mostly barons, like Roger, but there were also bishops and abbots. The Church was quite a big land-owner. Each tenant-in-chief had tenants of his own. These were the knights, the men who fought on horseback.

All the barons, bishops, abbots and knights were Normans. William made sure that the important jobs went to his own men. Many Saxon earls had been killed in battle but William didn't hesitate to get rid of most of those who were left.

Every knight divided up his land into smaller pieces. These were known as manors. The men who ran them were freemen and a few might be Saxons. Each manor was really a village. The men who actually worked the land were the Saxon peasants. Some were allowed to go on looking after a few strips of land. Others had no land at all. They earned a living by working on someone else's farm.

The feudal system was like a staircase with the king at the top, the tenants-in-chief on the next step down, and so on. Every man had to promise to obey the one above him. This was done at a ceremony. The man who was about to promise knelt in front of his lord. The lord took his hands while the man made the promise.

To pay for his land, each man had not only to swear the oath but, if necessary, to fight for his lord. He might also have to pay rent. Rent was not often paid in the form of money. It was more likely to be some of the things he grew or made. At the very bottom of the system, there were peasants who had to work on the lord's land for three or four days a week. They got no wages for this and had to try to do their own work in the time they had left. In return, the lord swore to protect his peasants from thieves, rebels or any other enemies.

Sometimes there were rebellions. These were usually the work of Saxons, angry at having their land taken from them. Only three years after Hastings, there was an uprising in Yorkshire. Some Danish ships arrived to help the rebels. William sent for his tenants-in-chief and the vassals, as the lesser men were called, to help him. When he had got his men together, he marched north. The Danes sailed for home as soon as they saw the size of William's army. William beat the Saxons and then went on to show them just what any other rebels could expect.

He ordered his men to burn the villages, food stores and haystacks. They drove off or slaughtered all the farm animals. Then the army went back to London.

Those rebels who had not been killed by William's soldiers were faced with starvation in the coming winter. It did not pay to make William the Conqueror angry.

7 The Domesday Book

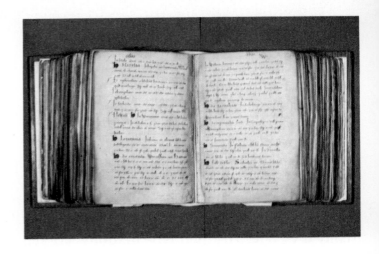

The Domesday Book is one of the oldest books of its kind in the world. You can go and see it in the Public Records Office in London.

Nowadays, we have to fill in forms for all sorts of reasons. Every ten years there is a census. The head of each household has to say how many people there are living under his roof. To run our country properly, we need to know how many of us there are. This is so that there will be enough schools, roads and hospitals for everyone.

We don't think William I made the Domesday survey just to find out how many people lived in England in 1086. He probably wanted to know exactly what everyone owned so that he could work out what taxes they ought to pay. The year before, William had called his advisers together at Gloucester. He asked them how he could find out what sort of country he ruled and what it was worth.

The advisers worked out a way of doing it. They told the king to send his commissioners to every county in England to ask questions. Let's imagine the scene in a village which is waiting for them to come.

It has been raining hard in Waldham. Now it is only drizzling but the ground is muddy and there are puddles everywhere. The reeve, or headman of the village, is in charge. His name is John. He had been hoping that the meeting could take place out of doors. Now it is raining, they will have to ask their questions inside his house.

'Which people are to be questioned, John?'

'I've been ordered to pick six of the oldest villagers with the best memories. They are waiting next door. I shall be here and so will the priest. In fact, I can see my boy running towards us. The commissioners must be coming.'

We question the commissioners as they dismount from their horses.

'What exactly are you trying to find out?'

'King William needs to know how much land there is in the village,' replies the elder of the two men. 'Is it good for growing wheat or grazing animals; is it woodland or waste? How much of each kind is there? How many ploughs? Is there a mill? What is it worth? How many pigs, cows and sheep? How many peasants? Who owns what?' 'Don't forget,' says the younger of the commissioners, 'that the jury must tell us more than that.'

'Why do you call them a jury?' we ask. *'And what else can they tell you?'*

'They must all swear to tell the truth and our word for "to swear" or "promise" is "jurer". As to the extra information, we are commanded by the king to ask not only what the village is like now but also what it was like when Edward the Confessor died. That's just over twenty years ago.'

'Won't that lead to arguments? And how are you going to talk to the jury? They can't speak French and you can't speak Saxon.'

Just at that moment the priest arrives and overhears what we are saying. 'I shall translate,' he says. 'The king's men can put their questions. I'll tell the jury what they are and then I'll tell the commissioners what their replies are. Ah! here are the monks. Perhaps you can tell the villagers we're ready.'

Soon everyone is sitting down and candles and rushlights are lit. The questioning goes on for hours. The monks speak French but they write the answers in Latin. 'Every educated man knows Latin,' one of them explains, 'no matter whether he is a Saxon, a Spaniard or a Norman like me. We write with quill pens. They are sharpened with penknives. We sprinkle fine sand over the wet ink to dry it. When every village has been visited, all these papers will be collected and copied on to parchment pages of very large books.'

At last they have finished. The weather isn't any better when they leave. It is still raining.

Although much of England was examined in this way, the work was never properly finished for William I died. It was to be over seven hundred years before England had another survey anything like it.

8 A Story

This is a story which Saxon peasants used to tell about one of their heroes. After the evening meal when they were sitting round the smoky fire, someone would say, 'What about Hereward the Wake?' and then they would all want to talk at once. Everyone has a different story. Quite a lot of the tales have been made up. A few are true but they happened to someone else. This is the story that most of them would agree about.

Hereward, they say, was the son of Earl Leofric of Mercia. His mother was Lady Godiva. When he grew up in Saxon England he rented a great deal of land. Most of it was in south west Lincolnshire and it belonged to the abbeys at Peterborough and Crowland.

Just four years before the Battle of Hastings, Hereward was forced to leave the country. No one seemed to know what he had done. He was abroad for eight years. When he came back, the Normans had already ruled England for four years.

He found that the kind old Abbot of Peterborough had been turned out by King William and that there was a new man in charge. His name was Turold. Turold would not allow Hereward to set foot on his own lands nor would he give him his belongings back. Hereward was thrown out of the abbey.

Promising himself that he would get his own back, he moved off into the countryside. He met two friends from the old days. One complained bitterly about the Normans. The other said that many Saxons had been made outlaws. They wanted to deal the Normans a blow. Would Hereward help them?

When he told them his own story, they took Hereward to their hideout. There were a great number of Saxons there. One of the men told Hereward that they were expecting a messenger from a Viking band. As soon as the man arrived they questioned him.

'We don't want to go back home empty handed,' said the messenger. Hereward asked him if the Vikings would like to attack an abbey as they had done in the old days.

The attack was arranged. The wicked Turold was killed and the Vikings rowed out to sea with their plunder. Hereward and his followers hid themselves on the Isle of Ely. They had chosen a good place. In those days Ely really was an island. There was firm, hard ground in the middle and all around it a maze of marshes and thickets of reeds. You had to be very sure of the paths if you wanted to get there.

A few pathways led to the island but they turned and twisted so much, it was easy to get lost. At times the path was no more than a few stones under the water. A foot on either side of the hidden stones and you could drown. King William sent a troop of soldiers to punish Hereward but they couldn't get to the island. They camped nearby. Next day they split up into small groups to try to find a way through the marshes. Only half of them came back to camp that night.

News of the rebels spread. Other Saxons went to fight alongside Hereward, including Earl Morcar and the Saxon Bishop of Durham. They raided Norman farms and still more Saxons joined them. After a year of these attacks, William himself was forced to lead a large army against the rebels.

The king camped at Cambridge and worked out a plan. His army would move to the edge of the marshes and begin making a causeway of their own to the island. William thought this could be done by ordering his men to drop lumps of stone into the water until there were enough to stand on. Then more lumps were to be dropped beyond where the men were working, and so on. He hoped that there would then be a straight, dry path right over to Ely.

Unluckily for the Normans, there wasn't enough stone to do this so William had to think of something else. It was late summer and the reeds were dry and brown. If the soldiers could start fires in the right places, they might smoke Hereward out. Making sure the wind would carry the flames towards Ely, William's men did as they were told.

Most of the Saxons gave in. They came across the pathways coughing and spluttering and yielded to the king. William was not as pleased as he might have been. Among the prisoners there was no sign of Hereward. The cunning Saxon had somehow managed to escape.

One ending of the story that the peasants told round their fires for years afterwards was happier than what probably happened. It is said that Hereward made his peace with William. Because he had been so brave and such a good fighter, he was allowed some of his land back again. Another ending says he died fighting Normans in France. We just don't know.

Chapter Seven   Norman England

1 William's Children

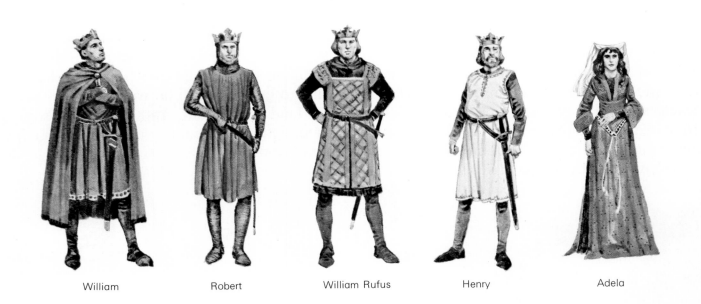

William   Robert   William Rufus   Henry   Adela

William the Conqueror's family was not a happy one. Richard, the first born, was killed in a hunting accident. William did not think too highly of Robert, the next oldest. He made Robert Duke of Normandy. He told his third son, also called William, that he was to be England's next king. He had one more son, Henry, and several daughters, one of whom was named Adela.

Robert rebelled against his father and had to be put in his place. It nearly went the other way. Robert and King William met in single combat in Normandy. William rode at his son but was knocked out of the saddle. Robert stood over him with drawn sword. William had to be rescued by one of his knights. When tempers had cooled, the two men made up their quarrel – but only for a time.

King William went back to Normandy again in 1087 to punish a French attack on his lands. He was nearly sixty. He captured the town of Mantes and had it burnt to the ground. As he rode through the ruins, his horse trod on a hot cinder and stumbled. William was thrown hard against the pommel of his saddle. He died of his injuries.

Robert had to be content with Normandy, while his younger brother William became King of England. William II had a nickname. People called him 'Rufus', which means 'red'. The name may have been given to him because he had a red face. He also had a hot temper. When something annoyed him, his face went scarlet. He was cruel and greedy too.

He even made money out of the Church. The Church had a great deal of land but when there was no bishop to receive the rent money, it went to the king. When a bishop or an abbot died, it was up to the king to pick a new man to take his place.

Rufus often pretended he couldn't make up his mind. The longer he delayed, the more rent money he could keep. After Archbishop Lanfranc died, the king would not name a new Archbishop of Canterbury for nearly five years. Then he only chose Anselm because he thought he was dying. He wasn't.

Rufus was always breaking his promises. He told the people of England he would make things easier for them. He swore to make punishments less cruel, but he made them even harsher. William the Conqueror had done away with hanging for some offences. Rufus brought it back. William the Conqueror had fenced off huge areas of forest for his favourite pastime of hunting. Some peasants had been hanged for daring to trap small animals there. Others had been turned off their land. Rufus gave his word that these peasants could have their lands back again. He broke his word.

In 1100 he was killed in the New Forest by an arrow. The king's body was found by a charcoal-burner. His death was said to be an accident but no one tried very hard to find out what had really happened.

The Rufus Stone

The king's younger brother, Henry, was hunting in another part of the same forest. Henry didn't stop to find out the facts either. He galloped off to Winchester, took charge of the royal treasure and had himself proclaimed king.

Robert, Duke of Normandy, was very angry. He thought his younger brother Henry had cheated him of the crown. He stirred up trouble in both France and England. Henry crossed to Normandy, fought against his elder brother and captured him. Robert was held prisoner for the rest of his life, a period of 28 years. He was 80 when he died.

123

2 A Village Year

Spring

Winter

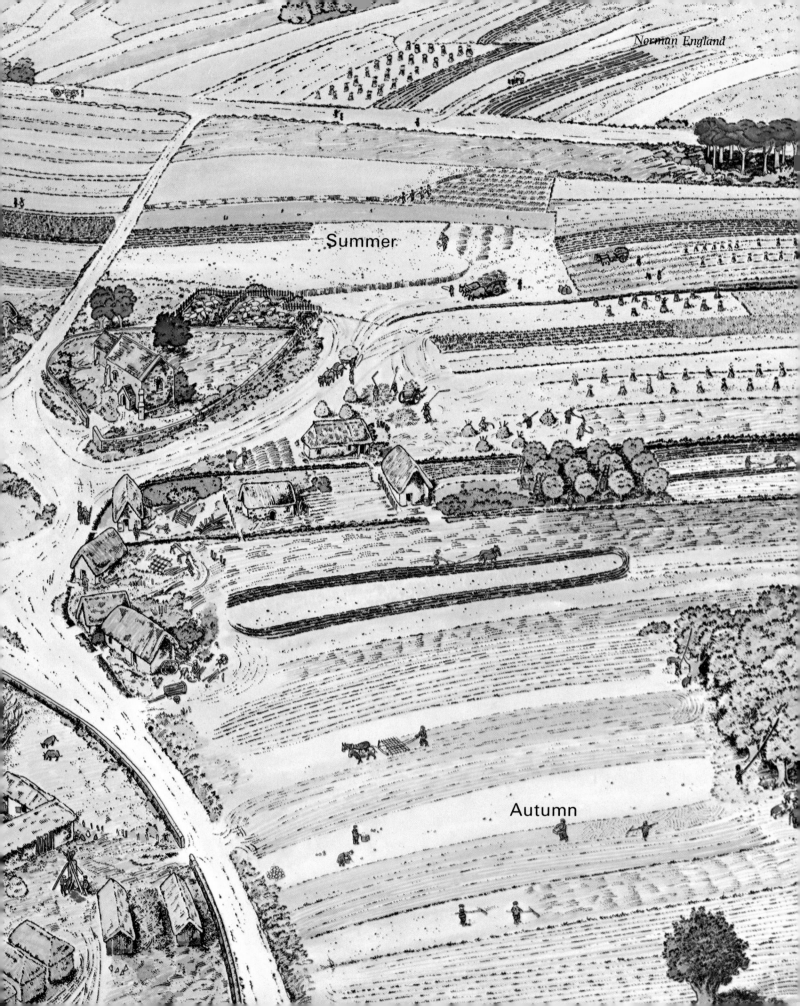

Norman England

Summer

Autumn

3 A Town

St. George's Tower today

The castle mound today

The Northgate Tower today

4 The New Church

This is the church at Adel, near Leeds, in Yorkshire. Most of what you can see now was built in Norman times. Norman building methods were different from those of the Saxons. You can compare the picture of Adel Church with that of the Saxon church below. The large picture shows what Adel church must have looked like as it neared completion.

DAN ESCOTT

5 Hunting and Hawking

This is a photograph of two men with their tame falcons. The men have trained them to catch and kill other birds. Seagulls, rooks and sparrows flock around rubbish tips, looking for things to eat. If there is an airfield nearby they are often a danger to planes. There are cases of planes crashing after colliding with birds in mid air.

It's strange to think of something which began as a way for Man to get more food ending up as a scheme to cut down air crashes. In Norman times, falconry had already become a sport. Hunting of all kinds kept the Normans fit for fighting.

In the England of nine hundred years ago there was plenty of woodland in which to hunt. Much of the country was covered with forest. There were many wild animals. From the reign of William the Conqueror onward, large parts of England were fenced off as royal forests. Hardly a region was free of them. The most famous was the New Forest. Almost all of Essex was a game preserve and there were well over a dozen others. The king's keepers patrolled the areas looking for poachers. Poachers were punished by hanging.

The creatures hunted for food included wild boars, hares, rabbits and several kinds of deer. They were hunted with dogs specially bred for the chase. There were mastiffs, greyhounds, spaniels and terriers. The larger animals were followed on horseback and the smaller ones on foot.

For stag hunting, the party moved out into the country early in the morning. They took food and wine with them and had a picnic while men cast about with the dogs for the scent.

A hooded falcon

Falconer's gear

Horns were blown as soon as the dogs picked up the traces of a stag. The hunting party mounted their horses and galloped off. The servants used the dogs to drive the animal into a clearing where the hunters fired arrows at it or finished it off with spears.

Hares were usually driven into traps or nets by greyhounds. If they were hiding in a cornfield, the dogs flushed them out and the hunters shot at them with crossbows.

As we have seen, a favourite sport was hawking or falconry. In the wild, hawks catch small mammals or other birds. They hover until they see their prey. Then they swoop down on it and kill it with their claws.

From the earliest times, Man had learned to tame hawks. He trained them to kill and then return to his wrist with the prey. The falconer wore a leather glove because his bird's claws were both strong and sharp. The falcon tended to get excited if it saw anything worth chasing, so the falconer put a little leather hood over its head until the right prey appeared. Favourite targets were ducks, pigeons, partridges or geese.

Women went hunting with their menfolk sometimes. Anything that could be caught would be welcome, especially in winter, when fresh food was scarce.

6 Stephen and Matilda

Adela

Stephen and his seal

Matilda and her seal

Henry I

Before he died, King Henry I had to decide who was to be the next ruler. In those days, a leader was expected to fight battles, so a man was almost always chosen. The death of his son had left Henry with only one child, a daughter named Matilda. He made everyone promise to accept her as queen after his death.

Poor Matilda! When her cousin Stephen claimed the throne, all the promises were forgotten. The churchmen and most of the barons said that they would have him as their next king.

A civil war broke out which was to last for years. The barons tried hard to make sure that their own lands, titles and castles were safe. When it looked as if Matilda's followers were winning, some of Stephen's men changed sides. The opposite also happened. One or two of the barons changed sides several times.

At one stage, Stephen ruled his half of the country from London, while Matilda made

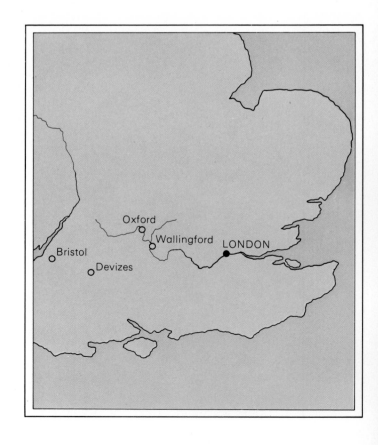

Devizes in Wiltshire her capital. In 1141, the queen's army fought a battle and Stephen was taken prisoner. He was thrown into the dungeons of Bristol Castle.

Matilda thought she had won the war but it wasn't as easy as that. She entered London but the Londoners drove her out again. It seemed that quite a lot of people didn't care much for either Stephen or Matilda, and the war went on.

7 Nineteen Long Winters

Not every part of England suffered. In some areas the peasants hardly noticed that there was a war on at all. In other places the peasants knew only too well. Their lands became battlefields. Their animals and crops were destroyed. When that happened, they faced starvation.

A monk from Peterborough wrote an account of what life was like in the Fenlands near his monastery. If we could ask him about it, he might say something like this.

'Even if there is no battle, ordinary people can still be ruined. It happens when the local lord takes advantage of the breakdown in law and order and behaves like a robber baron.

'He recruits farm-hands into his private army and even brings soldiers over from Normandy or France. His officers lead them on raids against the lands of other barons. To pay

An oubliette

their wages, he makes his own tenants give him more and more in taxes.

'He arrests all the men who can't or won't pay and tortures them. His soldiers drive the animals off the farms and take the corn without payment or permission. If the robber baron suspects that someone has money hidden, the victim might be thrown into a dungeon until he tells where it is. The dungeon is sometimes known as an oubliette.

'Not only do the robber barons strike terror into the hearts of all the common people nearby, they are a menace to everyone from the ruler downwards. No one knows how he stands, for a once friendly baron can change sides overnight.

'Almost all the powerful barons have built new castles and filled them with evil men and devils. Thousands have been starved and tortured for their savings.

Peasants are taxed until they have nothing left. When they can pay no more, soldiers burn their villages as an example to others.

'You can go a whole day's journey and not see a village with a person alive nor any field being tilled. Food is so scarce and dear, that men who were once rich are now begging.

'Even when a few peasants do return to their homes, they can't make a living because the soil has been ruined. It seems as though it is winter all the time.'

The monk ended his chronicle with the following words: 'And so it lasted for nineteen years while Stephen was king, 'til the land was all undone and darkened with such deeds, and men said openly that Christ and his angels slept.'

Part of the monk's chronicle

8 Escape from Oxford

A surviving tower of Oxford Castle

After she was driven from London, Matilda decided to move to the west of England where she had more supporters. Unluckily for her, Robert, her half-brother, was captured by the other side. To ransom him, she had to let Stephen go. Many barons who had come over to Matilda when Stephen was first taken prisoner, now went back to him.

At one point, Matilda found herself in Oxford Castle surrounded by an enemy army. The besiegers tried to break in but the castle was too strong. They put up their tents, lit their fires and got ready for a lengthy siege. The well in the bailey of the castle would go on supplying water but food stores, however large, would not last for ever.

The siege went on through the autumn and into the winter. The weather turned cold and snow began to fall. At last the defenders could hold out no longer. Matilda decided that she must try to get away.

She held a meeting with her officers to discuss how she could escape. The constable of the castle had an idea. 'You can't go out through the main gate,' he said. 'Your only chance is to climb down one of the towers at the back of the castle where they won't be expecting anything to happen.'

Matilda didn't think she could climb down the wall so it was decided to lower her on a rope. Three of her knights were to go with her. One of her ladies came up with an idea as well. 'Your Majesty,' she said, 'if you try to cross the fields in those bright clothes you will be seen at once. May I suggest that long, white cloaks are made to cover you and your men completely? Then you won't stand out against the snow.'

The arrangements were made and at about midnight, a sentry signalled that all was clear. The three knights swarmed down the rope and waited at the bottom for the queen to be lowered. Silently, the four picked their way carefully across the frozen moat. The rope was drawn up and they were on their own.

Dodging and hiding, they made their way to the bank of the River Thames. Crossing the moat had been easy but would the ice of the river bear their weight? They thought it would be better to cross one at a time, first making as sure as they could that there was no one about.

The ice crackled warningly under their feet but it held. After what seemed like hours, they reached the far bank and began to feel a little safer.

They had some miles to go before they could get horses. They daren't try to get them while they were still so near Oxford. It started to snow again. This was lucky in one way because their tracks would be covered. But the queen was already exhausted and half-frozen. Finally, they found a lonely barn in which to spend the rest of the night.

The next morning, the men hired horses for themselves and a litter for Matilda. She was so ill she had to be lifted off it when they came at last to Wallingford Castle. Matilda recovered from her ordeal but her cause was getting nowhere until she let her son Henry take over the fight.

The war went on for several years but the end came suddenly and rather strangely. In 1153, Stephen was forced to sign an agreement which said that he should be king for the rest of his life but that Matilda's son should take the throne after him. Stephen had wanted his own son, Eustace, to succeed him, so it was with a heavy heart that he put his seal on the treaty. It didn't really matter. The next year Eustace died and Stephen followed him a few weeks later.

Matilda's son was crowned as Henry II.

Chapter Eight   Monastic Life

1 Monasteries

Eustace, the son of King Stephen, died in a monastery at Bury St. Edmunds. A monastery was the only place for sick people in those days. There were no state hospitals then.

Care of the sick was not the only task monasteries had. They looked after the poor by giving them bread when times were hard. They ran schools for the brighter children. They repaired roads and bridges. They provided beds and food for travellers. They kept learning and order alive in an age of ignorance and lawlessness.

Monasteries and nunneries were not founded just to do these things, though. They were places where people could devote

The main monasteries of England and Wales

Eustace on his death-bed

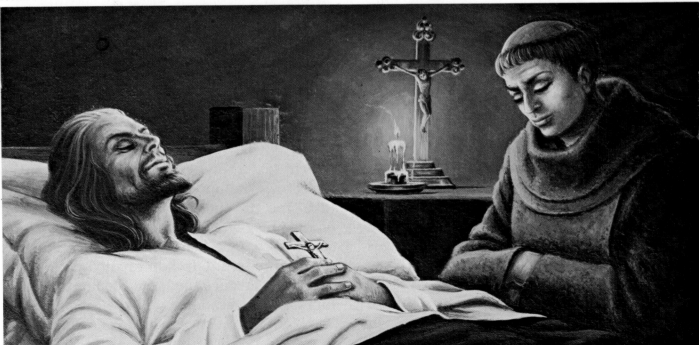

The fish that the monks caught was an important source of food for the monastery.

their whole lives to the worship of God. Nor were they new in Henry II's reign. They have a very long history.

The three main rules the monks followed were the vows of poverty, chastity and obedience. What did these things mean? Monks and nuns had to get rid of all their worldly possessions and promise not to own anything again. They vowed never to marry and always to do what they were told by those set over them.

Very often abbeys and convents had been founded by kings or members of their families. They had allowed the monks to build a chapel and somewhere to live. Lands had been given to them. The monks were expected to do a good deal of the work themselves but they still needed money. The rents from the lands were to help with the expenses.

As the years went by, a lot of abbeys found themselves getting richer as wealthy men and women left them lands and estates in their wills. St. Edmund's Abbey was already more than two and a half centuries old by the

A monastic school

time a man called Jocelyn of Brakelonde became a monk. It covered a large area, even at that date.

2 Jocelyn of Brakelonde

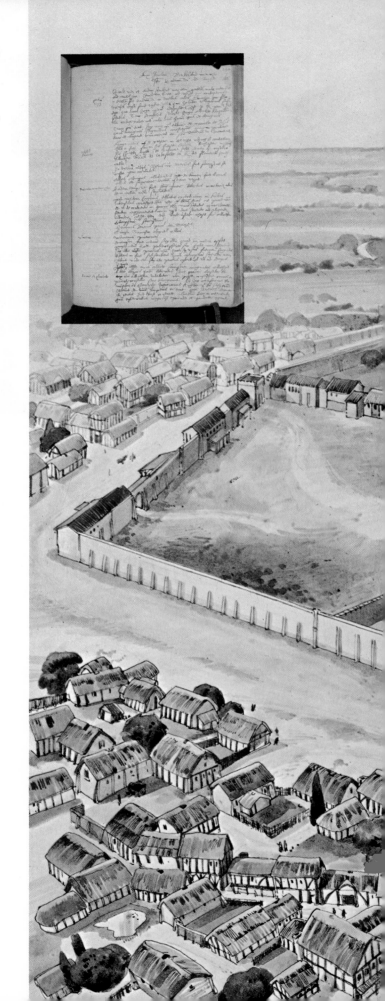

In the British Museum there is a copy of a book written by Jocelyn. He was a monk at Bury St. Edmunds in the reign of Henry II. His book was a kind of diary. Have you ever kept a diary? Did you make up your mind that you would write in it every day? Jocelyn kept his diary going for nearly thirty years.

He probably made short notes which he then turned into a book. We don't know for certain he did this. We don't even have the book, let alone the notes. The copy we have was made by another monk about a hundred years after Jocelyn's death.

It is a history of his abbey, or monastery, from 1173 until the first year or two of the next century. It was mostly about the abbot, whose name was Samson. Jocelyn disagreed with the way Samson ran the abbey. Jocelyn was at great pains to let the monks know what property the abbey owned and what rights they were supposed to have. Because of his vow of obedience, he felt he could not openly defy Abbot Samson. He hoped that if he wrote down everything that had happened, those who came after him would not let their rights be taken away.

It may seem strange to us that Jocelyn was so concerned about property, that is to say buildings, farms, land, villages and so on. Surely this is not what is meant by poverty? Of course, Jocelyn did not have any possessions himself; it was the abbey which owned everything. Here is a picture of Jocelyn's abbey.

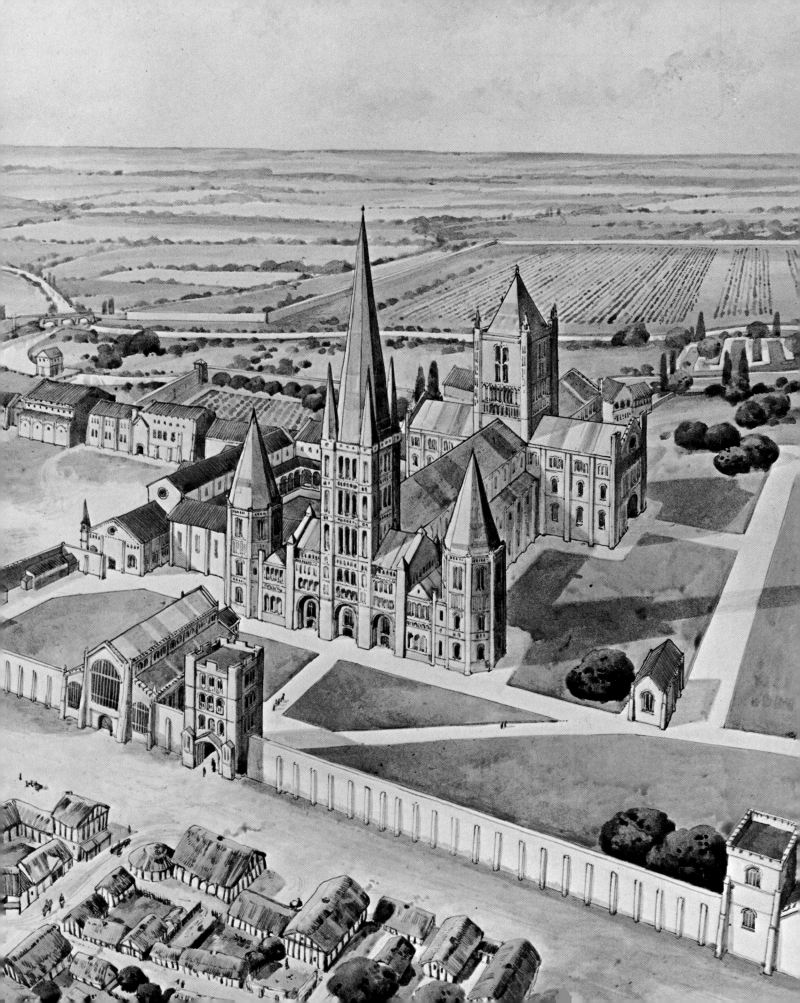

3 People of the Abbey

4 A Day in the Abbey

Time	Service or Activity	Place
Midnight	Matins	Church
1.00 a.m.	Lauds	Church
5.45 a.m.		
6.00 a.m.	Prime	Church
6.30 a.m.	Mass	Church
	Breakfast	Refectory
7.00 a.m.	Reading	Cloister
8.00 a.m.	Terce	Church
9.00 a.m.	Meeting	Chapterhouse
9.30 a.m.	Conversation	Cloister
10.00 a.m.	High Mass	Church
10.50 a.m.	Hand washing	Lavatory
11.00 a.m.	Dinner	Refectory
11.30 a.m.	Rest period	
12.30 p.m.	Work	
5.00 p.m.	Vespers	Church
6.00 p.m.	Meal	Refectory
6.30 p.m.	Walking	Cloister
7.30 p.m.	Bed time	Dormitory

The Sacristan's assistant wakes the monks in the dormitory. They go downstairs to the church for the service. There is a short pause at the end of prayers.

The service lasts about twenty minutes. The monks then go back to bed.

The monks are woken again.

A short service.

The service is attended by the lay brothers and abbey servants.

The choir monks, in the meantime, have breakfast of bread and ale. They are not allowed to talk during the meal. A book is read to them – perhaps the life of a saint.

Another short service.

The meeting lasts for about half an hour. Part of the founder's rule is read and monks who have broken it are given punishments. Notices are read, other business done and the day's tasks given out.

The monks walk in the cloister as they chat.

The main service of the day.

For washing only.

The meal consists of bread, vegetables, soup and wine or ale. There is more reading aloud by one of the monks. No talking is permitted.

The afternoon is spent working in the fields, gardens, cellars, scriptorium, etc.

The last service of the day.

A light meal is taken, again accompanied by readings.

In the winter, the monks stand round the fire in the warming room instead of walking.

The monks sleep until midnight when the programme starts all over again.

5 Books

Do you belong to a public library? How often do you go? Do you sometimes look for a book about your hobby? How do you find out where the book is? In most libraries, books on the same subject are together on the shelves. In Jocelyn's abbey the same kind of thing was done.

If you only have a few books in your class library, you may not need to keep them in any sort of order. How many do you need before you've simply got to arrange them properly?

At Bury St. Edmunds, the library probably had between one and two hundred volumes. They seem to have been divided into groups – Bibles, monastery rules, prayer and service books, lives of the saints, general religious books, medical books, sermons and so on. We

The library at Merton College, Oxford

belonging to other religious houses in England or Europe. All were handwritten, for in those days copying was the only way a book could be made. It was to be another two hundred years before printing was invented.

It is likely that the monks who were good at writing neat letters did little else. They worked at copying in a room called a scriptorium or in small rooms just off the cloister.

Monasteries like the one at Bury have been empty and silent ever since Henry VIII closed them down. Most are now in ruins. Luckily, many of the books were saved. Some went to libraries in private houses, others to colleges at Oxford and Cambridge. Some were taken by cathedrals but most ended up in the British Museum, where they still are.

don't know how they numbered all of them but each section was given a different letter of the alphabet: A for St. Augustine's books, B for Bibles, C for chronicles (histories), or S for sermons. Then all the A books were probably numbered in the order the abbey acquired them. There were over fifty by, or about, St. Augustine. It's just as well the monks had no more than two hundred books in all, or the system would have broken down.

Two hundred volumes does not sound much compared with modern libraries which stock several thousand titles but it was a large collection for the monks. Some of the books were bought or exchanged for different ones but a good many were copied from those

The monastery at Bury St. Edmunds today

Books

At Bury St. Edmunds, writing materials were bought from local craftsmen but other monasteries managed to produce what they needed on their own farms. Paper was dear, so they wrote on specially treated animal skins. Parchment, to give it its proper name, was made from sheep or goat skins. Vellum, which was of better quality, came from the skins of younger animals such as lambs or kids. The hides were cured with tannin. This stopped them going rotten. They were soaked in lime baths, then dried and polished with pummice stone. Tannin comes from oak trees and could also be used to make black ink.

After the skins were removed from calves, kids or lambs (*left*) they were 'cured' with tannin from oak trees. This was usually done in vats or wooden tanks (*right*). Then the skins were soaked in a lime bath to bleach and soften them and hung up to dry (*far right*).

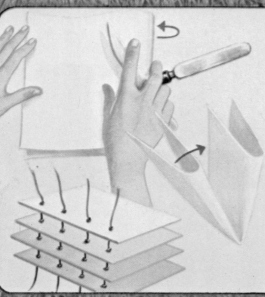

Left The vellum or parchment was carefully creased with a smooth bone or ivory blade. The folded sheets were stitched together and then slit with a knife to make the pages.

Right Strips of cloth were sewn to the pages and attached to thin wooden boards. These were covered with leather which was glued into place.

Ink was made by soaking oak-apples and mixing the liquid with flour and copper crystals. Other colours came from plants and clay.

The dry skin was stretched in a frame and polished with pumice to make it smooth and even.

AVTEM·MOYS·EN·
ET·LOQVVTVS·EST·EI·DN̄S

6 On the Move

This is a picture from a church wall at Chaldon in Surrey. It shows what people of the Middle Ages believed about life after death. They were quite sure that good people went to Heaven and that the wicked went to Hell. But most people are neither all good nor all bad. If a man were condemned to roast in Hell for the first small sin he committed, it wouldn't be worth trying to be good any longer. He was doomed anyway.

The Church gave its followers the chance to pay for their bad deeds while they were alive. A man was allowed to go to confession and own up to what he had done wrong. The priest forgave him, provided he promised to do penance.

A man's penance, or punishment, might be to kneel in the church and say the Lord's Prayer ten times. This was for a small sin. For something more serious, he might be sent on a pilgrimage. We know that St. Edmund's tomb attracted hundreds of people every year. So did the tombs of other saints, not only in England but also abroad.

Apart from penances, pilgrims, as they were called, went to pray at tombs for quite different reasons. Some went because they were ill, to pray for good luck, or to give thanks for past favours.

How did people get about in those days? The roads were not very good. Some main roads had been made by the Romans a thousand years before and were still usable for the most part. Not everyone could journey on main roads all the time and the minor roads were no more than pathways across the countryside and through the forests.

The only reason they were there at all was because so many feet had followed the same route that the grass had been worn away. If a lot of people, animals or carts went the same way, the 'road' was wide. If not many did, it remained a path. Both were hard, uneven and dusty in hot weather and a mass of slithery mud when it rained.

Those who had to make long trips tried to arrange matters so that they went only in the summer time. Of course, it rains in the summer too but the warmer air dries the mud more quickly.

We must remember that England itself looked very different then from the way it does today. Much of it was covered with thick forests. Towns were very small and a long way apart. It was possible to plan your route in such a way that you stopped in a town each night. Travellers could nearly always stay in the guest room of a monastery. There were even a few special inns for pilgrims only. Such a place was called a 'Maison Dieu' (House of God).

Monastery food was simple and plain. There was bread, porridge, cheese, vegetables and fruit in season. Occasionally there was meat but there was nearly always fish. The guests could drink ale or wine. They might even try water if the monastery had a pure well or spring.

The monks usually made no charge for what they provided but they expected something to be put in the collecting box. A poor man could always do a little work to pay for what he had eaten.

Not that poor people travelled very much anyway, unless they were tramps, outlaws or criminals. This was because they had to go on foot. Those who could afford it rode on horseback. There were carts but they were uncomfortable and very slow. The elderly or sick could be carried in a horse litter, as Matilda had been when she escaped from Oxford Castle.

If you were lucky, you could go by boat for part of the way where your journey lay near a river or the sea. Your boat would be hauled along the river by a horse, plodding along the towpath at the water's edge. Or you might sail along the coast to where you wanted to go.

On the whole, there were not very many people on the move in medieval England.

A traveller's meal at a monastery

On the Move

7 The Story of St. Edmund

In the little museum in the Town Hall at Kings Lynn is a sheet of parchment which tells us something about how the monastery came to be built at Bury St. Edmunds. The parchment is a charter, granting to the monks of Bury the right to look after the body of St. Edmund.

Edmund had been King of East Anglia in the ninth century. His kingdom had not long been Christian but Edmund had already built churches and founded a number of small monasteries.

Unluckily for him, the Danes were still a threat to peace and order. In 869, they came down from their town of York and camped at Thetford. Edmund didn't want them in his kingdom, so he gathered his army together and marched out to meet them.

The battle was fought at Hoxne in Suffolk. Edmund's army was beaten and he was taken prisoner. The Danish leaders, Ubba and Inguar, had him brought before them.

'Accept us as your overlords,' they said, but Edmund shook his head.

'Give up your religion and become one of us,' they demanded. Edmund said he would never do so.

The Danish soldiers took Edmund into the nearby woods and tied him to a tree. The archers aimed their bows towards the king. Ubba gave an order and an arrow whistled into the tree just above Edmund's head. Again the questions were asked and again the king said no. An arrow pinned a fold of his cloak

to the tree trunk. Another grazed his arm.

When they realized that Edmund would never give up his religion, Ubba and Inguar told the archers to shoot straight at their target. The king's body slumped in its ropes. The soldiers cut it down.

The news soon spread that the king had been slain. When the Danes had gone, some of the East Anglians went to look for the body. They were shocked when they found it. Before the Danes left, they had cut off the head and hidden it in the forest.

The people beat through the undergrowth looking for the head. Suddenly some of them heard a voice crying, 'Here! Here! Here!' They followed the sounds until they came out into a clearing. They could see a wolf with the king's head between its paws. When the wolf caught sight of them, it made off into the bushes.

They brought the head back to its body and the story began to get about that the shouting had come from the head itself, that

it had told the searchers where to look. People believed the story and came to pray at Edmund's graveside to have their illnesses cured or their sins forgiven. Men left their money and their land to the church where the miracle-working body lay. The king was declared a saint and he became a hero to the Saxons in their fight against the Danes.

Sweyn Forkbeard, the leader of a later Danish army, came to the church. He was annoyed at the way that St. Edmund seemed to be a greater enemy dead than he had been alive. He decided to take away the property and lands of the church and close it down. No sooner had he given the order when he dropped to the floor dead.

His son, Canute, didn't make the same mistake. He took the hint and put monks in charge of the shrine. From these small beginnings a monastery grew.

The charter at Kings Lynn on the left gives us written proof of what Canute did all those centuries ago.

Chapter Nine   The Crusades

1 Peter the Hermit

Pilgrims visited foreign shrines, as well as the tombs of English saints. Those of St. James in Spain and Saints Peter and Paul in Rome were popular. A few English pilgrims went on beyond Rome right down to the south of Italy. From there they sailed across the Mediterranean to the Holy Land. Sometimes they broke their journey at either Crete or Cyprus.

They were making the longest and most important pilgrimage of all. They were going to pray at the places where Jesus had lived and died. For several centuries, the Holy Land had been occupied by Arab peoples. They were followers of Mohammed, but they did not stop Christians going to Jerusalem or Bethlehem.

Then, at about the same time as the Battle of Hastings, a new race of people appeared in the Holy Land. They were the Turks. They too were Muslims like the Arabs but they were much fiercer and crueller. They captured Jerusalem in 1076 and from then on, Christian pilgrims could not go where they

Some crusader routes

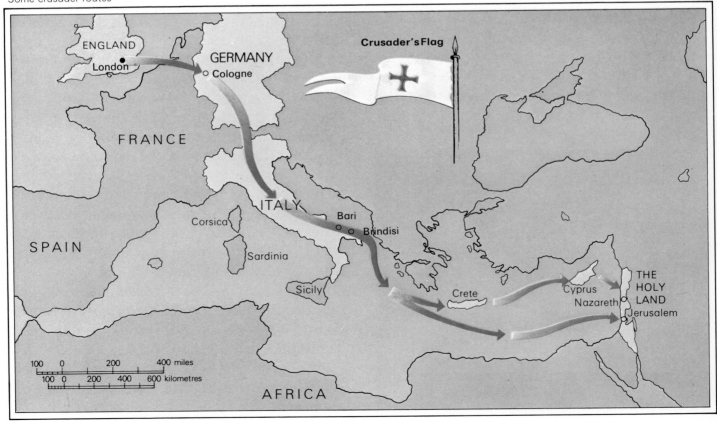

liked. The Turks turned them back, arrested them, threw them into prison and tortured them.

The Emperor at his capital city, Constantinople, sent a message to the Pope, telling him of the danger and asking for help. It was not just because pilgrims were having a hard time. The Emperor had seen how fast the Turks had conquered some of his own lands and he was afraid that Constantinople would be next on their list.

The Pope realized that if the Emperor was right, there would be nothing to stop the Turks sweeping across Europe. He urged all Christians to forget their own wars.

'It is a Christian's duty,' he said, 'to drive the unbelievers out of the Holy Land and free the holy places from their soldiers.' He said these things during a sermon he preached in 1095.

Among those who heard him was a French priest. The people called him Peter the Hermit. He made up his mind to bring the Pope's message to as many Christians as he could.

Let's pretend we are living in a small town on the banks of the River Rhine. What might we have seen?

The news has got around that Peter is expected this very afternoon. The people have gathered in the town square. Most of the craftsmen have shut up their businesses and are standing about in groups of two or three. Even the children know that there is something different about today.

Some apprentices have been larking about a little way down the road. One of them shouts, 'He's coming!' The rest stop their game and make way for Peter. He is riding on a donkey. He comes to a halt and gets down. He looks about him and sees a stone cross at one side of the square. He walks towards it and then faces the townspeople.

They all look at him. He is tall and sunburnt. Both his hair and beard are long and

uncombed. He wears a rough, one-piece garment with wide sleeves. It reaches to his ankles and would be even longer without the rope he wears round his waist to hitch it up. He fingers the crucifix hanging on his chest and begins to speak. His voice is very low to start with but it rises higher as he talks.

He tells the people what is happening in the Holy Land. He makes them angry at what the Turks are doing. He makes some of them weep. He makes them all proud to be Christians.

'The infidels must be driven out,' he shouts. Many of them join in the shouting.

'Take me with you,' cries one.

'I'll help you fight the Turks!' yells another.

On the next page, we'll see what happened to them.

2 Wars of the Cross

'Crusade' means 'war of the cross'. It comes from the same Latin word as 'crucifix' and 'cross' itself. It was a crusade that Peter the Hermit meant to wage against the Turks.

His army was not much more than a mob but they set out from Cologne on the Rhine full of enthusiasm. They left in April, 1096, making their way along the valley of the River Danube.

When they got to Hungary, many of them did stupid things. They thought they were already among the Turks just because they could not understand the local language. Fights broke out and men were killed on both sides. What was left of Peter's army reached Constantinople by July.

Peter thought they ought to wait until the proper soldiers arrived. Armoured knights would be coming to do battle with the Turks but they wouldn't arrive in Constantinople for several months. It wasn't so easy for the knights. They couldn't just pick up a pitchfork and set out for the East as Peter's men had done.

The Emperor did not want Peter's rabble to stay in his capital too long for fear they might cause more trouble. The men were so eager to fight they wouldn't listen to Peter. The Emperor sent them off in ships to the Holy Land. Of course, they were no match for

Peter and his followers were no match for the Saracen army.

the well trained Turks, or Saracens, as the crusaders called them. Peter's men were so badly beaten that few of them lived through the battle.

It wasn't until the following year that the knights got to Constantinople. They were much better organized and led, and there were a lot of them. Although they were sincere in wanting to do their Christian duty, there was another reason why some of them had come.

Many were the younger sons of nobles. A younger son knew that his elder brother would have the family lands when father died. Lands were not shared out between the children. Those who were left out jumped at the chance of setting up their own estates somewhere abroad.

After two years of fighting, the crusaders finally captured Jerusalem. Thinking that this was the end of the problem, a large part of the army packed up and went home. Those who wanted to stay set up a Christian kingdom with a Norman knight as their ruler. Several of the barons built castles on their new lands and tried to live the kind of life they had known back in Europe.

The Arabs and Turks did not like being ruled by Christians and did all they could to get rid of them. They were within easy reach of help for there were more Turkish soldiers not far away. There were not so many Christians and if they wanted help, it could take months to reach them.

The Turks attacked again and again and a second crusade had to be launched against them. It failed, and in 1187, the Turks recaptured Jerusalem. In spite of six more crusades during the next century, the crusaders never won it back again. In fact, the Turks were not forced out of the city until the First World War. This was over six hundred years later, in 1917, and in the lifetime of some people who are still alive now.

3 New Ideas from the East

In spite of themselves, some of the Christians had to admire the way the Muslims lived. The crusaders copied these ways and took them back to Europe. They brought back the carpets and wall hangings of the East and put them in their castles. A few improved their table manners. They stopped using their fingers and began to use forks as the Arabs did. They learned to use spices, such as pepper, with their food. This was to become very important later.

As trade improved between East and West, other new ideas appeared in Europe. Not all of them had been thought up by Arabs or Turks. Quite often they had just been passed on from places like India and China. They included better ways of sailing, telling the time and working out sums.

Our own numbers are based on those the Arabs copied from India. It was much easier for merchants to keep their accounts with the new figures. All the same, the new system didn't catch on straightaway. The old Roman letters hung on for centuries and are not completely dead even now. Do we not still write 'Henry VIII' rather than 'Henry 8'?

jewellery

rock crystal

ivory

glass

enamel

rice

perfume

astrolabe

mirror

cloves

ginger

nutmeg

porcelain

almonds

Arabic numerals

wall hangings

cloth embroidered
with gold

satins, silks, velvets and dyes

dates

raisins

green figs

gar

black pepper

fork

carpets

4 A Knight and his Family

As the years went by, the living standards of the rich slowly got better. The poor went on in the same old way. They had no fashions and few improvements in their homes.

Let's look at what a knight's life was like in the early thirteenth century. We'll just call him Sir John. He held his lands from the Abbot of Valle Crucis. He was not a great

landowner with huge estates and a title such as 'Earl' or 'Duke'. He was probably not allowed to build a grand castle, even if he could afford it, so he put up something smaller. It is a fortified manor house. The entrance is on the first floor. It is too dangerous to have the front door at ground level as an enemy could smash it down with a battering ram. For extra protection the courtyard is surrounded by a stone wall. The walls of the house itself are also made of stone and are quite thick.

The windows are still small and high up but some now have glass in them instead of oiled animal skin, or wooden shutters alone.

The manor lands aim to grow, make or produce everything the family needs – not only for itself but for the servants, soldiers, officers and guests. If this can't be done completely, there is always the possibility of buying what is wanted or taking it in the form of taxes from Sir John's tenants.

5 Family Affairs

This is Sir John, the knight who owns the manor lands, and his wife, the Lady Isobel. Their sons have been sent away to other families to be educated. This custom has gone on since at least the early Norman period. Sir John and his wife, in their turn, are bringing up two boys belonging to relatives. Their names are Humphrey and Guy. Sir John and Lady Isobel have only one child living at home with them. She is their daughter, Eleanor. There are two grown-up sons, Hubert and Theobold. But they are away on a crusade in the Holy Land.

Lady Isobel runs the domestic side of the house. She tells the servants what to do and is busy a good deal of the day with the preparation and cooking of food. In the days when there were no electric or gas cookers, no mixers or blenders and no fridges or deep freezers, everything took much longer to do. As well as the cooking, it is up to her to see that there is enough to drink in the buttery. A little wine is made but most is brought over from France. Ale and cider are made on the estate. Let's ask Sir John to tell us some more about life at the manor.

'Well, the girl servants and even Lady Isobel and my daughter all have to take a hand at spinning and weaving. We make nearly all our clothes at home. Most families do this, even the very rich people. It is only when we want something very special that we have to buy the cloth. My wife and daughter also embroider quite a lot. Lady Isobel gives Eleanor lessons on behaviour while they do their embroidery together. Humphrey and Guy are instructed at other times. For instance, they have to be taught table manners and how to behave in church.'

'What's the church like?'

'Well, it's really a chapel – just a small room at one end of the manor house. My family spend a lot of time at prayer in the chapel. They are all very religious!

'I'm afraid the family is a little sad today. I've told them that it is time I must join my sons, Hubert and Theobold, fighting for our Lord in the Holy Land. My wife doesn't want me to go, but she knows that she ought not to try to stop me doing my duty. And another problem is that we are rather short of money. A knight's fighting gear is very expensive. There are all my soldiers to equip as well. We've already had to find the money to send the boys to the war and I'm not sure how I'm going to pay for what I need. I could put up the taxes but even that wouldn't raise enough.

Silver and gold coins change hands at the market.

'My wife has another idea. I have a town on my land where there are merchants, traders and craftsmen. They are all much richer than the peasants who work for me. They are prepared to give me the money I need if I will give their town its charter. By doing this I would have no further claims on the money the townspeople earn.'

What money do you get from them at present?

'I can charge farmers for bringing the food they've grown into the town. I can make them pay me for putting up their stalls in the market place. I also take a share of their profits. If I give up these rights, they will give me the money for all the new weapons and armour that I need. There will also be enough gold to pay my expenses while I'm in the Holy Land. However, when I get home there will no longer be a regular income of tax money from the town. It's a difficult choice to have to make.'

6 Richard the Lion Heart

Henry II had ruled England so well that the country almost ran itself. It was just as well that it did, because the next king wasn't very interested in England. He was Richard I and he only visited his new kingdom twice in the whole ten years of his reign.

He came over from Normandy to be crowned and stayed here for less than four months. This was in 1189. Five years later he came back, this time for only two months. Then he returned to France. He was not to set foot in England again. His wife, Berengaria, holds a very strange record. She must surely be the only Queen of England never to have visited this country at all.

The reason why Richard was away so much was his love of fighting. He was a tall, well-built man who was extremely strong and yet light on his feet. He was an expert with nearly every kind of weapon and the only thing he liked more than a practice fight was a real war.

When he had the chance to take part in a crusade, nothing could hold him back. He stayed here just long enough to raise the money he needed for his expedition. He is said to have told someone that he would sell London if he could find a buyer.

By 1192, he had captured a string of towns and castles on the coast of the Holy Land but was never able to retake Jerusalem. In spite of Richard's many victories in battle, squabbles amongst the Christian leaders made it impossible for him to win the war.

Then news reached him that his brother John was plotting to take his throne from him. He set out for home but was shipwrecked. He had to try to make his way overland through

Richard's tomb in France

the territory of an enemy, the Duke of Austria.

He didn't get very far before he was arrested and thrown into a dungeon. The duke demanded a ransom of 150,000 marks from the people of England before he would set their king free. Afraid that Richard might be rescued, the duke kept the name of his prison secret. A story is told of Blondel, the king's musician, who travelled through Austria in disguise. When he came to a castle, he stood under the walls and sang Richard's favourite song. At last he was

rewarded by hearing a voice joining in the chorus. He had found his lord.

By this time, the king's subjects in England had raised most of the ransom, which in today's money might be about two or three million pounds. Richard was released and returned to England.

John thought it wiser to slip away to France. Richard had to raise an army and take it across the Channel to defend his lands in Normandy. He spent the last five years of his life abroad. He was killed by an arrow while besieging a French castle called Chaluz.

Richard was known as 'Coeur de Lion' which means 'Lion Heart'. He would have understood the first title better than the second, for although born in England, he spoke French and thought of himself as French. All the same. he was one of the bravest warrior kings we have ever had.

above Leopold of Austria

below Richard killed at Chaluz

7 Armour and Siege Weapons

The fighting man on horseback was an important kind of soldier during the early Middle Ages. His armour had changed little since the end of the Roman empire. Roman legionaries had worn strips of metal over their shoulders and round their chests. The tribes which had overrun their empire had used a different arrangement.

Barbarian warriors had worn coats of leather covered all over with little metal rings, discs or plates. They were sewn in place. The Normans wore something like this when they invaded England.

Linking the rings together makes chain mail. It was more expensive than the old leather coat style, for it took more metal and needed a great deal of skill to make. Crusaders had to wear a light linen coat over it to

Roman

Barbarian

Crusader

Detail of chain mail links

protect themselves from the heat in the lands where they were fighting. The coat was white with a red cross on it. There was a slit at the front and back to make horse riding easier.

Another drawback to any kind of metal armour, especially chain mail, was the fact that it rusted if it wasn't looked after. A Roman could wipe and dry his plate armour if it got wet. It wasn't so easy to do the same thing to a suit of chain mail with its thousands of little links. There was no stainless steel in those days so the knight's squire would have to protect the links by painting them with varnish.

Christian armies spent most of their time besieging castles and towns rather than fighting pitched battles against the Saracens. The Romans had worked out ways of attacking the defenders of a fort. They were very good at it, and the methods had not altered greatly in the centuries that had passed since their time.

The difficulty was the wall which formed the outer works of most castles. The attackers had to get inside somehow. There were three ways to to this. They could go over the wall, under it, or knock it down. Here are some of the 'engines' and methods the attackers used.

Undermining

Battering

Siege tower

Catapult

8 A Siege

9 Magna Carta

Richard Lion Heart died in 1199 and his younger brother, John, became king. The early histories tell us that he wasn't a very pleasant person. He had been spoiled as a child and it's hard to find something nice to say about him. His eating habits were disgusting. He often stuffed himself with food until he couldn't move, or drank himself senseless. He was just as uncivilized in other matters, leaving a trail of trickery and broken promises behind him.

John had a nephew named Arthur. Philip of France thought that John was treating the boy badly. War broke out between the two kings. John took Arthur prisoner. His barons asked him to set the boy free. John promised them that he would but he had Arthur murdered instead. Philip won the war and took most of John's French land away from him.

John then quarrelled with the Pope who promptly closed all the churches in England. This was a disaster for Englishmen. Most of them thought they were bound for Hell as a result. The Pope also said that John was not a fit person to be a king and asked Philip to invade England. John gave in and agreed to pay money to the Pope.

Biding his time, John collected an army and invaded France himself. He was badly beaten. This time his barons had had quite enough of him. Defeats and the heavy taxes needed to pay for the wars were too much for them.

They drew up a list of their complaints against the king and threatened to attack his castles and estates. John agreed to meet them at Runnymede in an open field alongside the Thames between Windsor and Staines. The field has changed very little since those days. There are few buildings in sight, so it's easy to stand there and imagine what the meeting must have been like.

It is a June morning in the year 1215. There has been a light mist but it has gone now. The sun shines from a clear blue sky, picking out the bright colours of the tents which have been put up. There is a carved wooden throne for the king to sit on, if and when he should come.

Some of the rebels are wondering if the king means to keep his appointment. Quite a few of the barons who had promised to come have not turned up. They know that John will never forgive those who have put this shame on him. The group at Runnymede is uneasy. Are they risking their lives by trying to force the king to rule according to the law?

There is a stir in the crowd. In the direction of Windsor some horsemen can be seen picking their way along the river bank. The king's party stops near the tents. Grooms hold the horses as they dismount.

The king sits on the throne. The barons and churchmen have drawn up a list of their complaints. It is on a sheet of parchment. One of them unrolls it and begins to read. There is a short pause when he has finished. John beckons a servant forward. Wax is heated over a flame and the parchment is spread out on a small table in front of the throne.

The wax is poured out and John presses

his Great Seal into it before it can harden. The meeting is over. The king leaves to ride back to Windsor Castle. The barons and churchmen will now have to have the Great Charter, or Magna Carta, as they call it in Latin, written out properly. The experts will get together and put it into the kind of words that lawyers understand.

The king has had to agree, among other things, not to interfere with the Church and not to imprison nor sentence a man without trial. He must give back the forest land he had enclosed without permission and defend the ancient rights of towns and cities. He must allow a baron to be tried by men of his own class, and not raise taxes without consent.

John had no intention of keeping these promises and even got the Pope to say that the Magna Carta was not lawful. When the barons realized that this was the case, civil war broke out. John did not live long enough to see what happened. He died after greedily eating a huge meal of peaches and cider. Some people muttered that he had been poisoned but no one knows for sure.

Magna Carta with John's Seal

Chapter Ten   Years of Change

1 Four Kings

HENRY III

EDWARD I

EDWARD I WAS ONE OF ENGLAND'S MOST WARLIKE KINGS.
HE CAME TO THE THRONE IN 1272. THE PEOPLE OF WALES
REFUSED TO ACCEPT ENGLISH RULE. EDWARD DEFEATED THEM
IN 1281 AND KILLED THEIR LEADER, LLEWELLYN, IN BATTLE.

TO KEEP THE WELSH IN ORDER, EDWARD BUILT
STRONG NEW CASTLES ALONG THE COAST OF
NORTH WALES.

EDWARD II

EDWARD II CAME TO THE THRONE IN 1307. HE WAS A GOOD
HORSEMAN AND SKILFUL IN THE USE OF WEAPONS, BUT HE
WAS MORE INTERESTED IN ENJOYING HIMSELF THAN FIGHTING

BATTLES. HE SPENT FORTUNES ON HIS FRIENDS, FASHIONS AND
ENTERTAINMENTS. EDWARD ALSO ENJOYED MAKING FUN OF
OF HIS BARONS WHOM HE CONSIDERED DULL-WITTED AND UNCOUTH.

EDWARD III

EDWARD III WAS ANOTHER WARLIKE KING. HE SPENT MUCH OF HIS LIFE
FIGHTING THE FRENCH. ONE OF HIS MOST FAMOUS VICTORIES WAS AT
THE BATTLE OF CRECY, WHERE HIS SON 'THE BLACK PRINCE,' WON HIS
SPURS. THE FRENCH LOST ABOUT 15,000 MEN. THE ENGLISH LOST 100 MEN.

WHEN EDWARD CAPTURED THE TOWN OF CALAIS FROM THE FRENCH, HE
SEIZED SIX OF THE CHIEF CITIZENS. THE KING WAS ANGRY THAT THE TOWN
HAD HELD OUT SO LONG. THE MEN WOULD HAVE BEEN EXECUTED IF THE
ENGLISH QUEEN HAD NOT PLEADED FOR THEIR LIVES.

HENRY III BECAME KING IN 1216 WHEN HE WAS ONLY NINE. HE ALLOWED THE POPE TO TAX THE COUNTRY VERY HEAVILY. THE KING QUARRELLED WITH HIS BARONS AND CIVIL WAR BROKE OUT. HENRY WAS CAPTURED AT THE BATTLE OF LEWES IN 1264.

ONE OF THE MOST IMPORTANT EVENTS OF HENRY'S REIGN WAS THE OPENING OF WESTMINSTER ABBEY. IT HAD TAKEN TWO HUNDRED YEARS TO BUILD.

SIMON DE MONTFORT WAS THE LEADER OF THE REBEL BARONS. HE FORCED THE KING TO PAY MORE ATTENTION TO A COUNCIL OF ADVISERS. THE COUNCIL CAME TO BE KNOWN AS THE 'PARLIAMENT.' SIMON WAS EVENTUALLY KILLED AT THE BATTLE OF EVESHAM BY HENRY'S ELDEST SON, EDWARD.

EDWARD OFFERED THE WELSH PEOPLE A RULER WHO SPOKE 'NO WORD OF ENGLISH.' HE HAD IN MIND HIS BABY SON WHO COULDN'T SPEAK ANY LANGUAGE. EVER SINCE, THE HEIR TO THE ENGLISH THRONE HAS BEEN CALLED THE PRINCE OF WALES.

EDWARD THEN DECIDED TO CONQUER THE SCOTS. HE CAPTURED THE STONE OF DESTINY ON WHICH SCOTTISH KINGS WERE CROWNED, AND BROUGHT IT TO LONDON. IT IS STILL SET UNDER THE ENGLISH THRONE.

THE SCOTS WERE CRUSHED AT THE BATTLE OF FALKIRK IN 1298. THEIR LEADER, WILLIAM WALLACE, WAS EVENTUALLY CAPTURED, HUNG AND QUARTERED.

ROBERT BRUCE, THE SCOTTISH KING, DEFEATED AN ENGLISH ARMY LED BY EDWARD, AT THE BATTLE OF BANNOCKBURN IN 1314. BEFORE THE REAL FIGHTING BEGAN ROBERT WAS ATTACKED BY ONE OF THE ENGLISH KNIGHTS, SIR HENRY DE BOHUN. KING ROBERT AVOIDED SIR HENRY'S LANCE AND SPLIT THE ENGLISHMAN'S SKULL WITH A BATTLE-AXE.

IN 1327 KING EDWARD II WAS CAPTURED BY A GROUP OF HIS BARONS. THEY KEPT HIM IN A DISUSED WELL FOR WEEKS AT BERKELEY CASTLE, AND EVENTUALLY MURDERED HIM. WHEN EDWARD'S SON WAS MADE KING HE EXECUTED HIS FATHER'S MURDERERS.

EDWARD III DIED IN 1377. TOWARDS THE END OF HIS REIGN THE FRENCH WENT ON THE ATTACK. THEY CAPTURED THE ISLE OF WIGHT FOR A TIME AND EVEN MARCHED INTO KENT.

EDWARD III'S SON, THE BLACK PRINCE, DIED BEFORE HIM. THIS WAS A GREAT BLOW TO THE KING, FROM WHICH HE NEVER RECOVERED. THE BLACK PRINCE IS BURIED IN CANTERBURY CATHEDRAL. THE NEXT KING WAS EDWARD III'S GRANDSON, RICHARD II, WHO WAS ONLY TWELVE WHEN HE WAS CROWNED.

2 The Wool Trade

One of the highest officials in the land is the Lord Chancellor. This is a picture of him in the House of Lords. Why, do you think, is he sitting on that cushion instead of a chair?

If you could look at England in the 1300s you might be surprised at what you saw. There were not as many towns as there are now and those that did exist were much smaller. The countryside was not divided by hedges into thousands of little fields and there was a lot of land that no one seemed to use or want.

Normally, three huge fields were spread out around each village. Sheep were everywhere. There were millions of them — far more sheep than people, in fact. If you thought that a lot of mutton was eaten in those days, you would be wrong. Sheep were not kept for their meat. Mutton was eaten, but the wool was more important. Most people made their own clothes. The wool for the cloth came from their own sheep. Even the spinning and the weaving were done at home.

Far more wool was produced than could be used in England, so the extra fleeces were sold overseas. English cloth was well made but rather coarse. If you wanted really good clothes, you had to get them from Europe. The strange thing was that, although the finest materials were woven in France or Italy, the weavers often used English wool.

All this means that there was a lot of travelling and trading to be done. Wool was sheared from the sheep and taken to the nearest town to be sold. It could be piled on to carts or slung over the backs of pack-animals. Whenever possible, it was loaded on to boats.

Foreign merchants travelled to England from France, Flanders and Italy to buy up the English wool clip and sell it in their own countries. After a while, English merchants began to take the wool overseas themselves and England soon came to depend on the money made from this trade. To remind important people where the country's wealth came from, cushions stuffed with fleece were made for them. That is why there is still a wool sack for the Chancellor to sit on in the House of Lords. One of the reasons why Edward III started the Hundred Years War was a French threat to the wool trade.

Let us follow an imaginary journey that an English merchant is making. John de Barnes has been on the road for several days now. He is riding a horse in company with two other travellers he has met on Watling Street. It is better for them to journey together. It is not safe to be out on one's own. There are too many cut-throats, outlaws and thieves about.

The travellers have been staying in monasteries or inns each night and this is their last day together. Tonight they will lodge at Stoneleigh Abbey in the Midlands. Tomorrow John will say goodbye to his com-

panions who are going on. He will meet the abbot in the morning and then go out to the sheep-folds.

To make sure he gets the first pick of the best wool, he needs to make the monastery an offer even before the sheep are sheared. Last year, he arrived too late and found the fleeces had already been sold to merchants from Flanders.

This year he is in time. The abbot is pleased to get his money and the shearing begins. It is done with hand-clippers. The fleeces are crammed into canvas bags which are then sewn up and taken by packhorse to the coast. John leaves his agents and servants to look after the packhorses and rides eastward to the port of Kings Lynn.

He is anxious until the wool arrives. The bags are weighed by the customs officers and stamped with his mark. They are loaded on to a ship as soon as John has paid the duty. The ship will sail to Calais in France. There John will put up his wool for sale. The buyers will take it to Ghent or Bruges and sell it to the Flemish spinners and weavers.

The profit John makes in Calais will be lent to a friend of his there, who will buy lengths of luxury cloth. These will be brought back to England in John's ship. When the rich materials are sold, John will have his loan returned plus a second lot of profits.

3 The Ship

4 A House in London

We catch up with John de Barnes on the road to London. He tells us that he is looking forward to seeing his family again.

'I've been away several weeks now, and I'll be glad to get home. The ship landed me at Dover. I rode here to Canterbury where I met this group of pilgrims. They have been to pray at the tomb of St. Thomas à Becket. Some of them have decided to stay here in Kent because there is a plague in London.'

'What sort of plague?'

'Well, every summer there is disease from which people die but the pilgrims say that this year it's much worse than usual. I hope they are exaggerating but I'm worried all the same. My wife and family are back in London. I pray they are all right.'

5 The Black Death

Black rat   Plague flea

The October sun is warm on his back as John rides over London Bridge and clatters on to the cobble-stones of the city. His horse picks its way past the heaps of rubbish which dot the streets.

He is relieved to see his wife at the door when he gets home.

'Don't worry, John', she says. 'The children are fine but several people have been taken ill in this very street and some have died. It's a new kind of plague, and it's all over London. Poor Mistress Bates has lost her husband and both her children.'

John finds out that his neighbours are beginning to call this new plague 'the Black Death'. This is because of what happens to those who are unfortunate enough to catch it. It starts with a sore throat and a runny nose, followed by really bad headaches and a high fever. Then dark splotches appear on the skin, rather like large bruises. Lumps swell up at the tops of the arms and legs. Within a few days, the patient dies.

There are doctors of a kind but they know neither the cause nor the cure. Today, doctors call the disease bubonic plague and they are sure that it was spread by rats and fleas. There are plenty of these in medieval England. It is quite likely that John's wealth has spared him and his family. His stone house does not have so many rats as the wooden, thatched houses of his neighbours.

John loses no time in moving his family

to a house he has in the country. He is lucky that the village is not visited by the Black Death. Because living conditions in the countryside are not so unhealthy as those in towns, many people have followed John's example and moved out. Some of them, without knowing it, have taken the plague with them.

We don't know how many people suffered but some experts say that as many as one out of every three English people died. Fields were not farmed and weeds grew everywhere. Stalls in market places were empty and ships stayed in port. Prices went up, for there were not enough people left to grow or make all the things that were wanted. Here and there whole villages were deserted as the people died or moved away.

The Black Death is thought to have been

above All that remains today of Tusmore, a village deserted during the Black Death

brought here from the East in 1348. It came back three times in the 1360s and continued to return every few years for the next three centuries.

6 The Peasants' Revolt

John Ball

Edward III died in 1377. The next king was his grandson, Richard II. He was only ten years old. Before he was fifteen, a serious rebellion broke out. It happened in 1381 and is known as the Peasants' Revolt.

There were several reasons for the rebellion. To begin with, the Black Death had killed so many people that the pattern of everyday life was upset. There were not enough people to work the fields but lords still expected their work to be done.

Parliament passed laws which tried to keep wages and prices down but they were not successful. On top of everything, the wars with France dragged on, costing more and more money. The peasants were taxed and taxed again. The last straw came when the government decided to raise a poll-tax. The word 'poll' means 'head'.

There were wandering priests who went round the countryside preaching that all men should be equal. One of these preachers was a man named John Ball. Let's listen to one of his sermons.

'My friends,' he says, 'your lives are miserable and poor. Things are wrong with England and they will not be put right unless you do something about them. Poor man hates rich man; rich man sets his face against poor man. Nothing will be better until the good things are shared out fairly.

'The rich man wears beautiful clothes and eats fine foods from silver plates. You wear coarse cloth and eat dry bread from a wooden platter. He drinks wine; you have nothing but water. He sleeps in a bed between linen sheets; you have to put up with mouldy straw on the ground.

'What makes him think he is better than you? We are all the children of Adam and Eve. How did he get rich at our expense?'

The villagers shout their agreement. John Ball tells them that they must be ready to act when the time comes.

The poll-tax did not bring in as much as the king's advisers expected. A lot of people dodged payment, so collectors were sent round. In some villages they were beaten up and dumped in the duck pond. The people armed themselves with pitchforks, knives and sickles.

At Brentwood in Essex, the officials sent to deal with the trouble were mobbed by the peasants. A few were killed by the angry countrymen. Their heads were cut off, stuck on long poles and paraded around the nearby parishes. Now there was no going back. The men of Brentwood sent messengers all over Essex to tell everyone that the time had come for change. Some rowed across the Thames to get help from the people of Kent.

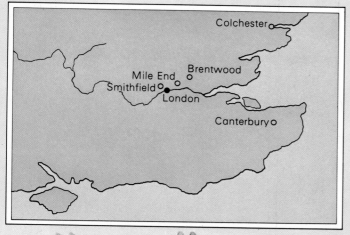

Groups of peasants began to move off westward from both Kent and Essex. They intended to march to London. The Kentish rebels chose a man named Wat Tyler to be their general. Later he became the leader of all the peasants.

Other bands of rebels captured the main towns in the two counties, including Colchester and Canterbury. In the last-named city, they smashed their way into the cathedral and the palace looking for the archbishop. They believed him to be responsible for their miserable condition.

The rebels got the idea that the boy king, Richard, did not know what was going on. They thought that as soon as he was told everything would get better.

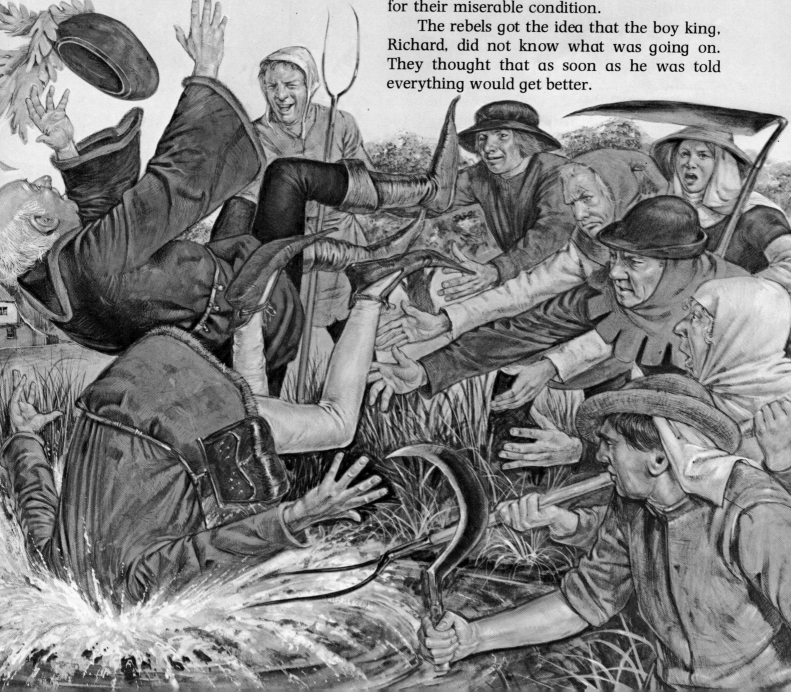

The Peasants' Revolt

On their way up to London, the groups of peasants broke into manor houses. They took food when they could find it, although Wat Tyler and John Ball insisted that they paid for what they ate. More often, they searched the houses for the parchment rolls which set out the details of the unpaid work the peasants had to do for the lord. They carried the piles of parchment outside and burned them.

The ragged army reached London and sympathizers inside the walls opened the gates to them. They destroyed the homes of the hated lawyers and officials and even hanged some of them. The rebels refused to go home until they had talked to King Richard II.

Finally, the mob met the king at Mile End. Richard promised to do what they wanted and set his lawyers to work to draw up the agreements. At Smithfield they met again.

Then things went wrong. Tyler seemed to threaten the king. The lord mayor struck at the peasant leader with his sword. He was pulled from his horse and hacked to death.

When Richard saw that Tyler was dead, he rode towards the mob, shouting to them that he would be their leader. By promising them a better life, he managed to get them to go home.

Later, soldiers were sent to round up the rebels and hang some of them. But the land-owners and lords had learned a lesson. Slowly, serfdom began to die out although it took a long time to disappear completely.

7 A King's Banquet

The boy king, Richard II, had a troubled reign in other ways. Eventually, he was forced to hand over his crown to his cousin, Henry. The new king, Henry IV, shut Richard up in Pontefract Castle, where he was later murdered. Henry left the Tower of London where he had been staying and was crowned in Westminster Abbey.

After the coronation, everyone went in procession to Westminster Hall where the banquet was to be held. The tables were covered with gold and silver dishes and the new king sat down surrounded by his courtiers, the two archbishops, seventeen bishops, all his lords and knights, together with the Lord Mayor of London and his aldermen.

The king's champion rode into the hall in full armour and offered to fight against anyone who dared to say that Henry IV was not the rightful king. There were no takers.

A small army of servants brought in the food. You can see what they ate from the menu on this page.

The decorations mentioned did not just come at the end of a course. They were put on or with any dish that seemed to need them. They were made of pastry, jelly or sugar, moulded into shapes, figures, or animals. Often they were gilded. Coats of arms, religious stories and hunting scenes in coloured sugar were popular.

No attempt was made to group the dishes in any sort of order. It was normal to serve a sweet in between two dishes of roast meat and the whole lot was washed down with wines from many lands. How different from the bread, cheese and porridge of the poor. No wonder there was a Peasants' Revolt.

First Course

Brawn in pepper and spice sauce · Royal pudding · Boar's head · Fat chicken
Herons · Pheasants · Cygnets · Date and prune custard
Sturgeon and pike · *Decorations*

Second Course

Venison in boiled wheat and milk · Jelly · Stuffed sucking pig · Peacocks
Roast bitterns · Glazed chicken · Cranes · Roast venison · Rabbits
Fruit tarts · Cold brawn · Date pudding · *Decorations*

Third Course

Beef in wine and almond sauce · Preserved quinces · Roast egret · Curlews
Pine nuts in honey and ginger · Partridges · Quails · Snipe · Small birds
Rissoles glazed with egg yolks · Rabbits · Sliced brawn · Iced eggs
Fritters · Cheesecakes · Small rolls · *Decorations*

8 In the Kitchen

Here is a recipe, in the original old English, fr

Storion in brothe.—Take fayre Freysshe Storgeoun, an choppe it in fayre water; þanne take it fro þe fyre, an strayne þe brothe þorw a straynoure in-to a potte, an pyke clene þe Fysshe, an caste þer to powder Pepir, Clowes, Maces, Canel; & þanne take fayre Brede, and stepe it in þe same lycowre, & caste þer-to, an let boyle to-gederys, & caste þen Safroun þer-to, Gyngere, an Salt, & Vynegre, & þanne serue it forth ynne.

On the right is a modern translation of the recipe.

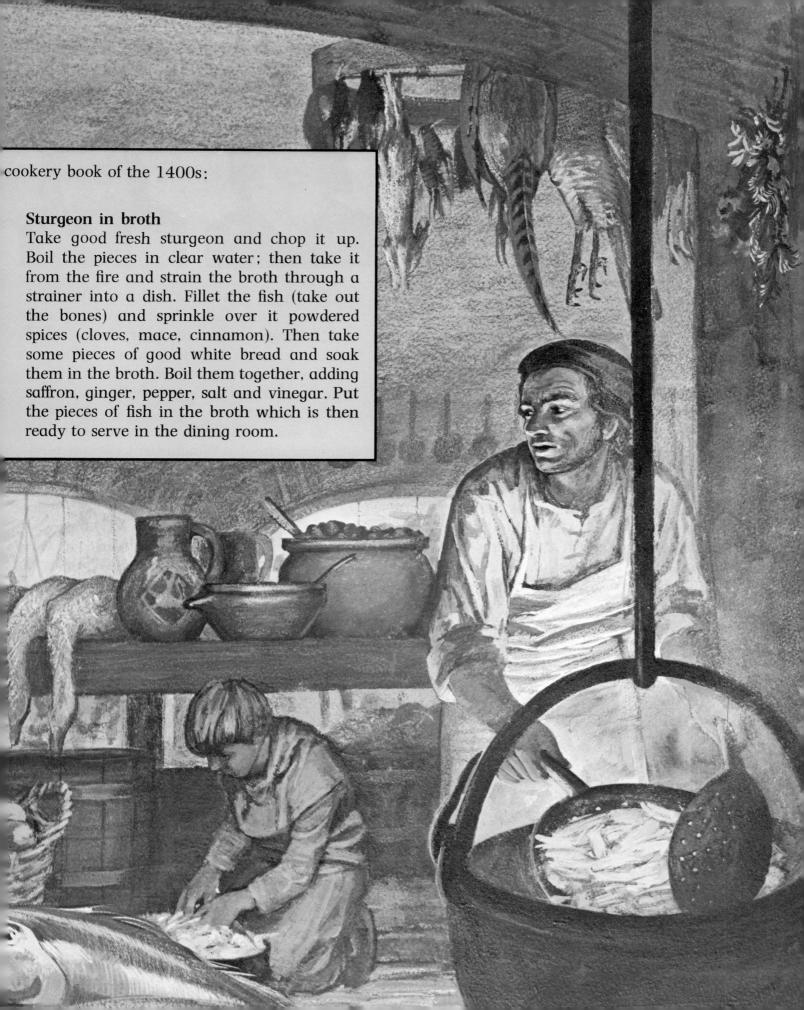

cookery book of the 1400s:

Sturgeon in broth
Take good fresh sturgeon and chop it up.
Boil the pieces in clear water; then take it
from the fire and strain the broth through a
strainer into a dish. Fillet the fish (take out
the bones) and sprinkle over it powdered
spices (cloves, mace, cinnamon). Then take
some pieces of good white bread and soak
them in the broth. Boil them together, adding
saffron, ginger, pepper, salt and vinegar. Put
the pieces of fish in the broth which is then
ready to serve in the dining room.

9 William of Wykeham

This is the story of William, a boy who grew up to be one of the most important men in all the land. He was born at Wickham, a little place about half-way between Southampton and Portsmouth. His father's name was John Long.

It seems likely that 'Long' was a nickname. In earlier times, few people had more than one name. Villages were small and it was enough to be known as 'John', 'Peter', 'Mary' or 'Alice'. As the numbers of people grew, this method no longer worked.

When you came to a large village looking for John, you would be asked which one you wanted.

'There are seven Johns here', you might be told. 'Do you mean John the son of William, John the son of Wat, John the thatcher, John the blacksmith, John the tailor, John who lives near the forest or John the tall man?'

In time, these ways of telling people apart would turn into Williamson, Watson, Thatcher, Smith, Tailor, Forest and Long. Our boy William ought to have been called William Johnson but he became so famous that his title as a grown-up was William of Wykeham. Wykeham was how Wickham was spelt in those days.

He was a bright boy and was sent to the grammar school at Winchester to be educated. This school was mainly for the sons of Winchester citizens and was not the same as the one King Alfred had founded 400 years earlier.

As a young man, William's first job was as secretary to the constable of Winchester Castle, Robert of Popham. He soon obtained

Building New College in Oxford

Winchester College has been a school for over 600 years.

a position with King Edward III. He worked well and was promoted. In 1359 he was put in charge of castle and house repairs along the south-east coast. The Hundred Years' War was being fought and French raids had damaged our defences.

In 1366, he was made Bishop of Winchester and the following year, Chancellor of England. He used a lot of the money he had made to found both a college and a school. He bought land for the buildings to stand on and more land to bring in an income. In this way, both school and college would be able to carry on after his death.

One of the reasons for his interest in education was his desire to replace the huge number of priests which the Black Death had carried off. He wanted his school, 'Seinte Marie College of Wynchestre', to send its best pupils to his new college at Oxford. The boys were to be the sons of parents who could not afford the money otherwise.

Wykehamists have been going on to New College ever since – a period of nearly 600 years.

New College today

10 St. Erkenwald

At the same time that William of Wykeham's school and college were being founded, a famous London landmark was being rebuilt. Everyone knows what St. Paul's Cathedral looks like now but the one we see today is only 300 years old. It replaced the one burnt down in the Great Fire of 1666.

    The first church on the site was probably a Saxon one, also burnt down. The Norman cathedral was started about 1250 and it had already taken over a century to finish. Just as Londoners were looking forward to its opening, a story in verse was written, retelling one of the legends of St. Erkenwald who had been a popular Bishop of London as far back as the year 675.

WORKMEN ARE DIGGING OUT THE FOUNDATIONS FOR THE NEW SAXON CHURCH WHEN THEY FIND A WONDERFUL OLD TOMB.

HE STANDS OVER THE COFFIN AND ASKS THE DEAD MAN WHO HE IS.

THE PEOPLE ARE AMAZED WHEN THE CORPSE OPENS HIS EYES AND ANSWERS. HE SAYS HE IS AN HONEST JUDGE AND HAS BEEN DEAD FOR 1,700 YEARS. HE SITS UP. HE SAYS THAT HIS PEOPLE HONOURED HIM WITH A FINE TOMB AND THAT GOD HAS KEPT HIS BODY FRESH BECAUSE HE WAS A JUST MAN. ERKENWALD ASKS HIM WHY HE DID NOT GO TO HEAVEN IF HE WAS A GOOD MAN. THE OTHER REPLIES THAT HE DIED BEFORE CHRIST WAS BORN SO HE COULD BE NEITHER BAPTISED NOR SAVED.

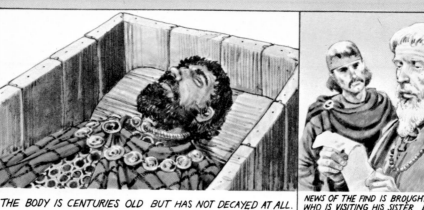

THE BODY IS CENTURIES OLD BUT HAS NOT DECAYED AT ALL.

NEWS OF THE FIND IS BROUGHT TO ERKENWALD WHO IS VISITING HIS SISTER, ETHELBURGA, ABBESS OF BARKING ABBEY.

HUNDREDS OF PEOPLE COME TO LOOK AT IT. THE MAYOR ORDERS THE COFFIN TO BE LIFTED OUT. THEY TAKE OFF THE LID.

ERKENWALD RIDES BACK TO LONDON AND PRAYS ALL NIGHT. HE HOPES THAT GOD WILL TELL HIM WHAT TO DO ABOUT THE BODY.

ERKENWALD IS SAD THAT THE MAN IS DOOMED TO SPEND ETERNITY IN DARKNESS, SO HE SENDS FOR HOLY WATER TO BAPTISE HIM. BEFORE IT CAN ARRIVE, ERKENWALD'S TEARS SPLASH DOWN ON THE CORPSE. THE DEAD MAN LIES BACK IN HIS COFFIN...

'YOUR TEARS HAVE BAPTISED ME INTO CHRIST'S LOVE,' HE SAYS. HE BLESSES ERKENWALD AND THEN, BEFORE THE STARTLED GAZE OF THE ONLOOKERS, THE BODY COLLAPSES INTO A HEAP OF DUST.

1 Heraldry

Do you ever go to football matches, or watch them on television? How do you know which side is which? You can usually tell by the colours the players are wearing. Sometimes your favourite team turns out in colours other than the ones you expect. This is often because the colours are too much alike. If Aston Villa plays West Ham, or Leeds is against Tottenham, such a change would be made.

Leeds United playing against Manchester United

left Their club badges

Knights in the Middle Ages had the same problems. When everyone wore chain mail and a helmet on the top of the head, the face could still be seen. By 1400, however, every part of the body was covered and you couldn't tell friend from foe. Something had to be done to identify them.

The Black Prince got his nickname because his armour was black, rather than bright and shiny. If other knights had copied his example and painted their armour in different colours, things wouldn't have been a great deal better.

This is because there aren't too many colours to choose from — at least, not many that can't possibly be mistaken for each other.

Silver, gold, red, blue, green, orange, purple, black or reddish purple could all be used. The only way to give each man a different appearance was to put two or more colours together. The shield was the obvious place to do this. You might like to work out how many shields you could make with just one or two colours. For pairs of colours, divide the shield like this.

There are nine colours mentioned above. You should put one on the left and the others, in turn, on the right. Then try a second colour on the left and once again pair it with each of the remaining colours — and so on. How many combinations can you get?

Of course, an upright line is not the only way to divide a shield in half. How about these?

You could repeat all the pairs of colours for each different pattern. The total you managed to get at first is now four times as big.

It won't take you long to work out that the shield could be divided into three, four, or even more parts. On top of this, the lines between the areas don't need to be straight — they can be wavy, zigzag, or a mixture of all three.

How many other ways can you think of? Already there are enough to give several hundred knights different designs. If you add extra shapes – diamonds, circles, fish, plants and animals – you have more than enough for all those fighting men who have a right to coats of arms. Often the designs were worn on a coat, which went over the armour, as well as on the shield.

Part of a herald's list: a register of knights and their colours

Heraldry

It wasn't just in battle where coats of arms were necessary, but also at the tournament. Two men would ride towards each other at top speed, in full armour, armed with lance, sword and shield. The idea was to knock the other man out of his saddle. If both men were unhorsed, they would fight on foot with swords.

Some of the judges and marshals took charge of the lists of knights. It was simpler for the officials to get competitors in the right place at the right time if they could recognize them easily. The men who looked after the lists came to be known as heralds.

They kept records of all those entitled to coats of arms. From this time onwards, the only men who could use coats of arms were the sons of men who had the same right. Few new knights were created and the heralds did their best to see that those who were not knights did not pretend that they were.

The work which heralds did was called heraldry and it still goes on today, even though men no longer fight battles in armour nor take part in real tournaments.

2 Henry V

One of the places a visitor to London ought not to miss is Westminster Abbey. Many English rulers are buried there, among them Henry V.

Henry V is one of England's most popular kings. Shakespeare wrote a play about him which was later made into a very successful film.

In some ways, Henry was England's Alexander the Great. Like Alexander, he fought his father's battles and then went on to conquer where all had failed before. Both men were handsome and athletic, both were fine soldiers and splendid generals. Both died young when on the edge of final success.

Henry became king at the age of 25 and spent most of the rest of his life trying to bring a victorious end to the French wars, which seemed to have gone on for ever.

In 1415 he took his army to France, demanding that all the lands which had once belonged to England should be returned. His own father had no real right to the English throne so it's hard to see how Henry could claim the French one as well, but he did.

He captured the port of Harfleur and challenged the Crown Prince of France to a duel. He marched inland but was cut off by a

much larger French army. The battle was fought and won at a place called Agincourt.

When the news of the victory reached England, the king became even more popular and money was raised to help him win the war. He won many towns and castles, and in 1420 signed the Treaty of Troyes. This said that he was to be the next King of France. He also married a French princess.

The Dauphin, as the French king's son was known, took no notice of the treaty and went on with the war. Henry drove his army back and it seemed as though nothing could stop him. Then, shortly afterwards, he was taken ill. He grew worse and died.

His body was buried in Westminster Abbey with his shield, saddle and helmet hanging over the tomb. He was just 35 years old.

Calais
Boulogne
Ruisseauville
AGINCOURT
Maisoncelles
ABBEVILLE
Eu
Somme
Corbie
Bapaume
Dieppe
Amiens
Péronne
Argues
Boves
Fécamp
Nesle
HARFLEUR
ROUEN
R. Sienne
Vernon
PARIS

English
French

J.Frey

3 An Archer in Henry V's Army

Most of you have tried to fire an arrow from a bow at some time or other. A tomato cane with a length of string tied to both ends makes a reasonable bow. A shorter piece of cane will do for the arrow. The arrow won't go very far or very straight but the game is still fun.

Archery has been popular as a sport for centuries. In an age when people had to protect themselves from attackers, every boy was taught to shoot a bow. In those days, they used yew wood to make the bow and hemp for the string. The arrows were made from straight branches of the ash tree. To keep them on course, goose feathers were trimmed and stuck around the butt end. Modern darts are 'flighted' in the same way.

By King Edward I's reign, the six-foot longbow was the one the English army used. Archers were also armed with short swords or daggers in case they got close enough to join in the hand-to-hand fighting.

Let's follow the fortunes of such an archer. We don't know many details of any real person, so we'll have to imagine some of them. We'll call him William – Will for short.

'I was born in a tiny hamlet to the west of London called Bedfont. As a boy, I worked with my father in the great open fields, ploughing, sowing and harvesting. Like my friends, I was fond of archery and won a competition at the age of twelve. I was easily the best boy archer in the district, so when I was sixteen, the lord of the manor was pleased to let me join the army.

'On the day I had to leave, I got a lift on a passing cart and waved goodbye to my family. I looked quite smart in my leather coat, new hose and leather boots. Later on,

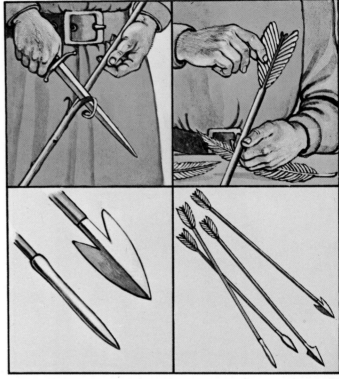

Making arrows

I may get a metal helmet instead of this woollen cap. Sometimes a knight passes on his old helmet to an archer. This usually happens when a new style comes in. Or I might be lucky enough to take a helmet from a beaten enemy.

'The first night away from home, I slept in an inn at Winchester. The next day I set out for the Hampshire coast. After asking several people, I found out where the army was camping. A man called Thomas Hamson took charge of me. We just called him Tom. Tom showed me a place where I could sleep and took me for a walk round the camp. He gave me some food and told me I was free until early next morning.

'I woke at sunrise. A quick meal of ale and bread and then it was time for drill. Tom asked me to show him the bow I had brought with me. I unwrapped it from its canvas cover. "Nice piece of yew wood," he said, "and the string is well waxed. Don't let it get damp. Perhaps we could find you a leather case for it." We went off to the butts where others were already shooting.

'I did well at the targets. Later I was taught to stand in line and fire on command. The morning ended with a distance competition. Most of the men could hit their mark if it wasn't more than two hundred yards away but an arrow can be fired much further. Tom won with a shot of almost a quarter of a mile.

'In the afternoon, we were given a quiver each in which we could carry thirty or forty arrows. They taught us about the different types of arrow head. The ordinary arrow is a good general one for straw targets and unprotected men. There is another kind with the metal head no wider than the wooden shaft. This will go straight through armour if you catch the right angle.

'Later that night, we were told we would be moving on to Southampton the next day and would cross the Channel to France as soon as both wind and weather were right.'

←Thomas Hamson's name on the Agincourt muster roll

4 Ships

It is said that Henry V's army needed more than a thousand ships to take it to France. Henry's father did not have a proper fleet of his own and the French were able to attack the south coast of England almost as they liked.

Henry V bought, borrowed and built ships until he had enough. They were not all exactly alike but the differences were not great. On the whole, ship design had altered very little during the previous few centuries.

The typical ship of the period still carried one oblong sail on a single mast. That was why Will and the archers had to wait at Southampton. Ships could only set out if the wind was blowing in the direction the captain wanted to go.

As you can see, the ship looks rather like the ones William I used to land his Normans in England some four hundred years earlier. The main difference is the built-up parts at front and back. These platforms were for the fighting men. They were called the forecastle and the aftercastle. The raised section at the bows is known as the forecastle to this day, even on a giant oil tanker.

Although gunpowder had been known for over a century, it was unusual to find guns on a ship. The English and French still fought each other at sea in the same way that the Romans had fought the ships of Carthage.

The archers and other soldiers stood on the castles and waited.

When the enemy vessel was near enough, the archers fired at the men on its deck. The ships then tried to get alongside one another so that the soldiers could swarm over the sides and fight with swords, daggers and pikes.

A few of the ideas the Crusaders had brought back from the East were mentioned on page 46. Some were to do with ships. The changes were slow to catch on and Will's ship didn't have many of them.

Of course, Will wouldn't have noticed the changes. He was a countryman and had never seen the sea before, much less a ship. All was strange and new to him. Let us see what happened at Agincourt.

5 Agincourt

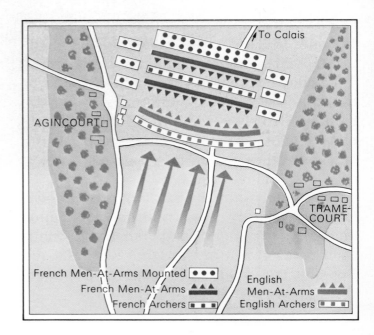

Henry's huge fleet set sail across the Channel. As well as the thousands of soldiers, there were large numbers of armourers, blacksmiths, engineers, cooks, orderlies, clerks, heralds, carpenters, messengers and many more. The knights took at least one horse apiece, plus grooms to look after them. Each knight had a complete set of armour and squires to keep it in good condition.

There were the usual weapons – pikes, arrows, bows, swords, daggers, battle-axes and clubs – as well as the things the king would need to capture towns and castles. On this list were siege towers, ladders, miles of rope, saws, hammers, chisels, adzes, portable bridges and anything else which might be useful.

Henry's aim was to capture a port as near as possible to Paris. It was all very well wading ashore to a stony beach but if the items mentioned above were to be landed safely, the docks and wharves of a port were

necessary. The one he chose was Harfleur.

It was small but big enough for his plans. Henry thought it would fall easily. Unluckily for him, it was a month before the citizens of Harfleur gave in. As it had taken longer than expected, Henry decided to spend the winter in the larger port of Calais, which was in English hands.

The army with all its equipment moved only slowly which gave the French time to collect their troops together. The French army kept out of sight of the English but marched in the same direction. French scouts and spies reported excitedly that the English army was losing more and more men from tiredness and disease.

The place the French chose for their attack was a tiny village called Agincourt, about thirty miles south of Calais. They were confident that the English soldiers could be wiped out and they would be revenged for their previous defeats.

The French knights should have learned a lesson from the times they had been beaten before, but they hadn't. They attacked in exactly the same ways that had been such a disaster at Crécy and Poitiers.

Henry V chose his position with great care so that the ground gave him an advantage. The archers were spread out with marshes in front of them and woodland on either side.

The English fixed six-foot long stakes in the soil with their points towards the French. The archers had plenty of arrows and there were boys to bring them more. They had to make use of the longbow's one advantage.

The French archers had crossbows, able to fire farther and more accurately. The only trouble was that they took a long time to load and aim. While the crossbowman was loosing off a shaft, the longbowman could fire at least five. The French had more archers than the entire English army but they hardly used them. The honour of destroying Henry's men was to go to the heavily armoured nobles.

Agincourt

Henry knew that his archers had only one chance. Provided that the French relied on their knights, as they had done at Crécy seventy years before, and provided that the knights attacked in close formation, there was hope.

The gap between the two patches of woodland was so narrow that only a few knights at a time could ride into it. Henry was lucky. The French did just what he expected. He waited until they were only a few yards away before giving the order to fire.

His bowmen loosed off their arrows so fast that the air was filled with them. Time after time the French knights attacked, only to be brought down in a hail of arrows. Henry had put some of his archers into the fringes of the woods so that they could shoot at the enemy from the side.

At last the battle was over and the almost impossible had happened. French soldiers had outnumbered the English by about seven to one but now they were lying dead in heaps.

It was a great victory but, as we now know, Henry didn't live long to enjoy it. He died seven years later, not much nearer to conquering the whole of France than Edward had been. His baby son did not grow up to be a warrior. Slowly, the French won back the lands they had lost. Joan of Arc inspired them to further victories. By 1453, both sides had tired of the war. The English nobles were beginning to quarrel amongst themselves about who should be the next King of England. The quarrels turned into a civil war which lasted thirty years. We call this the War of the Roses.

6 The Pardoner's Tale

Chaucer

Life went on during the war. People carried on with their daily tasks, soldiers left for France, merchants bought and sold things and bands of pilgrims trooped off to the shrines of saints. Geoffrey Chaucer, the greatest of the early English poets, who had worked for Henry V's father, tells of such a group travelling to Canterbury.

His pilgrims are of all sorts, good people and bad. One of the least attractive is the Pardoner. He pretends he can forgive people's sins and stop them going to Hell when they die. He will pardon anyone who can pay him.

The pilgrims take it in turns to tell the others a story. Thus the journey to Canterbury will seem shorter. The Pardoner sees his chance to make some money. This is the story he entertains his fellow pilgrims with.

WITHOUT STOPPING TO THANK HIM, THE THREE SCAMPER OFF TO THE OAK TREE. THE YOUTH GETS THERE FIRST. HE GASPS AND POINTS...

AS SOON AS HE HAS GONE, THE TWO MEN PLOT TO KILL THE YOUTH WHEN HE COMES BACK. THEN THERE WILL BE MORE MONEY FOR EACH OF THEM.

WHEN THE YOUTH RETURNS THEY DRAW THEIR DAGGERS AND STAB HIM TO DEATH. THE MEN LAUGH AND DRINK THE WINE.

LITTLE DO THEY KNOW THAT THE YOUTH HAS BEEN PLOTTING TOO, AND HAS POISONED THE WINE!

TWO MEN AND A YOUTH ARE DRINKING IN A TAVERN. A COFFIN PASSES BY. SOMEONE ASKS WHO THE DEAD MAN WAS. 'A FRIEND OF YOURS,' HE IS TOLD. 'LAST NIGHT, WHILE HE WAS DRUNK, A THIEF CALLED DEATH STOLE HIS LIFE AWAY. HE'S STOLEN MANY LIVES IN THESE PARTS.' ONE OF THE MEN SUGGESTS 'WE OUGHT TO HUNT DOWN THIS THIEF CALLED DEATH!'

THE THREE AGREE TO GO AND LOOK FOR DEATH. THEY MEET AN OLD MAN WHO TELLS THEM THAT HE KNOWS DEATH WELL. 'I'M SO OLD AND FEEBLE THAT I'M READY FOR DEATH BUT HE WON'T HAVE ME. IF YOU WANT TO MEET HIM GO TO THAT OAK TREE UP THE LANE. THATS WHERE I LAST SAW HIM.'

THE OTHER TWO SEE WHAT HAS STARTLED HIM. THERE IS A GREAT HEAP OF GOLD SPILLING OUT FROM THE HOLLOW TREE. THEY FORGET ABOUT DEATH AND GET VERY EXCITED OVER WHAT THEY WILL DO WITH THE MONEY.

'WE MUSN'T BE SEEN TAKING IT AWAY IN DAYLIGHT! WE'LL HAVE TO WAIT UNTIL IT'S DARK.' THE MEN SEND THE YOUTH BACK TO THE TAVERN FOR DRINK.

THE MEN CLUTCH THEIR THROATS AND COLLAPSE ON TO THE GRASS. NOW THERE ARE THREE CORPSES BY THE TREE.

THEIR WISH HAS BEEN GRANTED; THEY HAVE FOUND DEATH!

The Pardoner ends his story and tells the pilgrims that the drinkers were punished for their greed.

'If you good people want to escape Hell,' he says, 'I can let you have a pardon for the sin of greed. It won't cost you much!'

When the pilgrims realize that his story was not meant to amuse but to make money, they are angry at the way they have been tricked. They will not give him anything and it is quite a while before they will even speak to him again.

Chapter Twelve   Life in a Small Town

1   A Market Town

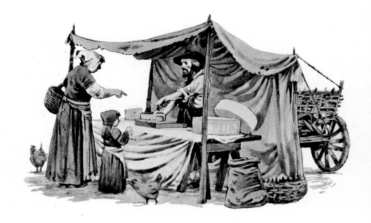

There were probably no more than about four million people in England in the Middle Ages. Today there are ten times as many. From this you can see that the towns in those days must have been much smaller than they are now. A town with one or two thousand people was quite a large one in the fourteenth and fifteenth centuries. Let's look at such a town.

Nowadays it is famous all over the world as the birthplace of Shakespeare but at the time in question, Stratford upon Avon was only a small market town. This means that it was a place where farm produce was sent for sale. Most countrymen grew all the food they needed and sold whatever they had left over. As the town got bigger, the farmers made sure there was enough surplus to send to Stratford by raising extra crops.

The town itself began as a good river crossing. Nowadays, we don't worry about bridges, nor even notice them very much, but centuries ago, travellers often had to go miles out of their way to find somewhere to cross a marsh or river. Sometimes there was a ferry or a ford, more rarely a bridge.

Those with goods to sell gathered at the bridge over the Avon. That was where they would expect to find customers. Business was good and before long, huts and storehouses began to go up. Then someone built an inn. The Falcon, opposite Stratford's Guild Chapel, dates from medieval times.

Slowly the town grew. The pattern of streets laid out at its birth still exists. Their names often tell what went on. Wood, Sheep and Rother Streets were where wood, sheep and cattle were sold. Rother Street is still the market of the town.

The houses were almost entirely made of local materials. There was a framework of oak beams, the spaces being filled in with basketwork panels. These were plastered and whitewashed. Shops were made in the same way and were really workshops. Articles were made on the premises and sold from an open window. The craftsmen and their families lived over the workshop. Such people did not have time to grow all their own food and it was they and the other town-

The Falcon Inn

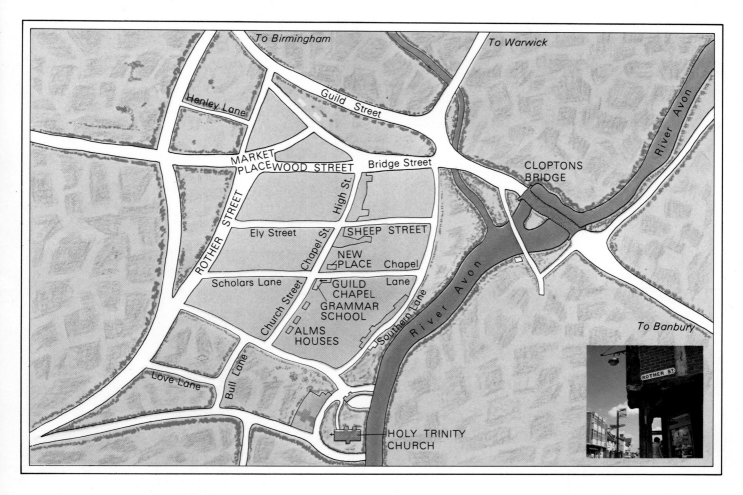

dwellers who bought from the peasants. All the same, it was a rare house or workshop that didn't have space for a cow in the back yard and perhaps even a few fruit trees in the garden.

Even though you could walk all round medieval Stratford in about twenty minutes, the houses were not crammed together. The gardens, orchards and open spaces saw to that.

Some of the country folk came into town on market days to sell their sheep, cattle, cheese, corn and vegetables. The money was spent on what they couldn't make or produce themselves, including ironware, barrels, leatherwork and some clothing.

It's not really surprising to find so many different kinds of things on sale in so small a town. Travel was not easy. Roads were bad and journeys were measured in days rather than hours. It could take a week to get to London by the fastest transport you could afford. Poor people hardly went anywhere very much. As walking was their only way of getting about they probably never journeyed more than a day's walk from where they were born all their lives.

Even the streets of the town were bad. There were no pavements and only a few cobble-stones here and there. Apart from that, Stratford had everything you could want – food, drink, shelter, clothing, entertainment, religion. The town had a fine stone church and a guild chapel, a school, four fairs a year, occasional visits from a band of actors and a weekly market. What more could anyone ask?

2 Medieval Tradesmen

Charcoal-burner

The woodcutters haul the logs to a clearing in the forest. The charcoal-burners chop the logs into small pieces. These are piled into a large heap and covered with turf. The men drop burning pieces of charcoal into the pile of wood which smoulders slowly for several days. When the wood turns black it has become charcoal. It is sold to those who want a smokeless fuel with no impurities. Rich men buy it for use in their kitchens and iron smelters burn it in their furnaces.

Cooper

The cooper needs as much wood as the wheelwright. It was discovered that wine and other drinks keep better in wooden containers than in clay pots. Early craftsmen may have tried to scoop out the inside of a large block of wood. This takes a long time and wastes a lot of wood. A better way is to cut a number of staves and fit them together with iron hoops. The barrel will be used to hold beer or wine.

Potter

The potter sends his assistants to dig clay from the pit near the river. They bring it back in a cart and pummel and knead it on a flat bench. The potter takes a lump of the clay and puts it on his wheel. He uses his feet to turn the wheel and his hands to shape the jug. Pottery in the Middle Ages is rough but not cheap. Some is glazed in green or combed in brown and yellow before it is fired in a kiln.

Wheelwright

The wheelwright also gets timber from the woodcutters. He needs three different types of wood — elm, ash and oak. The elm is used for the hub of the wheel which is huge and weighs several pounds. It has to be made carefully as it must be absolutely round and the eight holes for the spokes need to be cut very accurately. The spokes are made from ash. They are shaped and fitted into the hub sockets. The felloes are the pieces of oak which form the wheel rim. They fit on to the spokes and are fixed in place when the wheelwright nails strips of iron across the joints.

Medieval Tradesmen

Innkeeper

In the Middle Ages many peasants brew their own beer. Some make better beer than their neighbours so they produce more than they need and sell the excess. A few become innkeepers and provide drink and food for those who can afford it. At an inn travellers can get a bed for the night, a stable for their horses and, perhaps, a barn for their servants.

Moneyer

The moneyer and his helpers make coins. Poor people don't use money. They barter or exchange goods directly. This means that most coins are made of gold and silver for the use of the rich. The moneyer beats out the ingots of metal into sheets of the same thickness as the finished coins. He then cuts out the discs with a large pair of sharp shears. The disc is called a blank. The blank is set on top of a metal die and another die is placed over the top of it. The moneyer then gives the top die a sharp blow with his hammer. If it has been struck just right, the two dies will make the pattern on both sides of the coin at once.

Weaver

Just as most peasants brew their own beer, so most of them make their own cloth. For those who can't or don't have the time the weaver goes to work. He winds his threads of wool in a special way on his warping board to stop them tangling. Then he puts threads, one at a time, through the little eyes in the heddles and fastens them in bunches to the front beam of his loom. By pressing down a pedal with his foot the weaver can raise one lot of threads. This makes a space through which the shuttle thread is passed.

Miller

The peasant farmers all take their corn to the mill to be ground. The mill is leased out by the lord of the manor to the miller who is one of the wealthy men of the district. His mill stands alongside the river and the machinery is driven by a water wheel. The miller raises a sluice gate and the water pours past the mill and turns the wheel. The wheel makes the two millstones revolve against each other. The corn trickles down between the stones and is ground to flour.

3 The Cordwainer's Apprentice

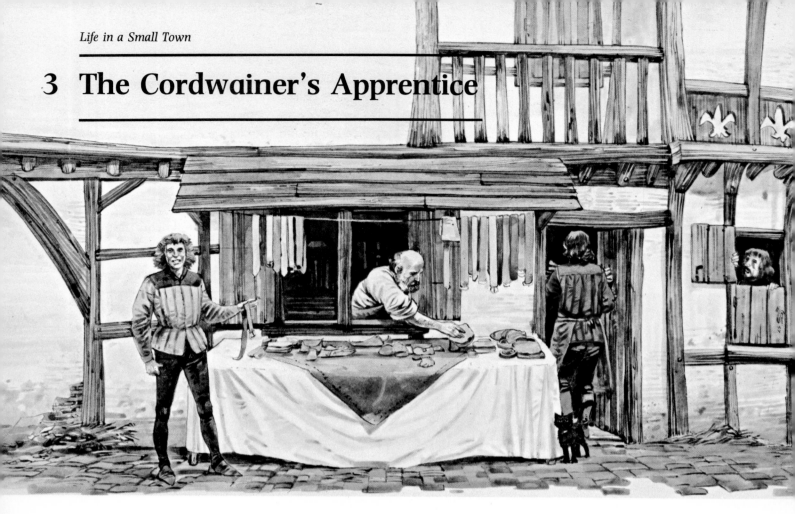

Towns in the Middle Ages were not large by our standards. If there were two or three thousand people in a town, it was considered to be a big one. Most people still earned their living by farming but town dwellers, on the whole, did not.

We have already seen that there were men in the Middle Ages who specialized in making just one thing. Most crafts of this kind were not open to everyone. You could not become a wheelwright, for example, without serving an apprenticeship. This meant that you would have to spend several years learning the job before you could open your own business.

Even today, apprenticeships have to be served for some careers. In the Middle Ages, this was true for almost any trade that needed the slightest bit of skill. To find out what an apprentice's life was like we shall ask the cordwainer's boy some questions. His name is Ralph.

'*What exactly does a cordwainer do?*'

'He is a worker in leather, but he is not a common cobbler or shoemaker. He does make shoes but rather fine ones. His main trade is in anything made of goatskin.' Ralph shows us some belts, purses and bags. They are made from what we would call suede leather. We still don't know why a leather worker should be called a cordwainer. Ralph will explain.

'The best goat-leather comes from Cordova in Spain. We call it Cordovan or Cordwain. I had to learn about these things when I first joined the trade. Luckily for me, my master means to teach me properly. Some masters don't do this and treat their boys as though they were cheap servants. You see, we don't get paid for what we do. On the contrary, my father has had to pay the cordwainer to teach me.'

'*When did you become an apprentice?*'

'Most boys start their apprenticeship when they are fourteen and it usually lasts seven years. By the time I'm twenty-one, I will know how to work with all kinds of leather, which kinds of stitching and thread to use and which types of buckles, clasps and ornaments to buy. There's a lot to learn about buying and selling and it isn't easy.'

As Ralph is speaking, one of the workmen starts to take in the goods on display and put up the shutters of the shop. It's only midday but it seems that all the workshops are shutting. Ralph explains what is happening.

'Today is a half-holiday for the apprentices,' he says. 'This afternoon we are going to play football.'

'*Are you in the team?*'

'Everybody's in the team!' he says in a surprised voice. 'You can watch if you like but, if I were you, I'd do it from an upstairs window.'

Later that afternoon, we take his advice. No one, apart from the apprentices, seems to be in the street.

The match starts near the middle of the market square. The ball is a small barrel of ale. There appear to be hundreds of players on each side. There are no rules as far as we can see and no referee. Linesmen are not needed, for the 'pitch' is wherever the 'ball' goes. Boys push the little barrel with their feet. They don't kick it for fear of breaking their toes. Every now and then, someone picks it up and tries to run. He doesn't get far before he is bowled over. The game surges all over the town and we can now see why all the shops close for the day. A mass of bodies is crammed into the narrow street where we were talking to Ralph. We realize that if the goods had still been on show they would have been scattered and trodden on. The whole stall would have probably ended up in pieces.

Some of the players are giving up. One has twisted his ankle on the cobble-stones and another has blood running down his forehead. The rest carry on. The game ends when the first goal is scored. The goals are at the end of Bridge Street in one direction and at the crossroads in the other. It's not often that the goal is scored and the game normally ends when it's too dark to see what is going on.

4 The Guild System

While we are waiting for the football match to finish, we ask Miles Collins, Ralph's master, about the guilds in the town.

'I expect you've heard about the Mercers' Guild? They are men who buy and sell cloth. Men who work at a craft all belong to their own special guilds. Just think of the things you need which you either can't produce yourself or perhaps you just don't have the time to make.

'For example, there are guilds for each type of metal worker. Blacksmiths turn out iron tools and implements while other kinds of smith work with lead, tin, copper, silver or gold. Most are concerned with everyday objects such as pipes, pots and pans but the last two, silversmiths and goldsmiths, make jewellery and fine table-ware.

'Then there are the various leather workers like myself. Tanners deal with the

Miles Collins

coarser hides and tawers with the finer ones, such as kid. There are boot-makers, cobblers and glovers and there are the men who make saddles and harnesses for horses. Even the stitching of cow hides into bottles and jugs has its own craftsmen.

'There's almost as big a group involved in woodwork of some kind. Separate guilds deal with furniture makers, plain carpenters,

Coats of arms of four of London's main guilds

sawyers, wheelwrights, cartwrights and so on. I could go on for quite a while.'

'What exactly is a guild? It sounds like a sort of club.'

'It is a club, in a way. All the members look after each other. If a man has the tools of his trade stolen, the guild will replace them. If a man falls on hard times or becomes ill, his guild will take care of him. It will see that his wife doesn't starve should he die. His fellow guildsmen will even pay for his son's apprenticeship.'

'Where does the money come from to do all this?'

'Oh, each member puts in a small sum. It adds up to quite a large amount when there are lots of members. Only masters have to pay the subscription.'

'How did you become a master?'

'I started as an apprentice, like young Ralph. I served my seven years and then I became a journeyman. That's a sort of skilled workman. Each apprentice has to pass an examination. He answers questions from a panel of masters and has to show them an example of his work. After a few years, if he works hard enough and saves his wages as I did, he may have enough money to start his own business.'

'Everyone seems to work very hard.'

'Oh it's not all work. You've seen the apprentices having their game of football. Of course, the masters don't join in but there are plenty of other pastimes we help with. Life is quite hard for most people so we seize any chance we get to have some merrymaking – a feast, a procession or a play. Our guild is rehearsing a play at the moment. Perhaps you would like to come and watch?'

Examples of guild craftsmanship

5 The Play

Miles is obviously keen on drama and knows a lot about the subject. He tells us something of its history.

'Guild members are good Christians,' he begins. 'You may have seen the guild chapel in Chapel Lane. We paid for that. You won't be surprised to hear that our play is religious too. The idea for a play started years ago in the days when hardly anyone could read or write. To help people understand stories from a Bible they couldn't read, some churches had paintings and carvings arranged around the inside of the church itself. Obviously, these were scenes from Bible stories. Then monks began to act out the scenes. They just did the actions with a storyteller to explain what was happening. Perhaps each playlet was put on near the picture or carving of the scene so that the audience would have to move round to follow the stories. After a while, the actors began to speak the lines and make up material which was not in the Bible.

'Audiences enjoyed the comedy which had crept in and more people crowded into the church to watch. So many came that before long, there wasn't enough room for them all inside. The actors moved outside to the churchyard and eventually to important points around the town.

'Each guild acts out its own part of the story and moves on to the next stage as soon as it is over. The guild performs several times in different places. Those watching can see the whole set, or cycle of playlets, by staying where they are.'

At last we come to the yard where the rehearsal is in progress. There is hardly any make-up and few special clothes or stage properties for the actors. Everyone seems to know their words. We watch what is going on.

The stage is known as the pageant and is almost head-high to an adult. It stands on four large wheels so that it can be pulled through the streets to the places where the play will be performed. Miles strolls over to have a word with the actors on the stage. Then Ralph comes into the yard. We ask him if he is in the play.

'Well, I was last year but not this. I said that I thought the Christmas play should be more like the one they do at Coventry. They do the same as we do for the birth of Jesus but they have this funny piece to start with about a thief called Mak, and the shepherds. Mak steals a sheep and hides it in the cradle at his house. The shepherds notice one of their flock has gone and call on Mak. They think the sheep in the cradle is a baby and Mak shouts at them for disturbing it and its mother. They apologize and leave but a minute after they have gone, one of them remembers that they haven't given the baby a present. So they decide to go back. One of the shepherds goes to the cradle with a sixpenny piece and discovers that the baby is really the missing sheep! They threaten to have Mak hanged but after a while, they let him off with their own punishment. Mak is put on a sheet of canvas and tossed in the air several times.'

Ralph is smiling as he says this until he sees the blank look on our faces. 'Well,' he says defensively, 'it doesn't sound so funny as it is when you see it.'

The Play

6 Hugh Clopton

Alderman's costume

Back in the thirteenth century, during the reign of Henry III, a man named Robert became the owner of an estate and manor house at Clopton. Clopton House still stands in parkland about a mile to the north of Stratford upon Avon in Warwickshire. From then, the owner called himself Robert de Clopton ('de' is French for 'of').

About two centuries later, the 'de' had been dropped and there was born at the House a boy who was known simply as Hugh Clopton. We don't know the exact year this happened but we do know that he went to London when he was still quite a young lad.

He was probably apprenticed to a high-class cloth merchant. By the 1470s, he had become very wealthy. In October 1485, he was elected alderman of the Dowgate ward. It was an honour to be chosen to sit on the Corporation of the City of London. It was fine to have the power to make rules for your fellow citizens to live by but it meant that Hugh had even less time to spend in his beloved Stratford.

This was a pity, for he had built a fine house in Chapel Street, Stratford, in 1483. It was timber-framed like most houses of its day but the gaps between the wooden struts were not filled with wattle and daub (plastered basketwork) but with good red bricks.

The Romans had often used bricks when they were here but after they left, the secret of making them had been lost, or else they had just gone out of fashion. It was to be a thousand years before they were included in buildings again. Hugh Clopton's house, New Place, as it was called, must have been one of the first houses in Stratford to have bricks.

Only eight years later, Hugh Clopton became Lord Mayor of London and was knighted. He may also have been elected to Parliament at about this time. In the short period he was able to spend at Stratford, he tried to make improvements to the town which would please the people who lived there.

He started with the guild chapel almost opposite New Place. He gave it a steeple and new glass windows. He arranged to have the inside decorated with paintings, some of which can still be seen.

One thing the visitor can hardly help noticing is the fine stone bridge over the River Avon. This too was the gift of Sir Hugh. The old wooden bridge had become rickety and unsafe. Sir Hugh paid workmen to drive closely-packed wooden piles in circles where the foundations of the arches were to go.

The men cleared away the mud and sand from inside the wooden pile rings and dug down to make holes for the foundations. Stone masons shaped and fitted the blocks together and finally it was done. Its fourteen arches were so well built that the bridge stands to this day.

above Clopton's bridge today

The building of Hugh Clopton's bridge

below The Guild Chapel in Stratford

The story of Sir Hugh Clopton is rather like that of Dick Whittington. Both were country boys who became mercers in London. Both were knighted and both were chosen as Lord Mayor. Both became rich and left money for the poor. There must have been many like them.

Another poor boy from the country made good in London and came back to pass his last few years in his native town. Towards the end of the sixteenth century, he bought New Place from the descendants of Sir Hugh Clopton. His name was William Shakespeare.

7 New Place

Clopton's fine house was pulled down in 1759. All we have left of it are a few sketches and the gardens that William Shakespeare set out when he moved in. Here is a picture of what the house must have looked like in Clopton's day. Walls have been cut away so you can see what is going on inside.

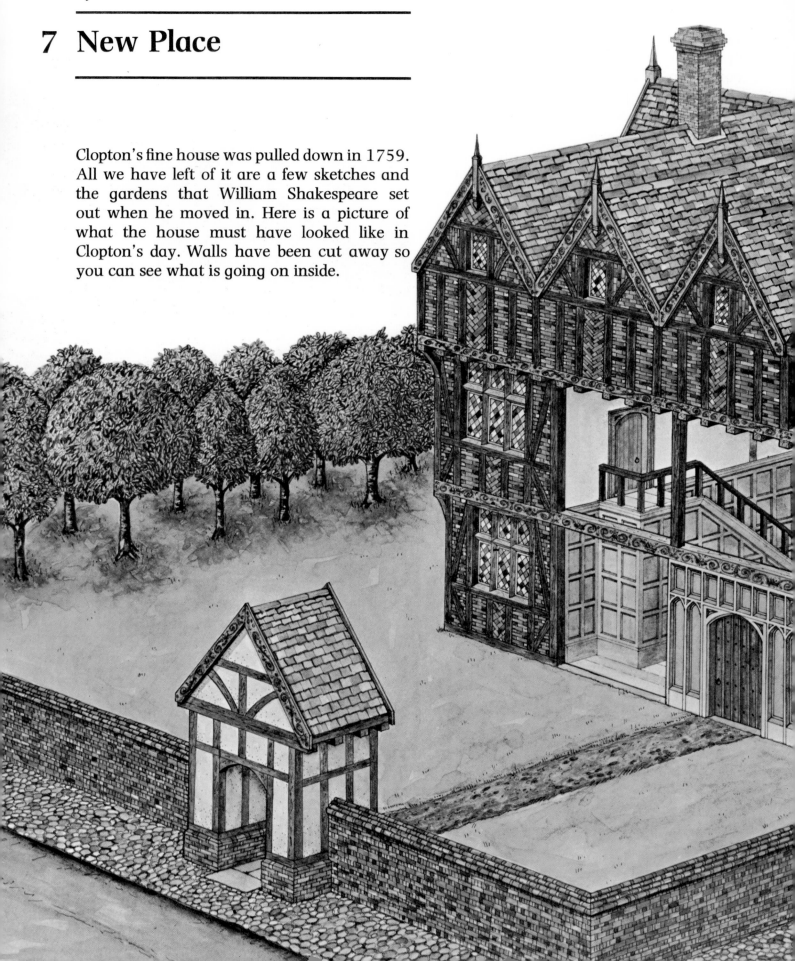

8 Family Chapels and Chantries

This is the inscription carved on Shakespeare's tomb in Stratford parish church. It was natural in a religious age for men to feel that they stood less chance of going to Heaven if their remains were scattered or destroyed.

Another way of making sure of eternal life was to have masses, or services, said for your soul after your death. The easiest way to make certain they were said was to leave land in your will, with instructions that the rent from it was to be paid to priests to pray for you.

Such an instruction set up what was known as a 'chantry' and because they cost

money, they were not for the poor. Peasants didn't have land, so they got a simple funeral service and that was that. The rich man's land was intended to provide the priest's wages for ever. When the priest himself died or resigned, the money was there to appoint someone else.

Wages were not the only expense. All the robes and vessels had to be bought, as did the ornaments and candles. The most expensive item on the list was the building of the chapel, or at least altering the church in which it was to be put.

The Clopton chapel in Holy Trinity Church, Stratford, is a good example of a family chapel. Although Sir Hugh died in London and is buried there, his money paid for a tomb altar in memory of him. Many other members of the Clopton family have tombs or memorials there.

Holy Trinity Church in Stratford

that didn't have a family chapel, or at least a chantry priest or two.

Some of the richer chantries also set aside money for charities. These might be schools, colleges, homes for orphans or almshouses for the aged poor. Those not rich enough to found colleges might arrange a chantry for a few weeks or months, or if that was too dear, then they could leave some money to buy candles for the parish church.

If a man were a member of a guild he might be lucky enough to share in a guild chantry paid for by all the members. In London alone, during the early 1500s, there were more than seventy such guild chantries.

A question you may be asking is, 'What happened to these chantries – why don't you hear of them nowadays?' You can of course visit any of the churches which have family chapels. Holy Trinity at Stratford isn't the only example – there are plenty of others.

The reason why you won't have heard of a priest being paid to do nothing else apart from praying for just one person's soul is simply that they don't exist any more. Henry VIII and his son Edward VI passed laws taking over all the land whose rent paid the salaries of the priests. As a result, the chantries had come to an end by the middle 1550s.

The Clopton chapel

The first chantry chapels were set up in the thirteenth century. By the fifteenth century, there was scarcely a parish church

9 King Richard III

This is the Tower of London. It is a grim-looking fortress. Many stories, some true, some merely legends, have given it a sinister reputation. A great many people have been imprisoned here. A number of them were executed, others were never heard of again. In 1674 the skeletons of two boys were discovered under the floor at the foot of the staircase.

Here are two pictures of Richard III. One is a portrait painted during his lifetime. The other is a famous actor playing the part of Richard in a Shakespeare play.

When King Edward IV died in 1483, his eldest son should have become king but the boy was only 12 years old. Richard was the prince's uncle. He promised to keep the lad safe until he was old enough to rule.

Richard was also appointed to run the country in the meantime. Instead of protecting the prince he put him and his brother in the Tower of London. Then he declared that neither of the two princes in the Tower could be the next king. Weeks later, he had himself crowned as King Richard III.

In Shakespeare's play about him, he is made to seem the worst villain that ever lived. There is certainly a strong chance that the skeletons mentioned above are those of the two princes and that their uncle had them murdered.

Those of Richard's subjects who didn't like the way he did things whispered among themselves that perhaps the exiled Earl of Richmond would make a better king. After all, he was a descendant of Edward III. Some of them were so disgusted with Richard that they went over to join the earl in France. In 1485, Henry, Earl of Richmond, landed with an army in Wales. He moved north and then turned inland. Richard III met him at Market Bosworth, about 12 miles west of Leicester. Henry had 5,000 soldiers but Richard had almost 15,000 — not that he could rely on all of them. In particular, Lord Stanley, who was in command of a large number of men, waited to see which way the battle would go.

Richard was anxious to fight against Henry man-to-man and tried to get at him. After a while Stanley gave the order and his men started to fight; unluckily for the king, they joined in on Henry's side. Stanley's soldiers surrounded Richard and hacked him to death.

The crown which he had been wearing fell off and rolled into a thorn bush. Lord Stanley picked it up and put it on Henry's head. Then he knelt before him and motioned to his followers to do the same.

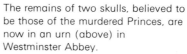

The remains of two skulls, believed to be those of the murdered Princes, are now in an urn (above) in Westminster Abbey.

Henry Tudor, Earl of Richmond, had become Henry VII. The new age which was about to begin is known as the Tudor period from his family name.

Chapter Thirteen Tudor England

1 Henry VII

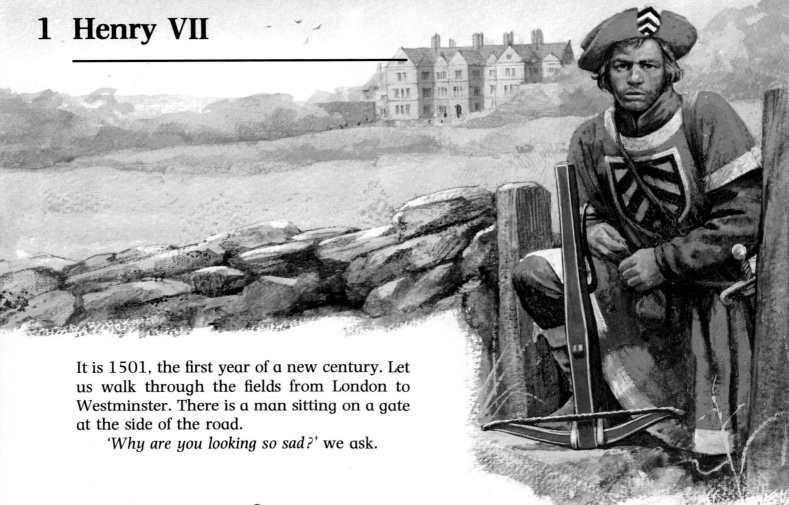

It is 1501, the first year of a new century. Let us walk through the fields from London to Westminster. There is a man sitting on a gate at the side of the road.

'Why are you looking so sad?' we ask.

Henry VII

'I shall lose my employment shortly and my fine uniform too,' he replies, 'and it's all the king's doing.' We ask him to explain.

'Well, King Henry VII has told all the great lords that they can no longer keep their private armies. He's also forbidden them to build castles without his permission. I can see why he's saying this. He still doesn't feel safe.'

'Why shouldn't the king feel safe?'

'For the last fifty years or so the great lords have been fighting each other to see who should be king. Fifteen years ago Henry won a great battle at Bosworth and took the throne.

He wants to stay on top. He keeps the lords weak so they can't make war on him. If they break his laws he brings them here to Westminster and tries them in his Court of Star Chamber. He makes them pay heavy fines. He even makes them pay fines if they've done nothing wrong!'

'How can he do that?'

'He calls the fines "loans", but they're not. My own master was forced to lend the king money. Many of the lords are so poor now that they just can't afford to keep paying wages to their soldiers. That's why I shall be out of work. I've no idea what I'm going to do. Soldiery is the only trade I know. I might even have to beg.' We wish him good luck and go on our way.

Henry VII wanted to make certain that the threats he faced when he became king did not grow into serious dangers. This is how he dealt with these threats:

| No castles | Treaties by royal marriages | No private armies |

2 Printing

Have you ever made a potato print or a lino cut? It is easy to make shapes and patterns but if you want words or letters, you will have to cut them back to front. You might like to try and print your initials on your belongings.

People have known how to do this for thousands of years. In the picture below is an example of an Egyptian seal. It is like a little roller with picture words carved into it. If a man wanted to put his name on a wine jar, he would wrap a strip of soft clay over the neck and then roll his seal across it.

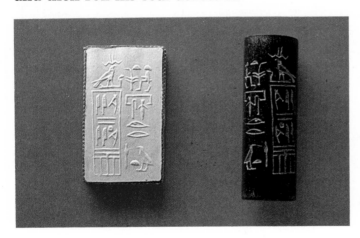

Roman potters stamped their names on their wares while the clay was still wet. There is an example on this page. It seems strange that no one at that time thought of printing books. The idea of doing so appeared in Europe and China round about the 1440s. Shortly afterwards, there were printers at work in both Germany and Holland.

William Caxton printed the first English book in England. He was a good reader but had grown tired of writing out the works he wanted to study. He was a rich London merchant whose business took him abroad from time to time.

He visited Bruges in what is now Belgium and saw the new invention of printing at work. He came back to England and set up his own press at Westminster in 1474. We call a printing works a press because the paper used to be pressed on to the type. Let's ask Wynkyn, the young man who works for Caxton, to explain.

'You have to make your own type,' he says. 'You start with some short rods of steel like these. You paint the letter you want on the end and then cut away the metal you don't want with a special chisel. Now there is a raised letter at the end of the rod. You can see that it's back to front.'

'Are they ready for printing?'

'Oh no! If you did that the letters wouldn't look alike. Printers who work with wooden types have found that out. Each time you carve a "B", for instance, it's slightly different.'

'What do you do then?'

'Well, you have to make a copper mould from each steel letter. Then you can pour hot lead into the moulds as many times as you like. Now all the "B"s, for example, will be identical. After trimming, they are ready. How many bits of type do you think we use?'

237

Printing

'All the letters of the alphabet: that's 26. Oh, and the numbers: that's another ten. Wait a minute – you'll need full stops, commas and things like that. About 40?'

'Look behind you,' he says. 'Every little wooden box has a different type in it and there are over two hundred boxes.'

'Why so many?' we ask.

'Because the letters on a page all have to be printed at once,' replies Wynkyn. 'If you wanted to set "these three trees" you'd need more than one of each letter. And the letters come in many different sizes.

'The printer puts the letters in his stick from right to left. He mustn't forget the spaces between words either. Then, a line at a time, he puts them into a frame and packs the blank areas with pieces of wood and wooden wedges. He taps the type gently all over with a small board and a mallet to make sure it is level. If it wasn't, not all the letters would show on the finished page.

'Then he locks the type tight with the wedges and a man called a "devil" dabs inky pads all over the typeface. We lay the paper over it and a pad next to the paper. A board goes on top. The whole lot is fed into this machine and pressed together. Now the work is done.

'My master, William Caxton, has already printed *The Canterbury Tales* and a history of Troy. This is only a beginning, you wait and see. What will the world be like when books are cheap and everyone can read and write?'

Wynkyn was right. Oxford University Press, which publishes this book, was set up only a few years after Caxton's business was founded and celebrated its 500th anniversary in 1978.

3 Sir Thomas More

Thomas was born in Milk Street, London, on 7 February 1478, the son of a judge. He was a bright, merry boy who was always fond of a joke. He did well at school and went on to Canterbury College in Oxford. Later he became a lawyer. After some years he was made a Member of Parliament and became one of the under-sheriffs of London.

When Henry VII died in 1509, his second son became king as Henry VIII. Thomas More was introduced to the new king in a rather strange way. He was appearing as a lawyer at the Court of Star Chamber when Henry turned up to listen. The king was not at all pleased when Thomas's brilliant speeches ensured that the Crown lost the case.

In spite of his annoyance, Henry saw that Thomas could be useful to him. Thomas rose rapidly in both the king's favour and the royal service. In 1529 he became Lord Chancellor.

But in those days it was dangerous to be one of the king's officers. There was a good deal of unrest over questions of religion. Many people protested at the way the Church was being run. They were known as 'Protestants'. Many people, including Thomas More, would have liked to see some changes made, but Thomas did not share the views of the extreme Protestants.

Then Thomas's loyalty was put to the test. The king had always wanted a son. His wife, Catherine of Aragon, had only borne him a daughter. Besides, he had fallen in love with Ann Boleyn, a lady of the Court. Henry thought he would divorce Catherine.

More and his family

The Pope was the only person who had the authority to grant divorces, and he refused to allow one to Henry VIII. Henry decided to break with Rome and make himself head of the Church of England. Then he could pass a law dissolving his marriage to Catherine.

King Henry wanted everything to seem lawful so he asked all his courtiers, officers and advisers to take an oath of loyalty to himself as head of the new Church. Most people thought it wise to take the oath, but Thomas either could not or would not.

The king went to Thomas's house in Chelsea. The two men walked in the garden and Henry did his best to persuade his friend to take the oath. But Thomas had a conscience. He had sworn to obey the Pope and could not break his promise. He offered to retire from public life.

Thomas was allowed to resign his office as Lord Chancellor. His wife, Alice, and his favourite daughter, Margaret, had done their best to make him change his mind. Alice loved her husband but she could not understand why he was being so obstinate.

Finally, the king accused Thomas of treason and had him shut up in the Tower of London. He was put on trial in Westminster Hall, found guilty and condemned to death.

Even as he mounted the scaffold, he was brave enough to make one last joke. 'Do not cut my beard,' he said to the headsman. 'It has committed no treason.'

4 Servants at Hampton Court

Who are all these people? A man named Nicholas comes forward to tell us. 'We are the servants at Hampton Court,' he says. 'Once our master was Cardinal Wolsey but he gave the palace to Henry VIII who is our new master.

'No one knows how many of us there are. The hundreds you see here all have different jobs. Would you like to know what some of them do?' We tell him that we would.

Servants at Hampton Court

Here are some of the servants we met. Nicholas says it is difficult keeping them all in order. 'Every time the king and the court are here, there may be anything up to 500 guests. We have to take on extra servants but we can't keep them once the visitors have gone.

'It's not easy to get good servants just for a week or two. Many of them are dirty or dishonest. I remember one who had to be rebuked for wiping his greasy fingers on the tapestries. Worse, I suppose, are those who take things with them when they leave. This place is so huge that the loss of something may not be noticed for months.'

Hampton Court – Clock tower

Hampton Court — Kitchens

Hampton Court — Wolsey room.

5 Loss of the Mary Rose

Everyone who likes history knows about Sir Francis Drake and the Spanish Armada but who has ever heard of the *French* Armada? Soldiers from France tried to invade England in the reign of Henry VIII, forty years before the Spanish expedition sailed.

The French Armada attacked the south coast of England to tempt the smaller English fleet out of Portsmouth harbour. At the same time, soldiers were put ashore on both the Isle of Wight and the Sussex coast.

It was an anxious time for the English. Most of their ships were driven by sails but the French had a lot of rowing galleys. Sailing ships were better when the wind was blowing but mostly the air was light and the sea smooth. This suited the galleys with their oars. They could move when sailing ships were becalmed.

Pewter jug from the *Mary Rose*

Listing the finds underwater

Arrows from the *Mary Rose*

Then, suddenly, a wind arose. The English ships set out from the harbour to fire their guns at the French. Unfortunately for Henry VIII, who was watching the whole thing from Southsea Castle, one of his vessels came to grief through sheer carelessness. This was the *Mary Rose*, a fine ship, only a little smaller than the *Great Harry*, the pride of the king's navy.

She had ninety guns on board and over 400 men. She probably hoisted too many sails too quickly and tried to make too sharp a turn. She heeled over and the sea poured in through the open gun ports. The extra weight of water made her list even more. Before the king's horrified gaze, she rolled over and sank.

Some of the lightly-clad seamen managed to swim away or were rescued from her topmasts, which were still above water, but most of the crew and all the soldiers in armour were drowned.

Eventually the French were driven off, in spite of their 200 ships and 30,000 men. There were some attempts to raise the ship but they were not successful. A few of her guns were brought up from time to time but after a while the masts collapsed, sand and mud piled up over the wreck and the very site was forgotten.

In 1965, Alexander McKee set out to find her. By then she had been at the bottom of the sea for over four hundred years. Most people said he was wasting his time; there couldn't be anything left after all those centuries, even if he could find the exact spot.

Mr. McKee wrote history books and was a keen diver. If he could only locate the wreck, what a lot it could tell us about life in Tudor times. Besides, the ship might not really be a wreck. It had only filled and sunk, not been ripped to pieces on rocks. If it was still in one piece, it was probably under the sea bed, not on it.

He managed to interest the local diving club and together they began the hunt. First of all, he had to track down every scrap of evidence that might give a clue to the ship's position. They dived for months, winter and summer, at every chance they got. They used echo sounders to try to pinpoint the site. Mrs. Margaret Rule, who had helped to excavate the Roman palace at Fishbourne, learnt to dive so that she could join in the search.

They found a low mound which they thought might be the grave of the *Mary Rose* and, after five years of searching, recovered some pieces of wood and a gun. Experts examined the cannon and declared that it really was a Tudor piece. The divers had beaten the odds and had actually found the *Mary Rose*.

The latest plan is to lift the vessel, to treat it so that it doesn't rot, and put it on display ashore. It will cost millions of pounds to do but the knowledge it will give us of everyday life in Tudor times will be worth every penny.

6 Rogues and Vagabonds

Imagine that you had to make a journey in late Tudor times. How would you travel? If you were poor, you wouldn't go far or very often because you would have to walk. If you were rich, you would ride a horse and take your servants with you to protect you.

There were a great many dangers. The roads were very uneven, unlit at night, and swarming with bad characters. There had always been outlaws and robbers lying in wait for travellers but there were more than ever in Tudor times. Why should this be so?

Enclosure for sheep farms was one reason. For years, landowners had been changing over from wheat growing to sheep farming, which needed fewer men. Another reason was the closing down of the monasteries. Henry VIII had ordered this to be done because he feared the monks would not accept him as head of the Church. Many lay brothers and

servants had nowhere to go. On top of that, poor people who had always relied on the monks for help now had to help themselves or starve.

There was no dole in those days. If you hadn't got a job, you had to live in any way you could. A lot of people could think of nothing better than robbing, begging, cheating and stealing. There were so many different varieties of rogues and vagabonds, we really need someone to guide us through the maze of types. Here we are, riding along a road in Tudor times and we don't know what to beware of. We see three men walking towards us. One of them looks important, so we rein in our horses and stop him.

'Oh yes, you've asked the right man,' he says. 'I'm the constable and I'm taking this wretch to the gaol in York.' We notice that one of the others has his hands roped together behind his back. 'We could rest awhile and answer your questions. We've covered several miles already today and we'll be glad to sit down.'

He tells us of the different kinds of villain he has to deal with.

'*Thank you,*' we say. '*How do you know which is which and how do you deal with them?*'

'If a man is on the road and can't tell you why, we reckon he's up to no good. We arrest all those we can. They may be whipped, burned, branded or hanged. They can be sent back to where they came from and . . .'

'*What if they really are poor and are just looking for work?*'

'We treat them all the same. It's impossible to tell who is lying and who isn't. Just recently, we've been told to try to sort out the genuine hard-luck cases from the villains and send them to special places being built for them. However,' he says, getting up and jerking the prisoner to his feet, 'it all takes time.' He looks at us shrewdly. 'I suppose you wouldn't like to help us on our way? No, not with money, although that's very kind of you. No, I was wondering if you'd lend us your horses — just for an hour, you understand.'

We tell him we'll do anything we can and he promises to leave the horses at an inn. 'It's in the village two miles up the road,' he says, 'We'll tie them up in the stables.' He waves goodbye as they mount up and trot away.

Alas! When we get to the village, there are no horses or any sign of the men. What were they — priggers of prancers or coney catchers? No wonder they knew so much about rogues and vagabonds!

Chapter Fourteen   The Sea and the City

1 The Spice Islands

The scene is Bristol docks in the late sixteenth century. Men are using hand winches to wind up bales, boxes and barrels from the hold of a ship. There is an extraordinary scent in the air, sweet, sharp and mysterious. If you were there, you might be able to recognize some of the different smells.

A lot of modern housewives use them when they are cooking – grated nutmeg on rice pudding, cloves in apple pies and so on. They make the food taste nicer. We call them spices.

In earlier times, spices weren't just a pleasant extra, they helped to hide the taste of food which wasn't quite fresh. There was no tinned food then, no fridges and no deep-freezes. It was very hard to stop food going bad. If it did, you couldn't just throw it away. There was hardly enough to go round as it was.

ginger

black pepper

nutmeg

cinnamon

cloves

Christians returning from the Crusades brought back with them the first eastern spices, which was good for those who could afford the high prices. They could use spices in cooking or smother their meals with them.

Most spices were grown on some islands to the south of Asia — half-way round the world. The growers sold them to traders who took them to the coast and sold them again. They changed hands over and over again before they travelled up the Red Sea to Egypt. There was no Suez Canal then, so the cargoes went overland by camel train to the Mediterranean. Then ships took them to Venice in Italy. From there they were sold all over Europe.

The Turks captured Constantinople in 1453 and conquered Egypt. The spice routes were cut and prices rose very rapidly. Some men began wondering if there was another way to the Spice Islands that didn't mean going through Turkish lands.

A man called Christopher Columbus was convinced the world was round, at a time when most people were just as certain that it was flat. They thought a ship would fall off the edge if it went too far. Columbus said that he could sail to the Spice Islands by going round the world, sailing westward instead of to the east.

The voyage was made in 1492. After several weeks of sailing, Columbus came to some islands. He brought back gold, cotton plants and 'Indians'. Yes, he called them Indians because he thought he'd reached the East Indies. It was only after he died that people began to realize that Columbus's islands and the Spice Islands were not the same place. Even today, we have to call them the East and West Indies to tell them apart.

Columbus found America, not Asia. His theory was right; he should have been able to reach Asia by sailing west. What he could not have known was that the American continent was in his way.

The first Europeans who actually reached the Spice Islands by sailing westwards were Magellan's men. They sailed right round the world. So did Sir Francis Drake a few years later.

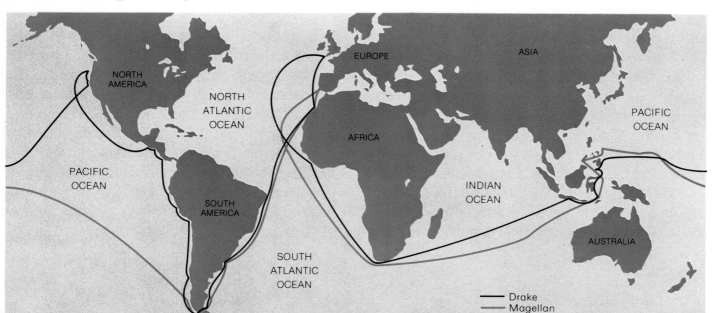

Drake
Magellan

2 Ship's Boy

This is a picture of Matthew Broadacre. He is eleven years old and was born on a farm in Hampshire. His father and mother worked very hard but were so poor they couldn't always feed their large family. As the children grew older, they were sent out to work on other farms.

Matthew never wanted to be a farm hand or a house servant, so just after his tenth birthday, he packed some bread and cheese in a large kerchief and set out to seek his fortune. Let's see what is happening to him.

He has always been fascinated by stories of far away places told by wandering pedlars and he wants to see some of these strange sights for himself. His footsteps lead him south to the coast. He trudges up Portsdown Hill. When he gets to the top, he sees the sea for the first time in his life.

Excited, he hurries down to the edge of Portsmouth harbour and wanders along it. A woman at an inn takes pity on him and sends out some pease pudding and a mug of ale. Her husband questions the boy and finds out that he wants to go to sea. The man knows someone on a ship in the harbour and rows Matthew out to it.

The wooden sailing ship looms huge above Matthew as they come alongside. Everything is strange and new. There seem to be several boys aboard. One of them, nicknamed Weasel, takes him to what is known as the 'slop chest' to get some clothes more suitable for a life at sea.

He is given a shirt and a short jacket. His cap is taken off his head and a loosely knitted woollen one is pulled down over his ears. His own knee-length breeches will do but he is advised not to wear the boots. He is used to going barefoot anyway.

He wonders what his duties will be. 'You might spend some of your time as a cabin boy,' says Weasel, 'but mostly you'll just be a ship's boy, like the rest of us. Come on, I'll show you round.'

They go up on deck and Weasel tells him the names of the masts and ropes and how the anchor is raised. They go below to the gun decks and Weasel explains that a boy called a 'powder monkey' has to keep fetching gunpowder and shot for the cannon when the ship is fighting.

Then they go to the crew's quarters in the fo'c's'le. It is stiflingly hot and quite dark. 'You wait till the winter,' says Weasel, 'you'll freeze in here. The only place you can have a fire in a wooden ship is on the bricks in the galley and that not often.'

They sit down to eat with the men. There is bread, cheese, dried fish and salted meat, washed down with ale. After a while at sea, the bread will run out and there will only be hard biscuit. Nearly everything else will be mouldy. Even the water will be green.

After his meal, Matthew hears the shrill notes of the bos'n's whistle calling the men to their stations. The sail setters swarm up the ratlins to the yards on the masts. Matthew goes with Weasel to help get the anchor up.

An endless loop of rope is tied in dozens of places to the anchor cable and led two or three times round the capstan. The cable is much too thick to go round it. The men sing as they turn the capstan with wooden bars and the boys have to undo the knots as they get near it, run to the bows with the lashing and make another fastening closer to the anchor.

The anchor comes up slowly, festooned with weed and smelling of slime. Men clean it and lash it to the cathead. While the sails are being set, Matthew is given a bucket and brush and told to clean the mess off the deck where the cable has dripped muddy water.

By the time it is done, the ship has cleared Southsea Castle and is beginning to roll slightly. There is an odd feeling in Matthew's stomach and he wonders, not for the last time, if he has done the right thing.

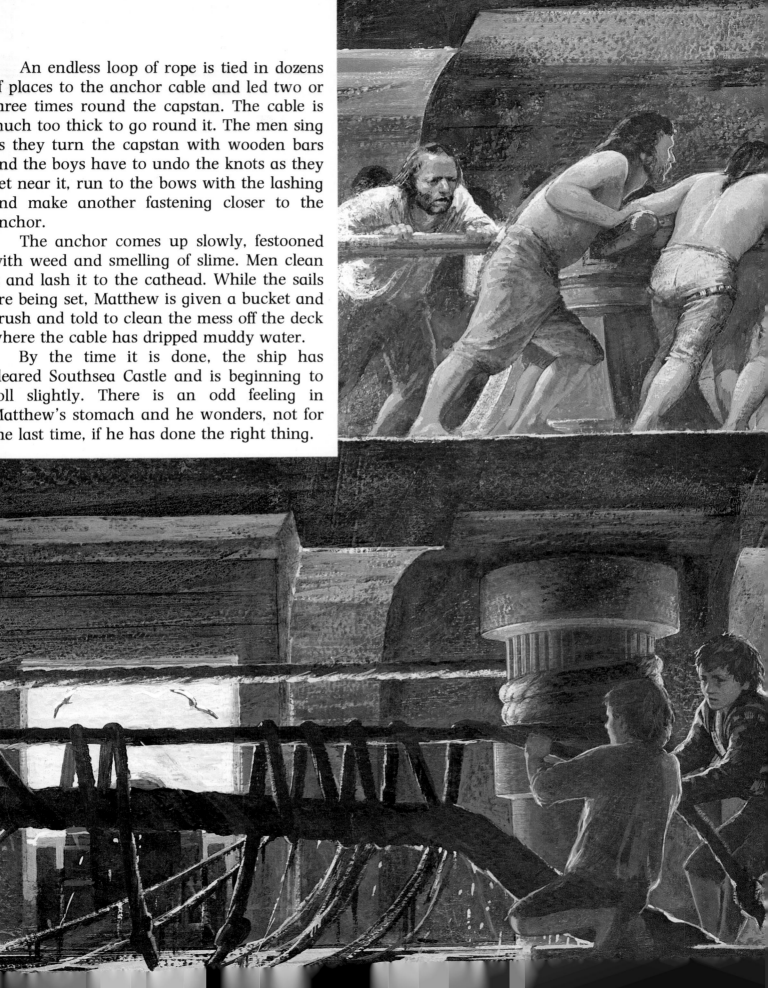

Ship's Boy

1 mainmast   2 foremast   3 mizzen   4 bonaventure   5 bowsprit
6 gallery   7 poop-deck   8 quarter-deck   9 forecastle   10 main gun
deck   11 capstan   12 helmsman using whipstaff connected to rudder
tiller   13 captain's cabin   14 main cabin—for officers and gentlemen
15 brig   16 lamp room   17 main hatch   18 galley stove   19 ships
stores i.e. sails, ropes etc.   20 ships stores food water, wine etc.
21 ballast—to help the ship's stability   22 keel   23 small deck
carronade   24 "beak"

3 Drake and Elizabeth

On board Matthew's ship is a seaman named Martin who once sailed with Drake. When he is 'watch below', Matthew loves to hear him talk about the great man.

'He is a Devon man,' says Martin proudly, 'like me. He sailed when he wasn't much older than you are, Mat, but it wasn't many years before he commanded his own ship. He made sure there was no bad feeling on board; the officers and even the soldiers had to help work the ship whenever there was need.

'From about that time, England and Spain were not at all friendly. Philip, the Catholic King of Spain, would like to remove Queen Elizabeth in order to put her Catholic cousin on the throne.'

'Who is that?' asks Matthew.

'Mary, Queen of Scots. She is a Roman Catholic but the Scots threw her out. She came to England but she is kept in prison because she keeps plotting to kill Elizabeth. A lot of people think that Philip must be behind the plots, so Elizabeth doesn't mind when men like Drake attack Spanish ships and lands.

'The Spanish ambassador used to complain that Drake was a pirate. Elizabeth pretended to scold Drake but she smiled as she did it. I think she is very fond of him and not just because he keeps coming back to England loaded down with Spanish gold. He's becoming a rich man. He has a fine suit of armour, many changes of clothes, silver dishes on his table and an orchestra to play to him when he dines aboard the *Pelican*.'

Matthew looks surprised at the name so Martin goes on. 'Yes, the *Pelican*. That was its name when I signed on. Drake changed it to the *Golden Hind* during the voyage.'

'The *Golden Hind?*' interrupts Matthew. 'Then you've actually sailed right round the world!' Martin nods. 'Tell us about it,' pleads Matthew.

'Well, we didn't know we were going round the world when we left Plymouth. Neither did the officers. The destination was kept secret. Only Drake and the queen knew that we were aiming at Peru on the far side of South America.

'There were four other ships besides the one I was on. Their names were *Elizabeth*, *Swan*, *Marygold* and *Benedict* but the *Pelican* was the only one to make it round the tip of South America and out into the Pacific. It was almost a year after we set out that we arrived at the Spanish colonies. It was a complete surprise. They weren't expecting us and we captured many ships and much gold.

'Then we sailed all the way across the Pacific to the Spice Islands, picking up a cargo of cloves there and setting sail for Africa by way of the Indian Ocean.

'We ran aground on some rocks and had to throw half of the cloves overboard. Some guns had to go too. I didn't think we'd live through it but we did. We got back to Plymouth in September 1580, almost three years after we had left.

'The Spanish were furious and wanted Elizabeth to punish "El Draque", or "The Dragon", as they called him. Our queen, bless her, would have none of it. She went aboard *Golden Hind* as she lay off Deptford in the Thames and knighted him.' Martin paused.

'As you know, Spain has decided we must be conquered. They'll be here before long, mark my words. You've joined the navy at an exciting time, Mat. You'll see as much action as you want then.'

That night Mat dreams of fighting at sea against the Spanish galleons. Before he is fourteen, these dreams will come true.

4 The Armada

Philip of Spain

In the summer of 1588, Martin's words look like coming true. Mary, Queen of Scots has been executed. Philip of Spain's only course is the invasion of England. He has collected together a fleet of about 130 ships: it might have been more but Drake sailed fire ships into Cadiz harbour the previous year. This has not only cut down the size of the Armada, as the Spaniards call it, it has also delayed the sailing.

Pope Sixtus V has blessed the Spanish ships which are to carry 30,000 men to England. Their commander is the Duke of Medina Sidonia. His plan is to sail up the Channel to the Spanish Netherlands and pick up another 20,000 men there. Then they will sail for England, destroying the English navy as they go.

Their method of doing this is out of date, according to the English admirals. Each Spanish captain aims to run alongside an enemy vessel, pull the two ships together with

grappling irons and use soldiers to capture the enemy. They have cannon but they mean to rely on small guns and muskets.

The English have given up this way of fighting. They hope that there will be fresh breezes so that they can get into the best position to fire their cannon at the Spanish without getting into danger themselves.

Matthew Broadacre is on board his ship at Plymouth. He is nearly fourteen now and has become a powder monkey. The admirals of the fleet are also at Plymouth. They are Lord Howard, Hawkins and Drake. They are waiting for the Armada to appear.

A small ship puts into port. The crew have sighted the Spaniards heading eastward. Beacon fires are lit on hilltops to tell our soldiers to stand by. Elizabeth goes to Tilbury to encourage her troops.

Drake doesn't want to get in front of the Spaniards – he prefers to pick them off from behind – so he must wait until they have passed Plymouth. He calmly goes on with his game of bowls.

Matthew makes sure everything is ready at the guns he will serve. Soon the order is given to put to sea. The weather is unsettled. It is not hot and calm as it was when the French tried the same thing over forty years before. The English seamen don't mind. They know that the weather favours them. They believe that they are better sailors than the Spaniards, or 'Dons', as they call them.

For a week they follow the Armada along the Channel. Sometimes the English captains sail their ships nearer to the huge galleons and fire at them. Then all is excitement on Matthew's ship. He hurries to and fro with the gunpowder while the gunners ram the shot home with long poles.

A glowing slow-match is put to the touch hole. There is a blinding flash and an ear-splitting explosion. The gun bucks, and swirls of gassy smoke billow across the deck. Other guns do the same.

One or two Spanish galleons are damaged

The Armada

but most of them come safely to anchor at the place where the troops are to be embarked. Drake decides to send in fire ships, just as he did at Cadiz.

Eight old vessels are filled with tar barrels, brushwood and gunpowder. They are drifted towards the Spaniards during the night. Their crews leave it to the last minute before lighting the fires and then escaping in the rowing boats.

The Spaniards panic. Anchor cables are cut before the crews are on deck. The galleons drift about and collide. Some run on to sandbanks. Drake's men keep up the bombardment. Matthew has run so much he can scarcely keep to his feet.

To add to the confusion, a southerly gale begins to blow and the galleons have to run before the wind, many of them badly damaged. Drake's ships follow them right up the east coast until they run out of shot and powder.

The proud Armada is scattered far and wide. Most find themselves alone the next day. Their only hope is to get back home safely. They have to sail right round the British Isles. Strong winds wreck more of them on the Scottish and Irish coasts.

In all, Philip has lost nearly eighty ships and over 10,000 men. He goes on trying to beat England but for Elizabeth and her people, the danger is over, thanks to Drake and the English seamen – not to mention the boys who also served.

5 London Life

Even in the sixteenth and early seventeenth centuries, London was fast becoming one of the great cities of the world. It had about sixty or seventy thousand people when Henry VII came to the throne in 1485. At Elizabeth's death in 1603, the numbers were three times as great. Cities were such unhealthy places in which to live that the new generation of babies hardly replaced the numbers who died. Most of these extra citizens had come to London from all parts of England.

The area of the old Roman city had been about half a square mile. Much repaired, the walls and gates still stood but there were houses and other buildings spilling out beyond, into the open countryside.

Many newcomers to London had to take lodgings if they wished to live inside the walls. If they wanted a new house built, it would probably have to be alongside one of the roads leading away from the capital or in Southwark, to the south of the River Thames. Here were the theatres, the bear-baiting and cockfighting pits. These were not allowed inside the city which was run by the guilds and merchants.

The streets were narrow and no cleaner than they had been in the Middle Ages. Houses were still mostly of wood, and in London were often three or four storeys high.

Let's walk along the streets of Tudor London as if we are tourists. We've come down from Colchester on the main road through the villages of Stratford, Bow and Mile End. We go through Aldgate (the Old Gate) and notice the pump at which people are queuing for water. Very few buildings have water laid on.

London Life

Straight ahead is the road leading to the Royal Exchange. This is where merchants meet to do business. It was built by Sir Thomas Gresham in 1571.

Just beyond is St. Paul's Cathedral. This picture doesn't look like the one we know. It is the old church, dating from the Middle Ages. Surrounding it are the booksellers' and printers' shops. All sorts of people have stalls set up here and along Cheapside. Almost anything you want can be bought from the stalls but there are also a great many pedlars, with their goods in barrows, on their backs or in boxes or trays slung round their necks on leather straps.

Everywhere there are churches and inns. The streets are full of people and animals. There are no dustmen or street cleaners. All sorts of rubbish and filth lie about on the rough dirt roads or clog up the cobblestones.

Of course, there aren't any empty tins or plastic bags; the rubbish is straw, bits and pieces of vegetables, shells of eggs or oysters and even bits of rotten meat.

Some rubbish is dumped in piles at the

Tower of London

London Bridge

end of the road. These attract rats and mice. Every now and then, the filthy conditions lead to outbreaks of the plague.

We'll head towards the river where the air may be fresher. All the way along the Thames, there are steps, landing stages and wharves. Here are landed all the things needed to keep London going.

All is bustle and excitement as men busy themselves with loads of corn, vegetables, fish and coal. Vessels are tied up the entire length of the north bank and the river is swarming with small craft.

In the distance we can see the grey outline of William the Conqueror's Tower. That is easy to recognize but what are the three odd-looking buildings on the south bank? One of them has a flag flying over its thatched roof. A mass of people seems to be making its way to the Globe, as the building is called. We could hire a boat to take us over but it's easier to go with the crowd and cross the Thames by the only bridge.

London Bridge stands on nineteen brick pillars and the space between any pair of them is only big enough for a rowing boat. As the tide turns, the river water pours through the gaps and forms waterfalls. You can hear the dull roar of the water as you walk between the houses that line the bridge.

The Globe

6 The Globe

When we get nearer, we can see that the Globe is a theatre. We would find the place very strange. The Tudors would be equally puzzled by the way most of us see plays. We sit in our own homes and turn a switch on the television. We settle back to watch. We don't often think of how the pictures get on the screen.

In the television studio cables snake across the floor, cameras move about silently, microphone booms hover over the set and batteries of powerful lights shine down. The pictures and sounds are turned into electrical pulses and broadcast. Miles away, the aerial on our roof picks up the signal and our TV set changes it back into voices and faces.

The actors in the studio aren't doing anything very different from what actors have done for centuries. Just before Tudor times they had started giving plays in the open courtyards of inns.

When special theatres were built, the designers used the inn yard as a pattern.

A television production of *The Tempest*

There was a flat, open space with a wooden platform sticking out into it. The bedroom verandas of the inn became the balconies of the playhouse.

The balconies surround the stage on three sides and a seat in one of them costs a shilling. A stool at ground level is sixpence. It is only tuppence to stand in front of the stage.

Most of the seats are taken, so we stand with the 'groundlings' and wait for the play to start. A trumpet sounds and the audience is still. There are no curtains and very little scenery. As there aren't any lights either, the performance always has to take place in daylight.

A man comes from a door at the back to announce the setting. The play is *The Tempest*. A few ropes are draped about to show that the first scene is on board a ship. Some of the cast are making noises off stage which are supposed to sound like a storm at sea.

It is not thought decent for women to appear in plays. Boys take the female parts. If they stay with the company, they will be able to play the men's roles when they grow up. At the end of each scene the actors all go off together.

Sellers of sweets and drinks wander round looking for customers. There may even be a pickpocket or cutpurse at work in the audience. They are often lucky because the playwatchers sometimes get so interested that they forget to guard their money.

By the time *The Tempest* has come to its end, the sun is beginning to set. The audience drifts out of the Globe and soon the theatre is empty.

The Globe

Chapter Fifteen   Years of Unrest

1 The Gunpowder Plot

Bonfire night! The frost in the air makes the flames seem even brighter. Rockets hiss upwards, bangers explode and sparklers make little pools of light. The children and their parents eat baked potatoes as they watch the guy burn.

Why do we call it a 'guy' and why do we burn one every fifth of November? To get an answer, we need to go back to the year 1606.

It is a bitter January day. A large crowd stands in front of the Parliament buildings. Some men are about to be hanged. We ask one of the spectators who the criminals are.

'The Gunpowder plotters,' he answers. 'They tried to blow up Parliament and now they are being punished.'

'How did they do that?'

'I'd better tell you the whole story,' says the man. 'When Elizabeth died, the King of Scotland was her nearest living relative, so he became James I of England – and also head of the Church of England.

'There are three main groups of Christians in the country now as there were before James became king. There are those who still look to the Pope as their head, the Roman Catholics, that is. The Anglicans accept the king as their head but they have made the religion simpler. The third group think that they have not made it simple enough. They don't want bishops, candles, robes, ceremonies or anything like that. They want the Church purified, they say, so we call them Puritans.

'When it seemed that James was not very sympathetic to the Catholics, a small, desperate gang of them decided to murder him and the whole of the government. A man called Catesby gathered the gang together and one of them, Thomas Winter, went over to Flanders to persuade a young soldier named Guido Fawkes to join them.

'Guido, or Guy, was born in York in 1570. He was brought up in the Church of England faith but his father died and his mother married again. Guy's stepfather was a Catholic so Guy changed his religion. He went to Flanders and became a soldier in the Spanish army.

'The plot was explained to Guy. Thomas Percy, another of the gang, had rented a house next to the Houses of Parliament. They were going to tunnel through into the basement of Parliament, and stack barrels of gunpowder in it. When the king, Lords and Commons met, they would blow the whole lot up.

'There was to be a rising of Catholics in the countryside. The plotters would take over the government and choose their own ruler.

The plotters in the cellar

'As it happened, they were able to hire a cellar under the House of Lords and the idea of tunnelling was dropped. They stored over one and a half tons of gunpowder there in thirty-six barrels and waited for Parliament to meet.

'Unknown to them, one of their number sent a warning to Lord Monteagle. The cellars were searched and Guy Fawkes was caught red-handed. He had a dark lantern and a fuse which he was going to light the next day — fifth of November, it would have been.

'He was taken to the Tower and tortured to make him give away the names of his fellow plotters but he wouldn't. Some of the others tried to start the revolution anyway but it came to nothing. Most were either killed or captured.

'The eight that were caught were put on trial. All were found guilty and sentenced to death. They were dragged here behind horses from the Tower this morning. Aren't you going to stay and see them hanged?' The man sounds surprised.

We murmur an excuse and push our way out of the crowd. We've seen all we need.

Now we know why the figure we burn is a 'guy'. As to bonfires, people have always lit them when they are glad. They were very pleased the explosion hadn't taken place.

Unfortunately for the masses of ordinary Catholics, feeling remained strong against them for over two hundred years. Some of them went overseas to start a new life in America where they could worship as they pleased. Strangely enough, so did many of the Puritans.

271

2 Witchcraft

King James I seemed to be a rather obstinate man who liked to have his own way. He thought he knew more than most people about a number of subjects. He even wrote a book called *Daemonologie*, in which he set out what he and most people believed about witches.

The word 'witch' nowadays most likely makes you think of an old woman in black, riding a broomstick and wearing a tall, pointed hat. Like elves and magic, witches are interesting to read about but nobody really believes they exist. Once upon a time, it wasn't only the children but their parents too, who believed in them.

For three hundred years, from about 1400 onwards, so-called witches were hunted down and killed in most Christian countries. Things

were not quite so bad for suspected witches in England as they were in Europe, but they were bad enough.

In those days, it wasn't so easy to get a living. There were no experts to tell you why your wheat had the blight, why your hens weren't laying or why your cows had stopped giving milk. Being human, you would look for someone or something to blame.

'What about that old woman who lives alone at the end of the lane? They say she's a widow but she's lived by herself for so long that no one in the village can remember her husband. Her only friend is a cat and she's often seen about the village muttering to herself as she gathers plants from the hedgerows. What does she do with them?' Probably no more than make simple medicines but you are ready to believe that they are wanted to make a magic brew.

It's whispered that she'll cast a spell on

someone for you if you ask her. Perhaps that was all there was to be said but people were much more ready to believe in magic than they are now. It took no more than a slight neighbours' quarrel to make her a suspect.

As soon as you told your friends that you thought the old crone had put a spell on your farm and its animals, there were sure to be some who would remember similar tales, each trying to tell a more dramatic story than the last.

Back in the Middle Ages, it used to be the Church's job to try the witch cases. Since Tudor times, it had been the ordinary courts that had to deal with witchcraft. When James became king, he made death the punishment for all kinds of witchcraft.

The victims were nearly always women, and elderly ones at that. Many of them didn't even know what was happening to them. Others seemed to enjoy the excitement of being the centre of attention and freely confessed to all the charges.

We don't now think that these poor old women had any special powers but people then lived in a world where magic was accepted. As far as we know, the only way a witch could harm you was to tell you that she had cast a spell on you. If you were so frightened and ignorant that you believed her, then some damage might be done.

Unfortunately, superstition was very strong and many witches were hanged. In Europe, witch hunts were officially organized and many thousands were executed. In England it was usually left to ordinary people to report their suspicions; there was only one occasion when officials went out looking for witches.

Matthew Hopkins and John Stearne travelled through eastern England for three years, beginning in 1644. An accusation was enough to prove guilt in their eyes. A confession tidied up the whole thing, so the two

'witchfinders' threw their victims into ponds to see if Satan would help them to float. If this didn't bring a confession, the suspects might be kept without sleep for days and nights on end.

Hundreds of arrests were made and dozens of witches were hanged. In fact, Hopkins got so good at 'sniffing out' witches, that people began to suspect that he was one himself. Finally, he was tried as a sorcerer and hanged in 1647. Witch trials went on for another seventy years after his death but the numbers of executions grew smaller until in 1736, the witchcraft laws were at last done away with.

3 The Colonies in the New World

In a churchyard at Gravesend on the Thames there is a memorial to a Red Indian princess who died in 1617 and was buried there. What was a Red Indian doing in England at that early date? To find out, we'll have to look at the beginnings of America.

You have already read about some English people going to the New World so that they would be free to worship God in their own way. It wasn't just religious men and women who went, however. Many were attracted across the Atlantic Ocean by the promise of riches.

The end of the war with Spain came in 1604 and it seemed to Englishmen that this was their chance to go and look for gold in North America as the Spaniards had done in South America.

In May 1607, three ships landed in Virginia with over a hundred colonists. Some were meant to set up a village of wooden huts, to clear trees and to plant food crops, while the rest went off to look for gold and silver.

The trouble was that everyone wanted to search for gold and none wanted to stay and work. Disease and starvation followed and many died. John Smith took charge of the colony but they had to rely on the local Indians for food. After a while, the Indians became less friendly and they took Smith prisoner.

The Indian chief, Powhaton, ordered him to be killed but his daughter, Pocahontas, pleaded with her father for the Englishman's life. The chief was merciful and Smith went back to Jamestown, as the settlers called their

village. Pocahontas went with him. Eventually she married one of the colonists, a man named John Rolfe. He took her to England but our climate was fatal to her and she died here. She was only twenty-two.

In the meantime, the Virginia Company in London decided to send out more colonists. Six hundred men, women and children were packed into eight ships which set sail for America. One of them, the *Sea Venture*, ran aground in Bermuda. Shakespeare read about the wreck and used some of the detail in his play *The Tempest*.

The rest reached Jamestown but were no more ready to work hard for the colony than the earlier party had been. Again, disease and starvation carried off many of them. Some even took to cannibalism!

More people arrived from Britain and in less than thirty years from the first landing, there were over 5,000 white settlers. Strangely enough, the thing which really saved Jamestown was the tobacco plant.

The Colonies in the New World

Raleigh was the first man to bring tobacco to England. He and other explorers had noticed how the Indians dried the leaves, rolled them up, set fire to one end and sucked smoke from the other. In Europe the habit spread. The leaves were chopped up and smoked in a pipe. The first pipes had a nutshell for a bowl with a straw for a stem, but before long, pipes were being made of baked clay. More and more tobacco was grown in Virginia and sold in England. Jamestown and Virginia went on to prosper.

Other European nations set up their own colonies in the New World; there was also another English colony. This was started by a hundred Puritans who sailed from Plymouth in the *Mayflower*. They were driven off their course by winter gales and landed far to the north of where they should have been.

In December 1620, they gave thanks to God for their arrival and for the freedom to worship Him as they wished. Their new land was on Cape Cod and they named their little village Plymouth.

Unlike the Virginian settlers, the Pilgrim Fathers, as we know them, were sober and hard-working. They built log cabins, cleared a nearby stream for a water supply and planted corn. Seeds and cuttings were set in the little gardens round the cabins but few survived: the first winter was very hard. Without the help of the Indians, they would have starved.

Indians showed them how to get by during the worst of the blizzards. They brought maize seeds to the colony and taught the Puritans about the local plants and animals. Slowly, the settlement grew. More colonists came to make a new life in 'New England'. In only a few years the settlement was doing more than just survive – it had become prosperous by means of trade and sheer hard work.

4 Civil War in England

James I died in 1625 and not many people mourned him. He had ruled for years without asking Parliament's advice and his son, Charles I, showed signs of doing exactly the same thing. English people feared that he would marry a Catholic princess and they didn't like the idea of a new line of Catholic kings.

Eventually, Charles married Henrietta Maria, the sister of the French king. England then blundered into a war with Spain but when Charles asked Parliament for money to pay for it, the members refused. Charles tried to carry on without them or the money.

The war went badly, so the king once more had to ask Parliament for funds. Again they refused. Charles tried every way he could think of to raise money. Even forcing people to lend it to him, or compelling them to feed his troops was not enough. Those who refused were put in prison without trial.

Parliament said that if the king would stop doing these things they would give him what he wanted. He agreed but the money was not well spent and the king was forced to make peace with Spain.

Not all the quarrels were about money. Parliament wanted a bigger say in the running of the country but Charles, like his father, believed in what he called 'the divine right of kings'. This, he explained, meant that as God had made him king, no one had any right to question anything he did.

Another disagreement was over religion. The members passed a resolution against the Catholic faith. The king sent them home and ruled without them for eleven years — but he still needed money as badly as ever. Most of the ways he had of getting it angered different groups of men. He charged landowners taxes on estates that had been in their families for generations. He demanded 'ship money' not only from those who lived on the coast but also from those whose homes were miles from the sea. Anyone who disagreed or refused was punished.

Then Charles tried to interfere with Scotland's religion, but the Scots would have none of it. They raised an army and invaded the north of England. Charles couldn't pay his own soldiers, many of whom didn't want to fight the Scots anyway. Parliament was called yet again. Before the king could ask the next Parliament for tax money, they passed a law saying that the king couldn't dismiss them if they didn't want to go.

Charles was very angry. He went with a band of 300 soldiers to arrest some of the more troublesome members but they had been warned and were not in the House of Commons.

Most of the members left Westminster for the City of London where they felt safer. The merchants and Puritans started to get ready for the struggle they felt sure would come. Some of the powerful landowners began to arm their tenants for the king's protection. The two groups began to refer to each other by insulting names. The king's men called the Parliamentary side 'Roundheads' from the short-cropped hair many of them wore. The Royalists were known as 'Cavaliers' which means 'swaggerers' as well as 'horsemen'.

The street mobs in London rioted and became so violent that Charles thought it wiser to leave the capital. He went north to York where he set about raising an army. He was not to see London again until the war was over.

5 A Royalist Family

What did the king's friends think of what had happened and what did they do about it? Perhaps we could ask one of them. We'll have to travel to the north-west of England because that is where his home is.

Sir Henry Moxon seems pleased to see us. He and his wife Ellen take us inside their large manor house set in acres of parkland. We are led into a richly furnished room. A servant brings wine and we sit down on comfortable leather chairs.

While we are waiting for the rest of the family, we look about us. There is a fine stone fireplace with glowing logs propped up on andirons. The walls are covered with oak panelling and the ceiling is beautifully moulded with leaf and flower shapes. There are two or three oil paintings hanging on the walls in gold frames.

The late afternoon sun slants in through the lattice windows and the light falls in hazy patches on to the rich Turkey carpets. The furniture is solid and heavy.

A Royalist Family

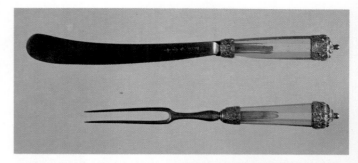

Jacobean cutlery

The light begins to fade as we sip our wine. Lady Moxon tells a servant to light the candles. The maid brings in a tinder box and strikes sparks with a flint and steel. She catches a spark in the tinder, a scrap of scorched cloth, and blows it into a flame. She thrusts a wooden spill into the flame. When it is alight, she closes the tinder box and lights the candles with her match, as it is called.

The candles are set in silver sconces fixed to the wooden panelling. The flames waver as the door opens. It is Sir Henry's son, Richard, his wife, Mary, and their three young children.

We are surprised to learn that there are two boys and a girl, for two are dressed as girls and only one as a boy. He is twelve and his name is Andrew. His brother is only three and it is the custom for young boys to wear girls' clothing until they are about six or seven. The two older children are dressed in the same way as the adults. Elizabeth, the girl, is nine.

We talk with the family while the servants lay the table for the evening meal. We can see from the fine, stylish clothes everyone wears that they must be very well off. We are sure of this when we glance at the table. Nearly everything on it is of silver.

The adults sit at the table and the children have bowls and spoons and a chair each by the fire. The meal is mostly meat dishes such as pork, lamb, venison, duck, pigeon and so on. The sauces are served in separate dishes and there is more wine. We end with almond and honey cakes, sugared fruits and cornflour pudding with jam.

'Well,' says Sir Henry, 'I believe you want to know why we are for the king? The reasons are quite simple. In fact, they all come down to only one reason and that is because he is the king. If a man takes up arms against his lawful sovereign, that is treason. There is only one way to deal with traitors.'

'That is true,' says Richard, Sir Henry's son, 'but my father has left out all the other reasons. We don't want a lot of low churchmen telling us how to lead our everyday lives. More important, we don't mean to let them interfere with our religion.

'My father and I have only a week left before we join the king's army. One of my cousins who lives nearby will move in here to look after our families. Another cousin . . .'

'Don't talk about him,' growls Sir Henry. 'He is no longer a kinsman. My brother's son feels that His Majesty is wrong to oppose the will of the people and has gone off to London to fight for the Parliamentary army. God will punish him for his wickedness.'

Soon after this, we take our leave. We don't tell Sir Henry but we are going to visit the armies of both sides shortly.

6 Royalist and Parliamentary Soldiers

The Roundhead, or Parliamentary soldier, nearly always fought on foot at the start of the war. He could be a pikeman or a musketeer. He wears a metal helmet with a flexible neck cover and face protectors. A leather coat and gauntlets to match, plus a high, plain collar go on the top half of his body. Some soldiers have a back and breast plate as well. The foot soldier wears knee breeches and woollen stockings but the horse soldier has long leather riding boots which hide the stockings. It is rather surprising to find that the boots can be worn on either leg. There was no shaping to the feet of shoes and boots in those days.

The cavalryman has a leather sword belt slung across his chest from the right shoulder. The sword sheath then sits on his left hip and the weapon is easier to draw out.

You will notice that complete body-armour seems to be less common now. Both sides have guns but most of the fighting is still hand-to-hand, so some protection is needed for the head and chest.

Cannon in the Civil War have not advanced much since Elizabeth's day.

Hand guns are complicated and not very accurate. The musketeer wears a bandolier over his shoulder. It is a belt from which hang little containers of gunpowder.

The musket is so heavy, it is hard to fire from the shoulder. The musketeer has to support the far end on a forked stick. Loading the gun takes time. First, the soldier has to stand the gun on its wooden stock. Then he empties the gunpowder from one of the containers into the muzzle and rams it down with a rod. The bullet is a round lead ball which is also rammed down. A piece of wadding is tapped into place to stop the ball rolling out and the powder spilling.

As the musket comes up to the firing position, some of the powder trickles into the pan at the side. The soldier pulls the trigger and a flint snaps down on to a grooved steel plate, rather like the action of the tinder box. Sparks shoot into the pan and light the gunpowder. The line of grains leads down to where the main charge is, behind the bullet. The explosion drives the ball out of the muzzle.

It takes several minutes to go through the drill. Clumsy as this weapon may sound, it is better than the old matchlock gun which many of the soldiers still have to use.

Prince Rupert is the commander of the Cavalier horsemen. He was only twenty-three when the war started but he is a daring and experienced soldier. To begin with, the Royalist cavalrymen did not dress very differently from the way they did when they went hunting. Apart from the pieces of armour that some of them wore, you could tell who they were from their bright, coloured clothes, the lace at their throats and wrists (and even over their boot tops!) and their plumed hats.

The cavalry played an important part on both sides. It was some time before the Parliamentary units were as large or as good as the king's.

Prince Rupert and his brother, Prince Maurice, were usually too good for the Roundheads to beat. They often drove large sections of Roundhead troops off the battlefield, only to find that the battle was over by the time they got back, and not always won for the king.

On 22 August 1642, Charles I set up his headquarters at Nottingham. The king's party was stronger in the north and west and in the countryside rather than the towns. The south and east, the seaports, and particularly London, were for Parliament. The king decided to strike at London and end the war quickly.

7 The Battle of Edgehill

At Nottingham Charles called on his loyal subjects to join him. When he first raised his standard, he had only 300 foot soldiers and not quite three times as many horsemen.

The recruits flocked in. As soon as he was ready, Charles moved westward to collect more men from the Welsh border area. Against him was the Earl of Essex, commander of Parliament's army. Let us ask one of his Roundhead troopers what happened to stop the king getting to London.

'My name is Peter Pike. I suppose with a name like mine I should have been a pikeman but My Lord Essex made me a musketeer when he found I could shoot.

'The king moved off to Wales to pick up his extra men. We were meant to stop his army but they got past us somehow and we didn't pick them up until they were on the way back from Shrewsbury to London.

'We followed so hard upon their heels that part of our rearguard got separated. We couldn't slow down, for the king's army had a good two days' start of us. We reached Kineton and could hardly believe our luck. The Royalists were camped only seven miles away. It was 22 October 1642.

'By now, there were as many Cavaliers as there were of us but they were all together in battle formation whereas some of our men were still miles to the rear.

'The king sat on his horse in his golden armour, surrounded by his own bodyguard. Between him and us were the lines of Royalists. On the king's right was Prince Rupert and most of their cavalry. In the centre were the foot soldiers, with a smaller group of horsemen on his left. More important, the army was at the top of a steep slope known as Edgehill.

'I suppose the Royalists thought we might surround them and starve them out. At all events, they left their hilltop and came down to our level.

'Rupert and the horsemen of the left charged before the rest of the army was formed up. We weren't ready for him and our left flank got pushed back. Luckily, one of our regiments that had arrived late met them in Kineton. John Hampden's foot soldiers they were, as I remember.

'Rupert struggled back to the battlefield with what was left of his squadrons and found that the king's infantry had taken a bit of a mauling — not surprising really, when you think that they had no horsemen to protect them.

'While Rupert and his men were away, the king's cannon were captured and so was his standard, at least for a while. Oliver Cromwell's regiment did well in the battle but when the Royalist horsemen came back, things were even again.

'After a while, both sides broke off the fight and took stock. No one had won and many men had been killed on both sides, perhaps as many as 5,000 of them.

'Lord Essex decided that the battle at Edgehill would have to be left as a draw and he ordered us to form up and march back south-eastward, so we could block the road to London. Charles took his army to Oxford, and set up his headquarters there for the rest of the war.

'There was talk of peace but Rupert struck at our army just before we got to London. There was a skirmish at Brentford Bridge and the king's cavalry stormed the town on 12 November. Then the Trainbands, or part-time soldiers, came out from London in strength. They formed up at Turnham Green and the Royalists retired to Oxford. It's the nearest they are going to get to the capital.'

Charles's headquarters in Oxford

Edgehill today

The Battle of Edgehill

The map shows the position of the two sides
at the beginning of the battle.

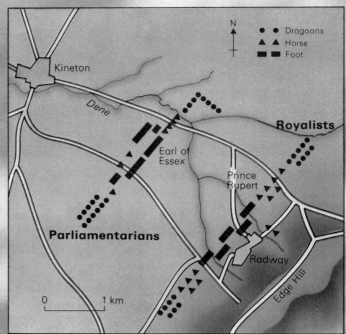

N

Dragoons
Horse
Foot

Kineton

Dene

Royalists

Earl of
Essex

Prince
Rupert

Parliamentarians

Radway

Edge Hill

0   1 km

OLIVER FREY.

8 Oliver Cromwell

What sort of a man was Cromwell? It's rather difficult to answer this question. For one thing, Cromwell was not a simple kind of man and for another, we know very little about his early life.

We know that he was born at Huntingdon in 1599, towards the end of Elizabeth I's reign. We think his father was a farmer but he might have been a brewer as well. Oliver attended the local grammar school where he was taught by a Doctor Beard. The good doctor drummed into him that God watches everyone and punishes wickedness. It was probably from Doctor Beard that Oliver got his first strict Puritan ideas, although his enemies were later to say that he wasted his time at school wrestling and playing cricket.

At the age of seventeen, he went to Cambridge to study law but his father died a year later and he went back to Huntingdon to farm the family estate. He married his wife Elizabeth when he was twenty. He must have had to work hard for he now had to support his wife, his mother and five sisters.

He still had time to help his neighbours when they got into trouble with the authorities so it isn't surprising to find him becoming a Member of Parliament for Huntingdon in 1628. There he spoke for the persecuted Puritans.

No one really knows where he learned how to command soldiers – perhaps it just came to him naturally.

If there was one person who learned a lesson at Edgehill, it was Oliver Cromwell. He saw the importance of well-trained cavalry. Back in East Anglia, he began to recruit and drill his Ironsides, as they were called.

Oliver Cromwell

They were mostly farmers and nearly all were Puritans. They took their religion seriously and, unlike most soldiers, agreed that they would not swear, gamble, ransack captured towns or get drunk. Cromwell worked them hard until they could fight or fire on command and break off a chase when ordered, something which Rupert's gallants never learned to do.

Cromwell demanded that only proper professional soldiers should lead the Parliamentary troops. Sir Thomas Fairfax was appointed Commander-in-chief and Cromwell was made Master of the Horse.

Training the New Model Army

Cromwell reorganized the troops so well, they were known as the New Model Army. It was to be a strong, well-disciplined body of men, dressed in uniforms and paid regularly at the rate of two shillings a day.

On 14 June 1645 came the last main battle. This was at Naseby near Leicester and the pattern was the familiar one of Rupert's cavalry dashing off after some of the Round-heads and leaving their foot soldiers without cover. Cromwell's own horsemen made short work of the Royalist infantry and Charles I had to be held back. He wanted to gamble his last few reserves and himself in the battle. His advisers persuaded him not to.

He rode north to Scotland, hoping the Scots would remember that his father was Scottish too. The Scots took him and sold him to the Roundheads but the army and Parliament couldn't agree as to what to do next. Cromwell was a member of both the army and Parliament and he tried to sort out the quarrels that arose over what form of government and religion there should be in England.

Charles, now in Carisbrooke Castle on the the Isle of Wight, tried to stir up the dis-agreements. He lost any trust either side might have had in him. He managed to get the Scots to invade England once more – this time as Cromwell's enemies.

Cromwell had to fight and win all over again. He was bitterly angry at what the king had tried to do. Those Members of Parliament who wanted to bargain with Charles were turned out of the House of Commons and Cromwell found himself in charge. Now neither king nor Parliament was ruling England. The army was in control and Cromwell was its leader.

Oliver Cromwell's hat

9 The Trial and Execution of Charles I

This is Westminster Hall. If you visit it when there are not too many visitors about you may be able to sense the ghosts of the past. It was the chief law court of England for over 600 years. Here Thomas More was tried for treason in 1535. Here, too, Guy Fawkes faced his accusers seventy years later. Both were found guilty.

In 1648, Cromwell's army was firmly in control of the country. The king was brought from prison in Hurst Castle and lodged at Windsor while workmen fitted out this very hall for the unusual trial it was to see.

Many members of Parliament no longer went to the House of Commons as they disapproved of what Cromwell was doing. The remaining Members appointed 135 commissioners as judges but only about seventy of them agreed to take part. The problem was that no one knew how the trial was to be run. Many argued that such a trial was itself unlawful for the king was to be accused of treason. How could a king be a traitor? Surely the word 'traitor' means one who is disloyal to his king?

But Bradshaw, the president of the court, Cromwell and a few others were determined to go ahead and nothing could stop them. Afraid of attacks by the king's supporters, Bradshaw wore a steel-lined hat throughout the trial.

A plate in the floor of Westminster Hall marks the spot where the king sat. The chair he used had been specially made for the occasion.

Bradshaw read out the charge of high treason and asked the king if he pleaded guilty or not. Charles replied that, as the court had no authority to try him for any crime at all, there was no point in his saying anything.

Witnesses told the court how Charles had made war on his own people. Charles repeated that the judges had no authority to try him and that he alone had the right to speak for his subjects. He insisted, 'A king cannot be tried by any superior jurisdiction on earth. If power without law can make laws, I do not know what subject there is in England that can be sure of his life or anything he calls his own.'

It didn't make any difference. Cromwell and Ireton, his son-in-law, had decided the king must die. Thomas Fairfax, who had been one of Cromwell's loyal supporters, withdrew from the trial. Lady Fairfax shouted from the gallery that it was Cromwell, not the king, who ought to be on trial.

However, fifty-nine of the judges signed the death warrant. Many protested later that Cromwell and the army had forced them to do it. On 27 January 1649 Charles was brought in to hear the sentence of the court. This time he tried to deny the charges but it was too late.

Three days later he was taken from St. James's Palace to Whitehall. At one o'clock in the afternoon, they led him out through a window of the banqueting house on to a wooden scaffold outside.

Thousands of people were waiting for him. Hundreds of soldiers were drawn up several ranks deep around the platform in case there was an attempt to rescue him. They had even provided ropes to tie him down if he struggled. Charles smiled calmly and scornfully at these. He said that he would die a good Christian, that he forgave his murderers and that he was dying for the good of the people. Then he arranged to signal the headsman when he was ready.

He knelt, laid his head on the block, said 'Remember,' and gave the signal. There was a groan from the crowd as the axe came down and a louder one when his head was held up for all to see.

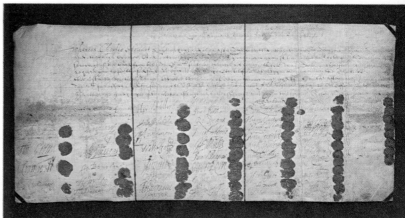

Charles I's death warrant

293

10 The Commonwealth

Even when the war was over, there were still three main Christian religions in England — the Catholics, the Anglicans and the Puritans. The freedom which the Civil War had brought encouraged all sorts of new ideas — some of them rather strange — in both government and religion.

For example, the Levellers wanted England to be a republic with complete freedom of worship. The Diggers thought they had a right to take land anywhere and farm it for themselves. They started to plough and sow seed on common and waste land but they didn't last very long.

Many of these odd sects thought that they alone had found the way to God and that everyone else was wrong. If you were not an

Anglican or a Catholic, there were many different groups to which you could belong.

They included Independents, Presbyterians, Baptists, Calvinists, Muggletonians, Fifth Monarchy Men, Seekers, Manifestarians, Family of Love, Ranters, Arians, Adamites and Libertins.

Most did not last more than a few years, although some thrived and are still in existence to this day. Among the surviving groups are the Quakers. In the next section, we will meet a Quaker family but before we do, we ought to see what had been happening after Charles I was beheaded.

Very often, the feeling of bitterness which leads to a civil war goes on for years after it is over. The execution of the king made that

feeling deeper and more lasting. Ireland and Scotland had immediately hailed his son as Charles II. Some of the colonists in America felt the same way.

Cromwell smashed the Royalists in Ireland and then turned to Scotland. Charles II, as we must now call him, promised to make allies both of the Catholics and the Scottish Presbyterians in his struggle against Cromwell.

Cromwell beat one Scottish army at Dunbar and defeated another at Worcester in 1651. Charles was forced to hide in an oak tree in order to give Cromwell's men the slip. He eventually escaped and managed to get back to France.

Within two years, England was called the 'Commonwealth' and Cromwell himself had become 'Lord Protector'. Some even wanted to make him king.

However hated Cromwell was by some people, it is true to say that he gave England a period of peace and made its name respected throughout Europe.

The Lord Protector

Charles hiding in the oak

11 A Quaker Family

This is a house built in the new style. Large timber beams for building have been getting scarcer. Houses from now on will mostly have to be made of bricks or stone, at least for the outside walls. Here, in a busy town not far from the capital, Isaac Penton, a well-to-do carpenter has moved with his family.

His wife is called Beth. His three sons are Josiah, Elias and Samuel. Among Quaker families, biblical names are often given to the boys. The girls are called by words which, until this time, were only used to describe someone's character. The two grown-up daughters are Prudence and Charity and the twelve-year-old girl is known as Patience. This is also a common practice in Quaker homes.

Isaac is a master craftsman. He makes cabinets, chests and furniture. He even does woodcarving, if his customers wish. He employs men to help him. Josiah works for his father but Elias, who is eleven, and Samuel, aged nine, are still at school.

The first thing you will notice from the picture is that the clothes are very dull. Gone are the bright colours and fancy lace-work of the Cavaliers. Most Puritans prefer not to show off with gaudy garments and long, curly hair but the Quakers nearly always dress in black or grey with touches of white here and there.

The Quaker movement was started by George Fox. He had become convinced that many people went to church on Sunday only because they had to and that they recited the set prayers like parrots, without really understanding them. He believed that each person could find his or her own way to God without the guidance of bishops or even priests and that this could be done through Christ's help, given to those who kept up a struggle against the temptations of a wicked world. Quakers thought deeply about their religion, prayed in their own words and read almost nothing but the Bible.

Fox travelled the country preaching the new life to all who would listen. He made many converts, among whom were the Pentons. They lead their lives according to the words and actions of Jesus, as shown in the New Testament.

The Pentons, like all Quakers, believe that there should be no ranks or classes in society and that all people are alike, as God's children. Once upon a time in England, a man might use the words 'you', 'your' or 'yours' when the person he was talking to was an equal or a superior, and 'thee', 'thou' or 'thine' when addressing an animal, child or servant. The Quakers use 'thee' and 'thou' to everyone to show what they think of this system. In the same way, the Pentons talk to each other and to strangers in the words of the Bible.

A Quaker Family

It is morning in the kitchen of the house. The walls are white, the doors of plain wood. There is a lattice window. A dresser with crockery stands against the wall. A long wooden table is laid for breakfast. There are earthenware dishes and mugs on it.

Beth serves out the boiled oatmeal porridge but before they eat, they all kneel on the stone floor to say grace. Everyone in the family takes a turn at thanking God and the others say 'Amen'.

After breakfast, the two youngest boys go to school. Josiah makes his way to the workshop at the back of the house whilst Isaac sits down to write out a bill for one of his customers.

Beth and the girls get on with the usual

George Fox, founder of the Quakers

household tasks. Unlike the housewives of our own time, she has to make many of the things we are content to buy from shops. As well as jam, preserves, butter and cheese, she also makes candles and even the ink her husband is using.

There is little time for play among Quaker children. Quakers don't approve of wasting time and they don't like amusements such as singing and dancing. If the girls sing at all as they work, it is a psalm or a hymn. Life is very serious in a Quaker family.

12 Crime and Punishment

We've already seen how strict the different kinds of Puritans were. Cromwell's Ironsides didn't drink, swear, gamble or brawl and the Pentons thought singing, dancing and the display of fine clothes were wicked. Soon, many of these ideas were put in the form of laws.

To see that they were carried out, Cromwell divided the country into eleven districts and did away with the old system of judges and juries. Over each district he set a major-general with a number of soldiers to carry out his orders.

Most people did not like this military rule, not only on account of its strictness but also because it interfered in the way people lived. Cromwell's government made the mistake of trying to force people to be good.

Cromwell's Parliament made new laws against bull- and bear-baiting, play acting, cockfighting, travelling or trading on a Sunday, and so on.

We can understand why cruel sports involving animals should be banned but it wasn't the cruelty the Puritans objected to, so much as the gambling and drinking which went with them. Besides, Parliament distrusted any gathering of more than a few people because they might be plotting against their rulers. This was perhaps why play-going was outlawed. Not only were there many citizens in the same place, they might also be corrupted by an anti-Puritan play.

Horse racing, playing cards or dice for money, even football and wrestling were forbidden. It seemed to those with no strong views on amusements that the Government was out to spoil their fun.

They could picture someone in a London office examining these and other pastimes one by one and asking, 'Do people enjoy this? If it pleases someone, it must be wicked and ought to be stopped!'

Local soldiers were often ordered to burst into private houses to see if any of these 'moral' laws was being broken and whether those inside were living their lives according to the Good Book.

There was no mention of May Day frolics in the Bible, so the troopers chopped down the maypoles. Nowhere in the New Testament did it say you should celebrate Christ's birthday by eating a lot of food. There were cases of troops seizing Christmas dinners as they were

Title page of a book attacking amusements

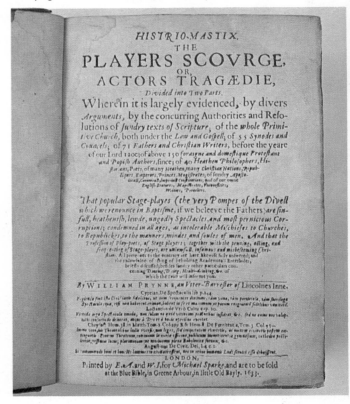

300

cooking and taking them away.

The main punishments for crimes such as theft, assault, robbery or murder, as well as the breaking of the new 'kill-joy' laws, included fines, imprisonment, the stocks or pillory and hanging. In those days many different offences could result in a hanging and at least one of the other punishments could also end in death.

For example, the Puritans believed that a public shaming hurt the offender as much as anything else. A village drunk might be put in the stocks or made to wear a wooden collar with a large 'D' (for 'drunk') painted on it.

Passers-by might jeer at a man in the stocks or sling mud at him but if they were really angry at what he had done, they could throw stones.

A man in the stocks could dodge some of them but the pillory didn't allow much movement. Sometimes the authorities nailed the criminal's ears to the wood to make sure.

Other sentences were slitting the nose, cutting off the ears and branding. It's strange to think of the love of God being used as an excuse to carry out these horrible punishments.

Stocks at Woodstock

13 The Countryside

We need someone to guide us through the counties of England in Stuart times. By good fortune, we are able to get Mark Rudge the pedlar to show us around. He is going to let us travel in his cart, so that we can see for ourselves what England was like just over three centuries ago.

'I'm sorry it's not very comfortable,' he says as he helps us up. 'The roads are very bad – all bangs and bumps in the summer.'

'Why just the summer?'

'Because the roads are mostly bare dirt. In winter, the sun doesn't dry up rainwater and the roads are seas of mud. Few people use them in the winter. Those who do, leave ruts in the ooze which are likely to bake hard when the weather gets warmer again. That's what makes the jolts; the wheels slip down into the ruts and pot holes.'

'What about springs on the axles?' we ask, but Mark doesn't know what we are talking about. 'We are lucky we aren't right behind another cart,' he says, 'or we would hardly be able to breathe for the dust.' He flicks his whip at the horses and we trundle on.

He shows us the hop-fields and orchards of Kent. It is blossom time and the trees are covered in pink and white flowers. We travel from village to village selling the things that the peasants can't grow or make for themselves. They are mostly luxuries such as fancy buttons, lace, combs, hair ribbons, toys and so on.

Mark says that the hop-field and orchard villages of Kent and Worcestershire are good places for him to trade because the farmers sell nearly all they grow and live on the money they get. Villages near large towns

grow wheat, barley, rye and oats and raise animals on a large scale. They too sell most of their produce and thus have money to spare.

'The villages that don't have a lot of coins to spend,' says Mark, 'are those that are too far away from the markets. They go in for what we call champion farming. I think it comes from a French word. It means they have huge fields and they don't really grow things to sell – only to eat. When we've been through London, I'll show you a village like that.'

A few days later, he is as good as his word. 'Here we are,' he says. 'Jump down and I'll tell you about it.' We wander round the tiny hamlet looking at the little cottages.

'The people here grow their own food and not much else. In a normal year they get by, in a bad one they go short but in a good one they may have a little left over to sell. That's where people like me come in. There are quite a lot of travelling salesmen.

'The tinker mends pots and pans. Then there are the sellers of hoes, sickles, scythes and spades. Some go about with barrels of tar, salted fish or salt on its own – anything, in fact, that the villagers can't get locally.

'They have a few long, narrow strips of land in each of the three big fields you can see. One field grows wheat, one barley and one lies fallow to allow time to get goodness back into the soil. The animals are turned into the fields to eat the stalks when the harvest is in.

'There's a meadow for hay: they cut that and store it to feed a few animals through the winter. Otherwise the cows and sheep graze on the common and the pigs root about in the woods.

'They are peasants and they live like peasants. It's lucky that I'm with you. A few years ago they'd have stoned you out of the village just because you're strangers. "Foreigners", they would have called you. They don't do that now but they aren't too friendly with folks they don't know.'

We are glad when Mark's business is done and we can leave.

Chapter Sixteen   The Restoration

1 Charles II

At first, the Puritans were admired by many people, particularly during the reigns of those rulers who had persecuted them. Unfortunately, the Commonwealth gave the Puritans the chance to show that in some ways they were just as narrow-minded and intolerant as their persecutors. They tried hard to force everyone into the mould they approved of.

There were disagreements between those who had won the Civil War: arguments between the different religions and quarrels between army and Parliament. After a few years many people had grown weary of Cromwell's rule, but there was little they could do about it. At least he kept the arguers in their place and prevented any one group from getting on top.

Just when it seemed that England might be getting back towards a better system of parliamentary rule, Cromwell died. One of the things he did before his death was to name his son, Richard, as the next Protector.

'Tumbledown Dick', as people began to call him, was not the man his father had been. He preferred to run his own estates in the peace and quiet of the countryside.

As soon as the different quarrelling groups realized that there was no one in control of England they began to make plans to take over. It looked as though there might be

Charles II on his way to London from Dover

Cromwell's death mask

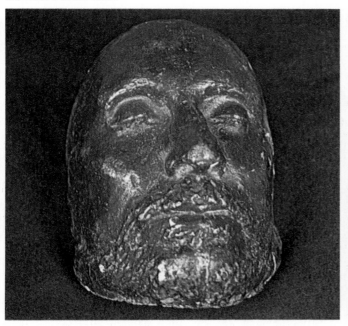

another civil war. It was then that General Monck took charge. He was a soldier who had fought for the Cavaliers at the start of the war but who had changed sides.

He commanded the Commonwealth army in Scotland and was trusted by most people. He marched his men to London and declared that there must be an election.

The new Parliament came to an agreement with Charles II. Many of the laws passed in Cromwell's time were to be cancelled. Charles said he would not seek revenge on those who had fought against his father. On one point his advisers were firm: the men who had actually signed the death warrant must be brought to trial.

With these things settled, Charles II set out to cross the Channel. General Monck waited at Dover. On 25 May 1660, Charles landed and made his way slowly up to London amid cheering crowds. They were only too glad to have someone who might be able to keep order and save the country from war.

The Ironside soldiers who had fought so fiercely against Charles I now stood to attention on Blackheath and saluted his son as he passed by. Then the new Parliament paid them off and sent them home. England had had enough of large peace-time armies.

When it came to punishing the killers of the late king, a difficulty arose. Fifty-nine men had signed and sealed the document condemning Charles I to death. About twenty of them had fled abroad, a similar number were already dead, leaving only about eighteen to stand trial.

To Charles II's credit, he did his best to see that as few men were executed as possible. In fact, only nine of those who had signed were put to death. To many Royalists, this seemed to be too small a number. Still thirsting for vengeance, some of them dug up the bodies of Cromwell, Bradshaw and Ireton and hanged them.

2 Charles's Court

In 1698 a fire burned down almost all of the old palace at Whitehall. The only part left was the Banqueting Hall from which Charles I had walked to his death. In spite of this, Whitehall before the fire had been one of Charles II's favourite palaces.

There were several other palaces at which Charles II could have held his court. There was St. James's which had been used by Henry VIII but Charles II didn't like it and it was not a royal dwelling again until the reign of his niece, Mary II. Hampton Court and Windsor saw the Royal party from time to time but the court was almost always to be found at Whitehall.

The palace covered twenty-three acres. If it had been a regular shape it might have measured 100 yards by 1,000 yards. In this maze of buildings there were about 2,000 rooms and many hundreds of servants.

We'll see if they will let us in. There are two main entrances. The first is on the river. You could hire a boat and land at Whitehall steps but we'll go the other way, down a narrow lane with a guarded gate at each end. Today we are lucky and the sentry passes us along. We have to go through another gate flanked by guards but soon we are in the Outer Chamber.

Here are all the rest of the men and women who have come to see the king. Sometimes the nearest the visitors get is the gallery of the Banqueting Hall. Every day at noon, Charles II dines in public. For many visitors, to catch a glimpse of the king eating was enough.

Some of those in the Outer Chamber are dealt with by minor secretaries. Those that are

Charles' Court

left are taken through into the king's Presence Chamber. Most of them are seen by senior advisers.

The king has a lot of these — the Lord Chamberlain, the Lord Steward, the Master of the Horse, the Earl Marshall and so on. We are not lucky enough to be shown into the Privy Chamber but after a moment, the king comes out of his office. He claps the man nearest to us on the back and laughs loudly. 'Well, Sir Peter,' he says, 'we shall give this matter some thought and let you know anon.'

We notice his striking appearance. He is tall with masses of dark hair, a small black moustache and a friendly smile. We don't have time to see much more. The king bows to two very beautiful ladies in fine clothes and has gone. The audience is over before it had properly begun. The courtiers get ready to leave.

On the way out, we fall into step with Sir Peter who guides us to the gate. We pass the queen's apartments, the tilting ground, the cockpit and the tennis court. 'His Majesty feels that his people went too long without pastimes under Cromwell,' says Sir Peter. 'He himself likes the things which the Puritans

Model of the Palace of Whitehall

stopped. Now the king and all his subjects can gamble, go horse racing, watch a play or even sing and dance if they feel like it.'

'The king is fond of dancing, then?'

'Indeed. He likes the ladies – and why not? Why should he not have beautiful people about him at court?'

'What exactly is a court?' we ask.

'It consists of the king and queen, their advisers, servants, friends and acquaintances. There are those who wait on the king because they want a favour from him – a grant of land, the right to trade, a title, perhaps, or something of that kind.'

We say goodbye to Sir Peter when we reach the exit. We wonder what sort of reign Charles II will have. His main occupation seems to be having fun but his eyes are those of an intelligent man. He won't be able to do as he likes with Parliament, though; the time when a king's lightest word was law has gone for ever.

The Banqueting Hall today

Key to Whitehall Palace: **1** King's private apartments **2** gate **3** tennis court **4** cockpit **5** banqueting house **6** formal gardens **7** horse guard yard **8** chapel **9** great chamber **10** kitchens **11** bakery **12** sawpit **13** coalyard **14** woodyard **15** privy stairs **16** bowling green **17** guard house **18** palace gate **19** River Thames **20** palace wharf

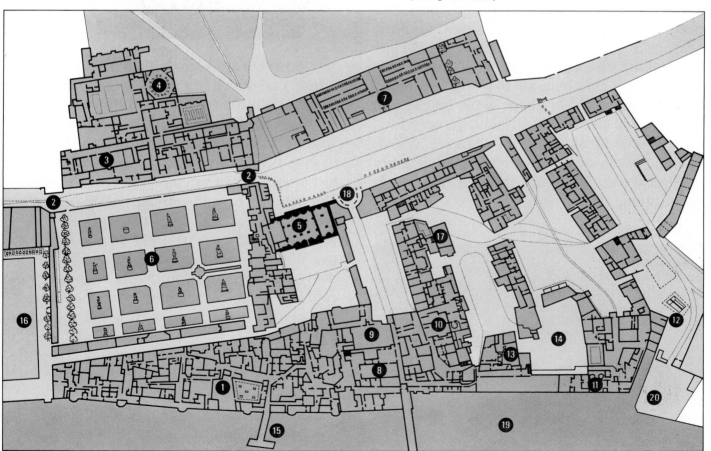

3 A Poor Family in London

These archaeologists are digging on the south bank of the Thames, almost opposite the Tower of London. They are looking for remains of the seventeenth century, not for traces of Stone Age men or Romans. One of them holds up a bowl. It is blue and white and known as 'Lambeth Delft'. Modern archaeologists are not the only people to have found Lambeth bowls at this site. There is one in the room shown opposite.

This room is in a London house at the start of Charles II's reign. The family which lives here are lucky that their room is at ground level. The house has four floors and many rooms, all occupied by different families. It lies in a narrow street near London Bridge.

Like the other buildings in this street, it is quite old and mostly made of wood. The inner walls are plastered to about waist height and lime washed above. The ceiling is very low. There is little furniture, as you can see. A bed, a couple of chests and a table are all roughly made of wood. There are three or four stools but only one chair.

Finds from the seventeenth century

An open fireplace will burn wood if the family can afford it. Coal is more plentiful but it doesn't burn as well without an iron fire basket. When there is a fire, mother can boil water and do simple cooking but if she wants to give her family puddings or pies, she must buy them from the cook-shop on the corner. She gets her bread from the baker's down the lane.

Apart from the iron pot on the fire, there are not too many cooking utensils. A good deal of the time the family eats cold meals in a cold room. Hot meals may consist of porridge for breakfast and soup with bread the rest of the time. Meat is very rare in this family.

There are wooden platters, rough earthenware bowls and wooden spoons on the table for the mid-day soup. On the chest under the window stands the blue and white bowl.

Now we'll meet the family. There are five members: the parents and three children.

A Poor Family in London

There is a baby, not much over twelve months old, a girl called Sarah, aged eight, and a boy of nine named Jem. Let's hear from the mother how the family manages.

'I look after the family as well as I can. I do all the usual chores such as cooking, cleaning and sewing. I also do some needlework for the neighbours.

'Father works long hours in a new brickfield a few miles to the east of the city near a village called Stratford-at-Bow. He wheels loads of roasted bricks from the ovens to the stacks and has to walk to and from his work. His wages are tenpence a day and the cost of living is rising. It's hard to make ends meet but he's lucky to have a job at all.

'Neither Jem nor Sarah go to school. Lessons cost money and there isn't enough to spare. I try to teach the older two to read. Sarah knows her ABC but Jem is bored with books and is happier roaming the streets.

'It's just as well I'm handy with my needle, for clothes are expensive too. I buy second-hand garments, cut them up and remake them. I can't make hats or shoes though. Sometimes we are given "throwouts" from richer houses. Otherwise we have to go without. Father is the only one who must have shoes. Fancy shoemakers are out of the question but even a pair from the cobbler's takes almost a week's wages. Hats are even more expensive. We don't wear these drab greys and blacks for religious reasons — we have no choice.'

Sarah and Jem help their mother about the room. Jem's task is to fetch water for the day from a nearby pump for cooking and drinking. There is no tap in the house. No one

in the family takes a bath, nor do they wash very often. Their thick clothes never get cleaned.

Jem can go out when he has brought the water. He may earn a copper or two running errands or holding gentlemen's horses. He also has a happy knack of finding things. It was he who found the Lambeth Delft bowl. If we go with him this morning, he will show us where he first saw it.

4 The State of the City

As we leave the house we glance back and are surprised to find that it isn't the familiar half-timbered type that we already know. The bottom part of the wall is made of stones and pebbles stuck together with stiff clay. Above it the whole side of the house is covered with overlapping boards, like a boat. Everything is tarred.

Our second surprise is the state of the roads. In some places there are cobblestones or patches of gravel. In others, someone has paved a stretch with flat stones. The rest is just hard-packed dirt. There are no pavements. It has been raining and there are puddles everywhere.

Jem doesn't seem to mind and splashes straight through them, his bare legs getting even dirtier. We pick our way across the drier patches. It would be difficult to do this at night, as there are no lamp posts to be seen.

One or two buildings have lanterns on brackets which are fastened to the walls but they only have candles and wouldn't give much light. It's a good thing Jem is leading the way, or we would quickly get lost. There are no sign posts, street names or house numbers.

There is rubbish everywhere, including a huge pile at the end of Jem's street. It doesn't smell very pleasant but the boy doesn't seem to notice. Above the stench of decay we can detect other scents every now and then – a wave of stale, drink-laden air from the ale-house, the pleasant aroma of baking bread and a general drift of salt, tar and spices from the direction of the River Thames.

Jem has agreed to show us round the city before we go to the place where he found the bowl. We follow him past the fish market at Billingsgate and hold our noses. We turn away from the busy, bustling docks and wharves, where all kinds of cargoes are being unloaded. We can still see the tops of the wooden cranes above some low warehouses as we climb a steepish street towards the end of London Bridge.

This is still the only way of crossing the river on foot, although Jem says you could hire any one of over 2,000 rowing boats to take you over. We come to the main road and plunge into the mass of people thronging it. This street is in better condition and there are lines of wooden posts at the sides. These are to stop the waggons and coaches crashing into the buildings.

If you wanted to feel safe, you could walk between the post line and the houses. You wouldn't get run over but you might get a bucket emptied over your head from an upstairs window. In any case, the ground nearest the houses is very muddy. None of the roofs has a gutter or drainpipe, so the rain-water just runs down the tiles and pours over the edge.

We glance curiously as a fashionable lady passes in a sedan chair. Street hawkers and traders all shout their wares at once. London is a noisy, dirty city.

Jem takes us to see the city wall and some of its gates. The wall is broken or crumbling in places. Elsewhere, the only thing holding it up is a shop or house built right up against it. The moat which once surrounded the capital has long been filled up with rubbish and built over.

At last we cross the bridge to a factory on the south bank. Alongside it is a long, low mound on which the workmen throw the pots and plates which are not good enough to be sold. Jem can't find an unbroken pot or bowl but suddenly he straightens up with a coin in his hand.

Hardly has he stood upright when another urchin snatches it from him and runs off. He is

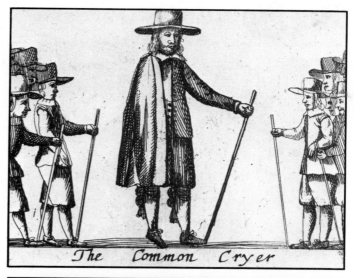

The Common Cryer

126

soon lost to sight. When we suggest telling the police, it is Jem's turn to look surprised. 'Police?' he says. 'What is that?'

5 The Plague

It is 1965. Mark, who is eight, has come to school early to show his teacher a curious object which he is carrying in a plastic bag. Some children in the playground are singing, 'A ring, a ring of roses, a pocket full of posies, atishoo, atishoo, we all fall down.'

'Hallo, Mark,' says Miss Fellows. 'What have you got there?' Mark shows her the object. 'My brother found it sticking out of the dirt in a front garden when he was on his paper round,' he says. Miss Fellows knows what it is and phones the police. A week later they go to the station to meet the police surgeon.

'You were right, Miss Fellows,' says the doctor. 'It's part of a human skull. We've done some tests and asked some questions and this is what we've found out.

'It was probably a man aged about twenty-five to thirty-five but he wasn't murdered. He died about three hundred years ago, possibly of disease. We think the house where your brother found it was built on top of an old plague pit.'

They thank him, collect the skull and later, put it in the school museum. Mark wants to know about the plague.

'Could you catch it from the skull, Miss?'

'No, Mark. It was passed from person to person by the fleas which lived on rats. We don't really know where the plague started – the Far East, perhaps. We think it was brought here by rats on ships. The piles of rubbish attracted the rats and they also built their nests in houses. People weren't very clean then and every summer hundreds died of Bubonic, as we call it now.

'In the summer of 1665, London and many other parts of Britain had their worst attack since the Black Death, over three hundred years before. This time hundreds of thousands died. No one knew what caused it nor how to cure it. Doctors thought that the bad smells might be responsible for the plague. They wore strange head-dresses stuffed with sweet-smelling herbs hoping they would be

Plague cottage at Eyam

Plague victims' graves at Eyam

protected. Some of their remedies were even stranger.

'As soon as a case was known, the house was closed and nailed up for forty days. The people inside could starve to death even if they weren't infected, unless they had friends who could supply them with food. There wasn't a street without at least a few houses boarded up and with a red cross painted on the door. Sometimes you could see where someone had scrawled underneath the cross, "Lord have mercy on us".

'So many people passed away that the bodies piled up faster than they could be dealt with. Carts rumbled through the streets at night, the driver shouting, "Bring out your dead." The corpses were buried in dozens or even hundreds in huge holes. This is where we think your skull came from, Mark.

'Some people tried to escape to the countryside but took the disease with them. The tailor at a village called Eyam in Derbyshire had some clothes sent to him from London. He died a week later. Within a month over twenty more people had died also. The village parson took a terrible decision. He talked the villagers into cutting themselves off from the rest of the world in case they spread the plague.

'Friends left food at the parish boundaries

and washed the money they got for it in vinegar baths. It was late in 1666 before the villagers were free of their year of terror and by then there were only about ninety of them left. Before 1665, there had been 350.'

Mark is very interested and goes to close the window to shut out the song the children are singing. 'Don't, Mark,' says Miss Fellows. 'Listen to the words. Rings of roses were the red spots on your body which told you that you'd got the plague. The posies were the flowers they thought would keep the disease away. Atishoo stands for the sneeze that was the plague's first sign. That little rhyme has lasted 300 years.

'And what,' Miss Fellows ends, 'what, Mark, do you think "We all fall down" means?'

6 The Great Fire of London

As well as the plague and the dirt, one of the drawbacks of living in a town in those days was the danger of fire. Most of the houses were made of wood and many of the roofs were thatched with reeds.

At that time, there was not much you could do if your house caught fire. If it was a small fire, you might be able to douse the flames with buckets of water, provided that there was a stream or pump nearby. When the thatch caught fire, the householder might try to pull down the bundles of smoking reeds with a long hook and stamp out the sparks.

A few families owned syringes like this one, but they didn't hold very much water. More often than not, fires were just left to die out of their own accord. On 2 September 1666, a fire started in London which could not be put out and which refused to die down for nearly a week.

The day before was a Saturday. That night, a baker named Thomas Fariner had stoked up his oven so that he could get a good start the next morning. He was woken up even earlier than he had planned.

In the small hours of Sunday morning, he and his wife coughed in their sleep and woke up to find the bedroom full of smoke. Quickly throwing on what clothes they could find, they shook their servant girl from her sleep. Escape seemed out of the question, as the staircase was already well alight.

Thomas and Mrs. Fariner made their way up to the attic, scrambled through the dormer window and slithered across the thatch to the next house and safety. The servant girl was too frightened to follow them and they never saw her alive again.

The baker's house was in Pudding Lane near London Bridge. The neighbours were alarmed but no one else was – there were always fires in London. However, there had been a hot summer and everything was as dry as tinder. To make matters worse, there was a stiff breeze blowing.

The flames reached the thatch and the wind carried wisps of burning reed to an inn standing on Fish Street Hill. Stores of hay and straw blazed up and the wind blew the sparks about. Within an hour or two, the whole street was ablaze and the fire was heading towards the warehouses by the Thames.

The Lord Mayor of London was woken by servants. So was Samuel Pepys, Secretary to the Navy, who later wrote in his diary for that day that although the fire was a large one, it was not near enough to cause alarm. Pepys went back to sleep again but the next day he went to have a closer look.

He hired a ferryman to row him along the Thames. By the afternoon of 2 September, dozens of houses had been destroyed, along with inns, stables, warehouses and even a church or two. Pepys asked the boatman to take him to Westminster. He reported to the king who told him to give orders to blow up

houses in the path of the fire. Pepys went back to tell the Lord Mayor. That night he watched what was happening from an inn on the far bank of the river.

Before it grew light the next morning, Pepys was alarmed to find the flames sweeping towards his own house. He took his best wine, all the documents from the Navy Office where he worked and a large cheese and buried them in the garden.

By 8 September the fire had been halted. Much of London lay in smoking ruins. The streets could hardly be seen under their piles of half-burnt timber and heaps of ash. Those who had fled at the height of the fire carrying their valuables now crept back in ones and twos to gaze sadly at the destruction. More than 10,000 houses and over eighty churches had gone, including St. Paul's, whose roof had rained molten drops of lead.

The strange thing was that only six people had died in a fire which had destroyed more than half of London. There wasn't a lot to be cheerful about but one good thing was that the fire seemed to have burned out the plague, for it never returned on the same scale again.

The last page of Pepys's diary

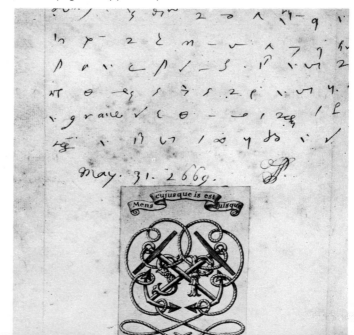

The Great Fire of London

7 Wren and St. Paul's

Nearly sixty years after the Great Fire an old man died, aged ninety. He was Sir Christopher Wren. Born before the Civil War when Charles I was still alive, he lived to see the end of the Stuart line. He died in the reign of George I.

In the days following the fire, his much younger figure was to be seen picking his way carefully through the smouldering heaps, pacing, measuring and taking notes.

Within a week he was able to show Charles II his plans for rebuilding the city. The design showed wide avenues of fine stone and brick buildings leading to a new St. Paul's as the centre of the capital.

Unfortunately, few of his grand ideas were realized. The rubbish from the fire took weeks to remove but as the streets were cleared, the owners of the land started to rebuild their houses and shops. Of course it would have been nice to get rid of all the narrow courts and winding alleys, but to broaden or straighten a road meant taking somebody's land away from them. Finally, most of the plan was dropped. Some tidying up of building lines was done but it was more like patching a torn garment than making a new one.

Something would have to be done about the places of worship, however. More than three-quarters of the city's 109 churches had gone. It was decided that there had been too many churches. In future there were only to be fifty-one and Wren was put in charge of designing all of them. After the first few, Wren found himself so overworked, he merely outlined his plans for the others in a general way and then left the details to his assistants.

St. Paul's Cathedral today

As Surveyor-General to Charles II, Wren had to make sure the new building laws were obeyed. These said that at least the main roads must be widened and that all new shops, houses and so on must be made of brick or stone if they were inside the city walls.

In six years, London was rebuilt, the money for the public buildings coming from a tax on coal. One building remained as a huge ruin from the Great Fire. St. Paul's Cathedral was beyond repair and would have to come down. This wasn't an easy task, for there were no power machines to help the workmen. Almost 50,000 cartloads of rubble had to be taken away.

Wren drew up his plans for a St. Paul's completely different from the old church. The work began in 1673 but details of the design were changed from time to time as the walls rose.

He lived in a little terraced house on the south bank of the Thames while the work was going on and perhaps wondered sometimes if he would ever live to see it finished. In the meantime, Wren went on with his designs for other buildings. Oddly enough, he had begun as a professor of astronomy at Oxford. He was not really an architect at all but he had started drawing up plans for buildings even before the Great Fire.

He was sixty-five before even part of the cathedral was finished. This was the eastern end and it was opened to the public in 1697, when William III ruled England.

Another thirteen years were to pass before the work was completed. At the age of seventy-eight, Wren had himself pulled up on ropes and winches to the top of the building, a height of more than 350 feet, so that he could see the last stone laid. The year was 1710, during the reign of Queen Anne.

He died in 1723, aged ninety. He had lived long enough to see England governed by no less than eight different rulers. He was buried in his own cathedral. A simple stone marks the place. It says: 'If you are searching for his monument – look around you'.

8 Art in Stuart Times

The making of beautiful things is one of the aims of art but during the Puritan Commonwealth, art was not encouraged. After Charles II's restoration, it is not surprising to find that English artists were in short supply. Portraits were popular in the late seventeenth century but the painters were mostly foreigners. Milton was the most important writer of the time.

Painting of Charles I by Van Dyck

Frontispiece of Poems by Milton

Wood carving by Grinling Gibbons

Painting of Nell Gwyn from the Studio of P. Leley

Painting of Samuel Pepys by T. Hays

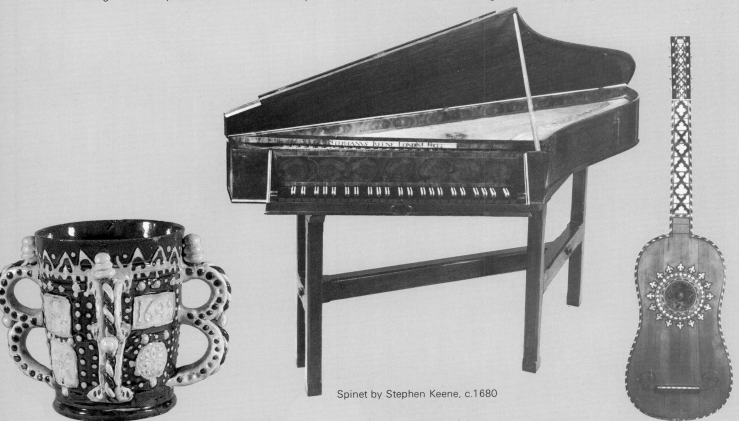

Lead-glazed four-handled cup

Spinet by Stephen Keene, c.1680

Guitar attributed to Jean Voboam, c.1680

9 Architecture in Stuart Times

If there was no outstanding painting in the Stuart period, there was certainly a great deal of good architecture. The rebuilding of the London churches destroyed in the fire was in the hands of Wren and Hawksmoor but Vanbrugh and Winstanley were designing magnificent country houses for the great landowners.

Sir Christopher Wren by G. Kneller.

Quebec House, Kent

Rufford Old Hall, Lancashire

St. Mary-le-Bow, 1671–80

Interior of St. Mary-le-Bow

St. Andrew's, Holborn Circus, 1686

Sudbury House, Derbyshire

Blickling Hall, Norfolk

Audley End, Essex

Castle Howard, North Yorkshire

327

Chapter Seventeen   The Last Stuarts

1 James II and the Monmouth Rebellion

Charles II died in 1685 and, although he had several children, none of them could claim the throne, for none were the children of his own wife. One of them, the Duke of Monmouth, was quite sure his mother had been married to Charles and he did not see why he should not be the next ruler.

He had been the king's favourite son and did not take kindly to the idea that his uncle James should be the king. However, Parliament thought otherwise and Charles II's brother ascended the throne as James II. There was nothing Monmouth could do; he was out of favour and living abroad in Holland when his uncle became king.

James II

His friends argued with him that, as James II was a Catholic, a lot of people would support a Protestant like himself and would help him gain the throne – by force if need be. Help was promised in fitting out ships and finally the duke agreed to a rebellion against his uncle.

Three ships were to sail to Scotland to stir the Scots up against James, whilst the Duke of Monmouth would head for the west of England where there was supposed to be a better chance of getting recruits.

The Duke of Monmouth landed at Lyme Regis in June 1685. Straightaway he sent men about the town to tell everyone that James was not the rightful king and that they should fight for the duke.

Monmouth was handsome, popular and, most important, not a Catholic. Men came to join him by the hundred. Soon he had about 6,000 followers.

They may have been keen but they were not really an army. A few had been soldiers but most knew nothing of fighting and had few proper weapons. Worse still, the leaders couldn't always rely on the men to do exactly what they were told. All the same, there were enough of them to frighten the townsfolk of Axminster and Taunton, which they captured.

The news alarmed both James II and his Parliament. The duke was declared a traitor and an outlaw. A reward of £5,000 was offered for him, dead or alive. James collected what troops he could and ordered them down to the west country.

A playing card of the time

Unluckily for Monmouth, he didn't realize that there were several deep ditches between his men and the king's camp. One of his rebels stumbled into a ditch and his gun went off. This was enough to alarm the regular soldiers and the ditches stopped the two armies grappling with each other straightaway.

In the end there could only be one result. The king's soldiers stood their ground and shot down Monmouth's peasants by the hundred. When the battle was over, the duke's dreams were ended. Nearly all the Sedgemoor rebels were taken prisoner. A few, including the duke himself, tried to escape. He was captured near Ringwood in the New Forest and executed on 15 July 1685. His rebellion had lasted about five weeks all told.

The rest of the prisoners were tried by the hard-hearted Judge Jeffreys. Something like two hundred of them joined their leader on the scaffold. More than eight hundred were shipped to Barbados in the West Indies and sold into slavery.

To this day, surnames in Barbados can be traced back two hundred years to the west of England and 'Monmouth's Rebellion'.

The king's army caught up with the rebels on Sedgemoor. By this time, Monmouth had heard that the Scottish part of his plan had failed, so he made up his mind to launch a surprise attack at night.

Duke of Monmouth pleading for his life

2   The Glorious Revolution

James II managed to survive one attempt to force him off the throne but he wasn't so lucky the second time. He was not a clever man but he was a stubborn one. Once he got an idea in his head nothing would shift it.

He became a Catholic late in life and looked for ways to change the religion of England. His first wife had been a Protestant and James's two grown-up daughters, Mary and Anne, were the same.

By now, England was a thoroughly Protestant country and wanted nothing to do with the Pope in Rome. This didn't stop James. Even though he knew there were laws to stop Catholics being officers in the army or navy, he appointed several of them to senior positions.

He increased the size of the army and went to inspect the soldiers at their camp on Hounslow Heath. Parliament was alarmed at the things he was doing, and protested strongly. James decided to copy his father, Charles I, and rule without a Parliament.

His elder daughter, Mary, was already married to a Dutch Protestant prince named William of Orange. A few important people slipped quietly over to Holland to ask his advice about what James II was doing. What should they do? Surely William and Mary as Protestants were also alarmed at the way James was trying to bring back the Catholic religion?

The general opinion seemed to be that it was better just to wait. James was nearly sixty, after all. When he died, Mary would be the next ruler. Of course James was an unpleasant and rather stupid man but they wouldn't have to put up with him for long.

A William and Mary plate

Then, suddenly, everything changed. James II's second wife, Mary of Modena, gave birth to a son. As a boy, the new baby became heir to the throne over his half-sister Mary. Everyone realized that the boy would be brought up as a Catholic, like his parents.

Now there was no point in the Protestants waiting for James to die. They could see in their mind's eye a long line of Catholic kings stretching away into the future. They lost no time in sending a letter to William of Orange, inviting him to bring his army to England and drive Catholic James out. The letter was carried to Holland by Admiral Herbert, disguised as an ordinary sailor.

William began to get ready for the invasion. When James heard that William had gathered together 14,000 men and over 500 ships with which to transport them to England, he panicked. He tried to undo the mistakes he had made during his three-year reign but it was too late.

William landed at Torbay on 5 November 1688. James II's army was almost twice as big. It was marched a short distance towards the west country and made camp near Salisbury. It looked as though a tremendous battle was going to take place.

In fact, there was no battle because many of James's army leaders took their men and deserted to William. All over the country there were revolts and demonstrations against the king. James II saw that the position was hopeless and left the country. On the way, he dropped the Great Seal of England into the Thames, hoping that this would hinder the running of the country.

Both Parliament and people acclaimed Dutch William and his wife as William III and Mary II. There would never be a Catholic ruler again, nor would any future king be able to rule England as he liked. From now on king and Parliament would work together.

3 Science

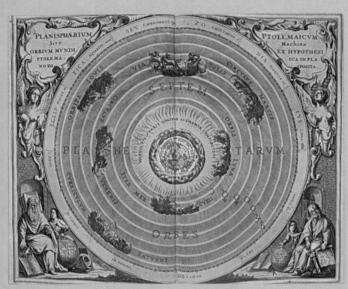

The old view of the universe with the earth in the centre

The Copernican view of the universe

Not long before the Stuart period, most educated men had believed that each planet was fixed to a huge, hollow crystal ball and that all these spheres, as they called them, revolved round the earth.

We know now that these ideas were wrong but in those days, such matters came under the heading of religion, not science. Science, as a way of getting to know what makes things work, was not yet accepted.

The universities were not interested in the scientific method. Whenever a problem arose, the official way of solving it was either to argue the thing out or to give a ruling that everyone had to accept. It never occurred to most people that it's best to get the facts right first. Copernicus and Galileo had already shown that the strange movements of the planets could be explained by accepting that the sun, and not the earth, is in the middle of the system.

The Church in those days imprisoned, or even put to death, those who said they believed in the new theories. But by the middle of the seventeenth century, quite a number of people were beginning to think it was silly to debate the truth when you could find a way of showing it. Isaac Newton explained why the moon and the planets kept travelling in circles. His very important discovery was the Law of Gravity.

One reason why people's thinking was changing was because population numbers were rising. This led to more trade and travel and more ships. The captains wanted to know how to find out where they were when they couldn't see land.

It was easy enough to measure the angle of the sun or a star above the horizon and from that to say how far north or south of the Equator you were. But there was no simple way to work out how far east or west you had

Sir Isaac Newton

Newton's reflecting telescope

travelled. However, a careful study of the moon and stars helped mathematicians to draw up tables which sailors could use.

Growing numbers of people needed more and more coal so the mines had to be dug deeper. Some of these filled with water and couldn't be worked. Several ideas were tried to get the water out of the pits but the only one that worked at all during the 1600s was Thomas Savery's 'Miner's Friend'. Before the Stuart period was over, Thomas Newcomen's steam pump was clearing some coal mines of water.

These practical things were based on an immense amount of pencil and paper work and the experiments by a new kind of man, to whom we must now give the name 'scientist'.

Charles II was very interested in science and allowed a group of thinkers to call themselves The Royal Society. They met regularly

from 1662 and talked about the work they had been doing. Other members could point out where somebody had gone wrong or repeat their experiments if they wished. Something new had been learned when several men got the same results from an experiment.

Quadrant for measuring the angle of the sun or stars

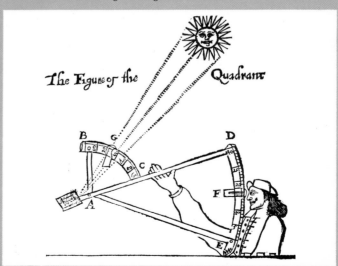

Science

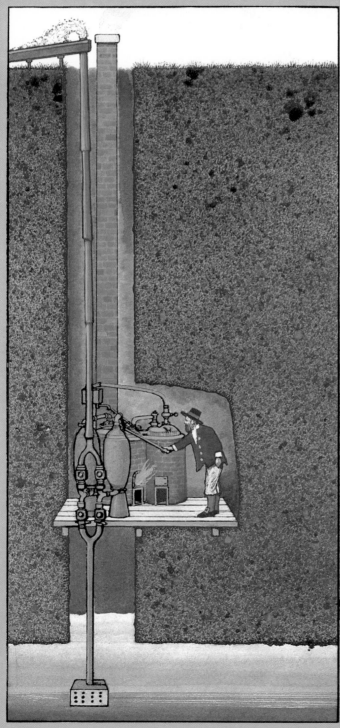

Savery's mine pump

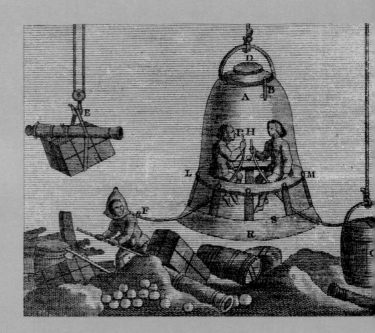

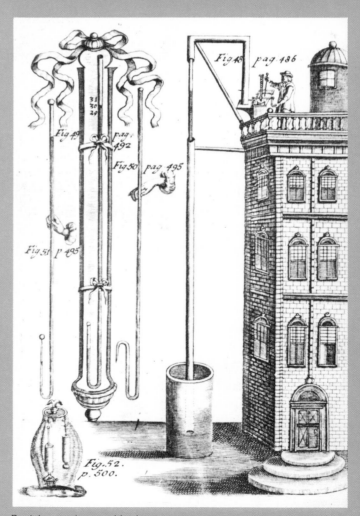

Boyle's experiment with air pressure

above Edmund Halley
above left Halley's diving bell
above right The comet named after Halley
right Boyle's vacuum pump
far right Boyle
below Hooke's microscope

An experiment with light (Newton)

335

4 Law and Order

If your house is broken into and burgled, what ought you to do? The most sensible thing would be to tell the police. A detective will probably come round to look and to ask questions. If you are lucky, the thief will be caught and you might get your valuables back.

It wasn't like that in those days. Let's ask a gentleman of the early 1700s to tell us what happened when he was robbed.

'It's a long time ago now,' he says, 'and I'm not sure I can put all the details in the right order but I'll try. I came downstairs one morning about eleven or twelve years ago to find that a thief had got in during the night and stolen a pair of silver candlesticks and some other odds and ends.

'My first thought was to call in the Charlie, or watchman, but he didn't know anything and hadn't seen anything. Not surprising, really, for he was at least seventy and most of his nights were spent in his little watchman's hut. He did patrol from time to time, calling out the hour and the weather, but a criminal had only to wait for him to pass to be safe for at least an hour.

'I reported my loss to the parish constable but he held out no hope. I had no witnesses, he told me. So I resigned myself to the fact that I should never see my candlesticks again.

'Imagine my surprise when a gentleman called to see me about a week later. He had a strong, perhaps even coarse, face but dressed and spoke quietly. He offered his services as a "thief taker" and finder of stolen goods.

'He persuaded me to set a reward and made me promise not to prosecute the thief if he should be found. "It's easier like this to get stuff back," he said. "Very well," I replied, "I agree to your terms, Mr. er — ?" "Wild. Jonathan Wild."

'I then forgot about him and my silver until three weeks later. He called, gave me my candlesticks back and claimed the reward. I was delighted and paid up. Before he left, he gave me a sheet of paper on which was printed his name and portrait, together with the address of a new office he was opening in London.

'A friend of mine went there once and a clerk took down the details of what he had lost. He, too, got his property back. I remember thinking what a good thing it was that this lawless city of London had men like Jonathan

Wild. At least there was one man fighting crime.

'Several years went by and rumours began to be heard that Wild wasn't the honest man he pretended to be. Everything came out at his trial. Far from tracking down the thief, he had actually ordered him to rob my house. Provided I promised not to lay charges against the robber, the thief was safe and so was Wild.

'What a foolproof scheme he had! Thieves all over England, let alone London, brought their loot to him and he only pretended to try and trace it, so he and his crony could split the reward money and I could get my goods back. If he couldn't return things, they were altered and perhaps sold abroad. He had no

mercy on a robber who disobeyed him or complained about his share. Wild thought nothing of turning him over to a constable with enough evidence to hang him.

'Wild himself was hanged at Tyburn in 1725 but I must say it didn't make the crime figures drop. It's still unsafe to walk the streets at night and sometimes even in daylight. Because of the highwaymen, you can almost rely on being robbed if you are upon the road.

'All the government does is to make hanging the punishment for more and more crimes but the criminals just laugh. So few of them get caught, it doesn't really sink in that they might end on the gallows.'

5 A Country Parson

Let's visit Parson Clegg at his new parsonage. The house is new but Thomas Clegg is old. He has lately come into some money after being poor most of his life and has had the old house pulled down and this new one put up in its place.

It is brick built as timber is getting scarce and expensive. Even wood for the fire is beyond the means of most of the villagers. They burn dried turf or do without.

The windows are the new sliding sashes with larger panes of glass. The windows are set in straight lines, unlike the ones in the old parsonage, which appeared here and there in the walls, seemingly without pattern.

Thomas Clegg is celebrating his seventieth birthday this very day. He is waiting for the guests who are coming to take tea with him. His wife died many years ago but his two married daughters are expected any minute. They will have their husbands and children with them.

His unmarried daughter keeps house for him. His son is an officer in the army and is away fighting with Marlborough against the French. The only other caller is Squire Johnson who rode over from the Manor House earlier in the day.

The visitors arrive and are ushered in through the front door. We'll follow them in to see what the new house looks like inside.

The hall runs through to the back of the house and is quite wide with doors opening off it on both sides. Like most of the rooms, the lower half is panelled in wood with white painted walls above. The staircase is also wide and faces the front door.

On the ground floor are the dining, drawing and sitting rooms. On the top floor are the servants' quarters, the bedrooms and the parson's study. This is where he writes his sermons and the whole room is lined with leather-backed books.

In the drawing room, the guests are served tea in china cups. Surprisingly, these have no handles. Even less to our taste, the tea is weak, with no sugar or milk. This is a new habit at the parsonage, for tea is very expensive, costing up to £2 a pound – or about six weeks' wages for a workman. The farm workers in the village can't afford tea, even those who do have jobs or strips of land to farm.

After tea, the children play in the garden; the two married sisters exchange gossip while their husbands talk about crops and the weather. Parson Clegg and the Squire stroll across the garden to the churchyard. Beyond it is the decaying tithe barn, where the villagers have to bring part of their harvest each year. A little farther off is the glebe which is the parson's own land.

The Squire is talking but Thomas has gone off into a daydream. He sees the grave of his dead wife and remembers when he met her. His own father, although a cattle dealer, had been rich enough to send Thomas to Cambridge where he took his degree. His first post was as a curate and he had met and married the vicar's daughter.

He has been master of his own parish here for nearly fifty years. He has seen governments come and go and he has managed not to upset any of them. He and his wife had seven children but three of them died young, one a baby only four months old.

The Squire is asking him about new ways of farming and what they might do for the poor. Thomas doesn't want to talk about these things and can hardly say he wasn't listening, so he thinks of something he knows will amuse his friend. 'Did you know,' he begins, 'that you can split the name "Shak-speare" into two parts, with four and six letters each. If you count 46 words from the beginning of psalm 46 and 46 from the end, a most amazing . . .' His voice fades out as the two men continue their walk.

6 Public Health

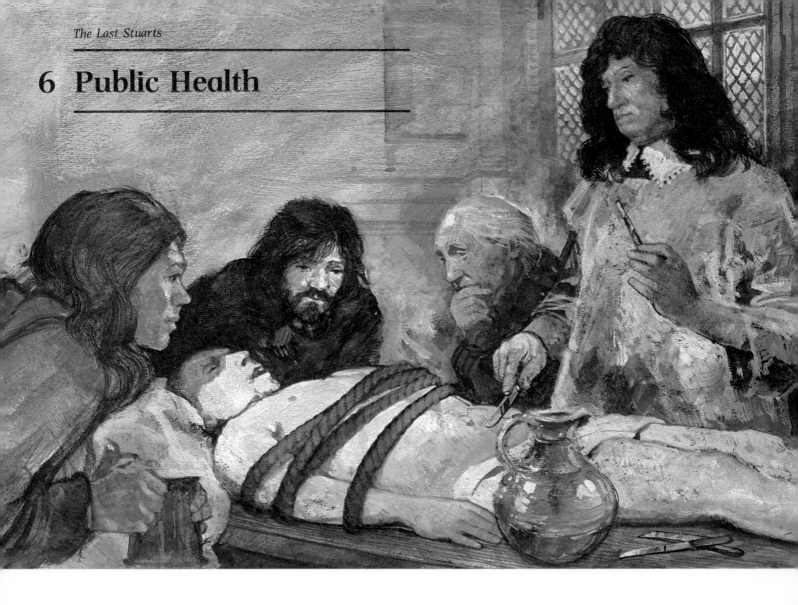

Neither William nor Mary had very long reigns. Mary died of smallpox in 1694 and William was killed in 1702. His horse stumbled on a molehill while he was out riding at Hampton Court. The couple had no children, so Mary's sister, Anne, became queen.

War had broken out between France and England at the beginning of Anne's reign. Everyone thought that France with its magnificent army would win easily but the English under John Churchill, later Duke of Marborough, won victory after victory against them. The war was to last to the end of Anne's reign.

It was a pity that men could do no better than fight each other when they might have fought against the widespread diseases of those days. The state of the people's health was extremely bad.

The Plague had almost vanished after the terrible summer of 1665 but there were plenty of other diseases. Smallpox was a killer, too. Sometimes the victim recovered but was marked or handicapped for life. Even Queen Mary II could not be saved from smallpox by her doctors. Typhus, or jail fever, also claimed many lives.

Many doctors had few, if any qualifications, had passed no exams and were simply men who were interested. The most a patient could expect was that his doctor had served some sort of apprenticeship. In fact, doctors were looked upon as being no better than any other kind of craftsman.

Housewives tried to look after the health of their families with simple herbal cures and common-sense nursing but there was a good deal of ignorance and superstition. If a person had no garden or no skill in picking the right herbs, he could go to apothecaries who sold pills, potions and ointments which they made themselves.

The barber-surgeons would take out teeth and perform other simple operations, as well as shaving and cutting hair. If a leg or an arm had to come off, the patient had to be made drunk, knocked out or tied down. There was no way in those days to make him unconscious with injections or gas.

No one knew anything about germs. Even a century and a half later, when Pasteur tried to show that diseases are caused by germs, there were many people who refused to believe him.

The main reason why health was bad was the conditions in which people lived. Their drinking water came from rivers which were also used as dumps for waste. There were still no dustmen to collect rubbish from houses. Personal habits rarely included washing or taking a bath and (even in the richest families) laundry was only done once a month at best. Among the poor in the slums, clothes were scarcely washed at all.

It took more than 150 years for men and women to realize that disease starts in dirt and can then be spread to the not so dirty. What hope did ordinary people have of escaping killer diseases, when the royal family could not?

Queen Anne had no less than fifteen children, all of whom had died young. The eldest had survived only to his fourteenth year. When the queen herself passed away in 1714, the Stuart line came to an end. The next ruler was George I, a German-speaking prince from Hanover and a descendant of James I.

A modern operation

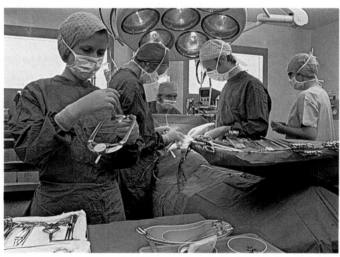

7 The Jacobite Risings

top Queen Anne
above George II

top George I
above Bonnie Prince Charlie

The two risings which happened in 1715 and 1745 are actually called the Fifteen and the Forty Five. When Queen Anne died in 1714, the throne passed to a German prince from Hanover. He and the three kings who came after him were all named George. They ruled England for over a hundred years. The Stuarts tried several times to take the crown away from them but they never managed to do so.

James II's son tried in 1715. His name was also James but his enemies called him the Old Pretender. He wasn't a very inspiring leader and didn't even land in Scotland until his cause was almost lost. Six weeks later his supporters, or Jacobites, as they were called, watched him sail away again. The Fifteen had petered out.

Thirty years on, his son, Charles Edward, made the second main attempt. This was known as the Forty Five. Charles Edward was a very different person from his father. The English dubbed him the Young Pretender but his friends knew him as Bonnie Prince Charlie, or the Young Chevalier.

He landed in the Hebrides in July 1745 with only a handful of followers. His good looks and charm soon made him many more friends. When he raised his standard in Glenfinnan, the clansmen of the Highlands flocked to join his army in large numbers.

In less than a month, Edinburgh had surrendered to the prince. Four days after its fall, the Highlanders beat an English army at Prestonpans. Everything seemed to be in the prince's favour – the English had their hands full with a war in Europe and the time seemed to be ripe for an invasion of England. Just two things were needed before they could be sure

of success: some help from the French and a few thousand English volunteers from across the border.

They waited but no help came from France. Charles could delay no longer and set off for the south with 6,500 men. It was late in the year before they left and well into December by the time they reached Derby.

There were signs of panic in the capital, for the Highland army was no more than 125 miles away. Charles knew this was his last chance and wanted to press on but his advisers pointed out that this would be unwise. English soldiers had been brought back from Europe and English Jacobites had not come forward to join the Highlanders. With a heavy heart the prince gave the order to retreat.

Duke of Cumberland

Once back in Scotland, they beat off an English attack at Falkirk but could not hold Edinburgh. Finally they came up against an English army under the Duke of Cumberland, George II's son. The two armies met at Culloden near Inverness on 16 April 1746. The battle was a fierce one but the Highlanders were tired, cold and hungry, and were routed. A thousand of their dead were left on the moor after the fighting had ended.

It is easy to see why the Scots called the English general 'Butcher' Cumberland: he had the stragglers hunted down and slaughtered and even the wounded and prisoners were killed. The government in London passed laws to make sure that the old clan life of the Highlands was finished for ever.

Charles managed to get away from the moor and spent the next five months dodging the redcoat patrols. Such was the loyalty of the Scots, that not even a reward of £30,000 could tempt any of them to betray him. He finally escaped to Europe in a French ship.

Over forty years later, he died in Rome, a hopeless drunkard. Perhaps he drank to blot out the memory of all those gallant men who had died in his cause.

His younger brother, Henry, became a cardinal in the Roman Catholic church. With his death in 1807, the direct line of Stuart descent came to an end. If things had been different, he might have become Henry IX.

Bonnie Prince Charlie shortly before his death

Sweet William

Stinkwort

After the battle the English named a
flower after the Duke of Cumberland.
The Scots renamed a weed
'Stinking Billy'

Index

Acknowledgements

The publishers would like to thank the following for permission to reproduce photographs:

A-Z Collection; Aerofilms; Malcolm Aird Associates Ltd. (photo: Robert Estall); A Anholt White; Ashmolean Museum; Barnaby's Picture Library; BBC Copyright Photographs; Bibliothèque Nationale; Birmingham Museum and Art Gallery; Bodleian Library; Janet and Colin Bord; Jack Bricklebank; British Airways; British Library; British Museum; British Tourist Authority; Vernon Brooke; J J Brookes; Cambridge University Collection: copyright reserved; Central Office of Information; Charter Trustees of the town of King's Lynn (photo: Colin Shewring); The City of Manchester Art Galleries; Clerk of the Records, House of Lords; Colchester and Essex Museum; Bruce Coleman Ltd. (photos: Jane Burton and C. James Webb); Cooper Bridgeman Library; Corinium Museum; Master and Fellows of Corpus Christi College, Cambridge; Cromwell Museum; Crown Copyright; Daily Telegraph Colour Library (photos: John Marmaras and Patrick Thurston); Michael Dixon; The Trustees of the Dorset County Museum, Dorchester; East Sussex County Council; Werner Forman Archive/National Museum of Iceland; Fotomas Index; W. F. Grimes; Fay Godwin; Guildhall Library, City of London; Guildhall Museum; Sonia Halliday Photographs; Michael Holford Photographs; Holy Trinity Church, Stratford upon Avon; J T Jackson; Kobal Collection; Kunsthistorisches Museum, Vienna; Leeds United AFC; Manchester United FC; Mansell Collection; Mary Rose Trust; The Master and Fellows, Magdalene College Cambridge; Musée des Antiquités de Rouen; Museum of London; The National Gallery, London; National Museum of Antiquities of Scotland; National Museum of Ireland; National Portrait Gallery; The National Trust; New College, Oxford; Oxford Mail and Times; Parks Canada; Robert Pendreigh; Photographie Giraudon; Photoresources; Michael Poulton; Public Record Office (Crown copyright reserved); Reading Museum; Ann Ronan Picture Library; Royal College of Music Museum; Ronald Sheridan; Society of Antiquaries of London; Alison Souster; Southwark and Lambeth Archaeological Excavation Committee; Alan Spain; Statens Historiska Museum; Sussex Archaeological Society; Syndication International; Jeffrey Tabberner; Trinity College Library, Cambridge; University and Society of Antiquities of Newcastle upon Tyne; Verulamium Museum; Victoria and Albert Museum; Vikingeskibshallen, Roskilde; Dean and Chapter of Westminster Abbey; Terry Williams; Woodmansterne Ltd.; Geoffrey Wright; York Archaeological Trust; Yorkshire Museum, York.

Special thanks for help with photography are due to the staff of the Ashmolean Museum and to the National Photographic Record.

Illustrations by Victor Ambrus, Peter Andrews, Robert Ayton, Dick Barnard, Howard Beavan, Nicholas Brennan, Norma Burgin, Stephen Cocking, Michael Cole, Peter Dennis, Richard Eastland, Dan Escott, Brian Evans, Oliver Frey, John Flynn, George Fryer, David Godfrey, Mary Hampson, John Higgins, Richard Hook, John Hunt, Gwyneth Jones, Margaret Jones, Peter Kesteven, Gordon King, Leslie Marshall, Christine Molan, Tony Morris, Peter North, Michael Oakenfull, Trevor Parkin, Roger Payne, Ken Petts, Martin Reiner, Trevor Ridley, Ian Robertson, Colin Shearing, Tudor Art Agency, and Michael Whittlesea.

The cover illustration is by Richard Hook.